Managing Residential Child Care

Managing Residential Child Care

A Managed Service

Richard Whipp
Professor, Cardiff Business School, UK & Pro Vice-Chancellor Cardiff University, UK

Ian Kirkpatrick
Senior Lecturer, Leeds University Business School, UK

Martin Kitchener
Assistant Professor, Department of Social & Behavioural Sciences, University of California, San Francisco, USA

First published 2005 by
PALGRAVE MACMILLAN
Houndmills, Basingstoke, Hampshire RG21 6XS and
175 Fifth Avenue, New York, N.Y. 10010
Companies and representatives throughout the world.

PALGRAVE MACMILLAN is the global academic imprint of the Palgrave Macmillan division of St. Martin's Press, LLC and of Palgrave Macmillan Ltd. Macmillan® is a registered trademark in the United States, United Kingdom and other countries. Palgrave is a registered trademark in the European Union and other countries.

ISBN 1–4039–3560–2 hardback

This book is printed on paper suitable for recycling and made from fully managed and sustained forest sources.

A catalogue record for this book is available from the British Library.

Library of Congress Cataloging-in-Publication Data

Whipp, Richard.
    Managing residential child care: a managed service / Richard Whipp, Ian Krikpatrick, Martin Kitchener.
        p. cm.
    Includes bibliographical references and index.
    ISBN 1–4039–3560–2
        1. Children – Institutional care – Great Britain. 2. Institutional care – Great Britain – Management. I. Kirkpatrick, Ian, 1965– II. Kitchener, Martin, 1966– III. Title.

HV1144.W48 2005
362.73'2'068—dc22   2004052106

10 9 8 7 6 5 4 3 2 1
14 13 12 11 10 09 08 07 06 05

Printed and bound in Great Britain by
Antony Rowe Ltd, Chippenham and Eastbourne.

Contents

List of Tables and Figures

Tables

Figures

Acknowledgements

The project on which this book is based received help and support from many sources.

The research was commissioned by the Social Care Division of the Department of Health. Throughout the project, the team was given wise counsel by Carolyn Davies in Research and Development. We are extremely grateful for not only her patience and diligence but, above all, for the way that she championed this example of the introduction of management scholarship into her field. Her colleague, John Rowlands, was a valued provider of questions and promptings as well as sharing with us his statistical knowledge of the sector.

The project team also had the advantage of a Department of Health advisory group during the course of the research. The group included David Behan, Valerie Brasse, Carolyn Davies, John Rowlands, Lionel Took and Dorothy Whittaker. We are indebted to the group for the range of its advice and the appreciation shown of the particular demands of the project.

As newcomers to the field of children's care, we have been the beneficiaries of generous assistance from many established scholars in the sector. Jane Aldgate, Lesley Archer, David Berridge, Roger Bullock, Leslie Hicks, Michael Little, David Quinton, Wendy Rose and Ian Sinclair are deserving of special thanks for sharing their expertise so readily and engaging with our work so fully.

Professionals in the sector were equally forthcoming with their knowledge and experience. Phil Green and Ruth Newton of the SSI were kind enough not only to support our work but also to respond to our findings as they emerged during the project and, in particular as they were presented at regional events organised by the inspectorate. Moira Gibb, in her capacity as Chair of the Association of Directors of Social Services, was notable for her backing of our study and for using some of the results through the Association.

The authors are also grateful for the fieldwork carried out by Dianne Owen, prior to her retirement from the project due to ill health. Lesley Plowman and Gill Powell provided excellent secretarial assistance.

Thanks are also due to the comments received on the initial manuscript during the anonymous refereeing process organised by Palgrave

Macmillan. We would also like to record our appreciation of the work of our editors at Palgrave Macmillan, Briar Towers and Jennifer Nelson, in bringing this book to print.

Notwithstanding such welcome help, the responsibility for the text remains, of course, with the authors.

1
Introduction

The institutions that are responsible for the 6900 children in residential care in England, Scotland and Wales are the source of major concern. High profile cases of institutional abuse have scandalised the public for over a decade. 'Looked after' young people account, in due course, for almost a quarter of adult prisoners (Parker 2000). Few people need convincing of the need for concerted reform and re-working of the residential care system. Successive official inquires have highlighted the need for change in almost every aspect of the operation of children's homes. It is only recently, however, that attention has moved towards the managerial features of the system. This book reports the results of the first attempt to study the external management of children's homes in England and Wales in its own right.

This chapter introduces the study and contains two main parts. The first part explores the development of concerns about residential care and the state of current understandings of the management of children's homes. The second part of the chapter outlines the book's purpose and structure.

1.1 Children's homes and their management

Residential care

Residential care has been a controversial subject for most of the post-war era, although its acute notoriety has developed mainly in the last ten years. Before dealing with the role of management in this area it is useful to gain a sense of the characteristics of children's homes that are often lost beneath the extreme prose used to report well-publicised episodes of malpractice.

In 1996 almost 130,000 children were in some kind of residential setting. 20,000 in special boarding schools, 12,000 in hospital and 7,000 in

1

children's homes. From 1971 the reduction in the number of young people in children's homes had been of the order of 80 per cent, down from 41,000. The decline in numbers has affected all types of permanent care institutions in education, health and social care. Turbulence has become commonplace for many people involved given the changes in need amongst children, the growth of scepticism about the efficacy of children's homes or the succession of social policy initiatives. The climate created by the uncovering of abusive regimes in children's homes in Leicestershire, Staffordshire and Clwyd, and extensively reported in the results of the Waterhouse Inquiry in 2000, has been a' major challenge for those working in the sector.

Yet a sense of proportion is required. As the Utting inquiry observed (DH 1997), and the subsequent chapters of this book will show, there are many excellent institutions and staff looking after children in residential settings. The specialisation of children's homes has made progress: 35 per cent of homes offer respite care, 28 per cent are devoted to children with disability and 19 per cent concentrate on observation and assessment (DH 1998: 10). The notion of a continuum of services has spread whereby health and local authorities now seek to blend their services in a complementary way and residential services are being recast accordingly.

Management

Given the reshaping of residential care during the past two decades, the management of children's homes by UK local authorities has undergone extensive change. Reflecting broader shifts within public administration, key alterations have included the emergence of mixed economies of provision, the search for more efficient and responsive forms of service delivery, a complex process of labour force restructuring and the installation of new forms of organisational accountability (Langan 2000). Each of these moves has tended to be developed through, and supported by, an enhanced role for new forms of public management.

Nevertheless, the problems associated with the organisation of residential care stand out. Weaknesses have been identified in: the inability to match the needs of children and the resources required, the failure to maintain adequate controls and safeguards and the general under-achievement of local authorities when trying to raise standards of residential care. Awareness of such difficulties has grown at national level through a range of official inquiries and related reports (see Section 2.1). Taken together, the findings of these investigations point to inadequacies in the management of residential services in general and the specific external management of children's homes. The list of deficiencies is wide ranging.

The creation of specialised residential provision, which can meet the particular needs of users, has been slow to emerge. Planning of resources so that the appropriate placements of individual children to homes are made has been weak. Residential homes and their staff have been found to be isolated in relation to the rest of their social services department, given ineffective communication and line management. Little attention has been devoted to the management of those who work in children's homes with the result that recruitment, training and employment conditions have suffered.

This book presents findings from the first study to address these themes directly. The intention is to tackle head-on the way the service is managed and to confront the implications for the standard of residential care. The opportunity will also be taken to identify which management practices are more or less effective in the external management of children's homes by local authorities.

Previous studies

In spite of the problems associated with residential care, the study of external management has been conspicuous by its absence until recently. Bullock *et al.*'s (1993: 3) literature review suggests that the management of children's homes received limited attention in the 1970s and '80s. Instead, research concentrated upon the technical implications of institutionalisation and the importance of child-centred regimes (e.g. Tizard *et al.* 1975; Millham *et al.* 1978).

Since the 1990s, studies conducted by research teams from the Universities of York, Luton and Bristol (Dartington Social Research Unit) have begun to address some of the issues raised by, for instance, Utting (DH 1991a) and Warner (DH 1992) in connection with the external management of children's homes by local authorities. Whilst these studies have not researched this subject as a separate entity, it is important to recognise their indirect findings on management. Examples include the work by Dartington on *The Structure and Culture of Children's Homes* (1996a) which drew attention to the organisational instability in the sector and the weakness of planning. Sinclair and Gibbs (1996) studied *The Quality of Care in Children's Homes* and concluded that homes experience 'less trouble' when the head has a clear remit and compatible roles for those who run the home. *In Children's Homes Revisited* (1997), Berridge and Brodie returned to the homes involved in a 1985 study to discover that many had closed or changed function and that few were now 'better managed' by the local authorities in question. In 1998, Whittaker and colleagues reported in *Working in Children's Homes* on the need for line managers to consult unit mangers over policy implementation, to reduce unplanned admissions and to mediate the relationship with external inspectors. (See also the studies reported in *Caring for Children Away from Home: Messages from Research*, DH 1998a.)

Beyond these examples and their attention to the issues of management, systematic research into the external management of children's homes remains sparse. Some observations have emerged though within analyses of broader administrative changes across the public sector.

When commentators have, in passing, considered management within the context of residential children's services, a sceptical or cautionary approach has predominated (Holman 1993; Ballard 1994; Hearn 1994; Jones and Bilton 1994). Some have attempted to draw comparisons with organisational arrangements in care of the elderly services (SSI 1996a: 1). As a consequence, much is made of the complexities of arrangements to commission and provide services (Hood 1997). A number of studies discuss the complex and often unsatisfactory nature of the relationships between field and residential social workers (Berridge 1985; DHSS 1988; DH 1991a). The problems are rooted in a variety of differences in values, practices, perspectives and professional ethos, arising out of a range of social, cultural, political and historical processes.

Other academic work in the area has provided valuable insights into organisational issues such as: the cultures within homes (Whittaker *et al.* 1996; Dartington Social Research Unit 1996a), leadership (Berridge 1985), and formal roles, tasks and organisational structures (Billis 1984; Challis 1990). This research offers less in the way of insights into the ways that conflicting managerial and care demands are reconciled, or, the significance of relationships with senior managers within the organisation responsible for running the home and external agencies (Dartington Social Research Unit 1996a: 23). In one broader approach, Packman and Hall (1996) recognise that the operation of an SSD depends on the organisational structure, the values of managers and social workers, the traditions of service delivery, the political context and the expectations of council tax payers.

The project

Beyond these general observations, however, little attention has been given to embracing the management of children's homes as a totality. By contrast, the aim of this study is to improve understandings of how social services departments (SSDs) manage residential units, and to evaluate the appropriateness of their actions in the light of current models of management, legal obligations and official guidelines. The Audit Commission, in its report *Seen but Not Heard* (1994: 69), highlighted the importance of balancing different needs and service elements, as well as ensuring 'clarity of purpose in process and outcome … at strategic, operational and individual case levels'. The Commission was concerned that there should be a 'managed service'; what constitutes a managed service is a question which is at the heart of this study. The project arose from the Research Initiative on Residential Care (see DH 1998a for an overview). The research brief was to explain the external management process, with particular regard to the relationship between the home and line management. As a result, a three year study was conducted, between 1996 and 1999, covering England and Wales and using a research design based on different types of local authorities and contrasting approaches to the external management of homes.

The goals of the project were to understand the models of management within social services departments and how they impact on the external management of children's homes. The intention was also to offer alternative solutions and recommendations for improving management practice. There was a separate concern to discover what techniques of monitoring performance and remedial intervention were in use. In pursuing these goals it was hoped that the study would construct a framework for understanding the external management of children's homes which was sensitive both to the public sector context and the needs of those in care. Subsidiary objectives included the need to extend the existing research reported earlier and to form the first sustained link between management and organisation scholars with experts on residential care. Chapter 3 in particular explains how these aims were met. The following section summarises the logic behind the arrangement of the chapters in the book and their relation to the project's goals.

1.2 Book structure

There are nine further chapters in the book.

The purpose of Chapter 2 is to address the issue of what is management in the sector where the problematic issue of residential care is located. Management is first defined in very broad terms and then its particular form in the public sector is specified. We explore the institutional circumstances in which management operates in social services departments and reveal the constraints involved within a 'professional bureaucracy'. An appreciation of such contextual features and the limits they give rise to are vital to the development of the finer grained account of managerial tasks within the external management of children's homes that follows.

Chapter 3 presents the main aims of the project and the research design. Care is taken to share with the reader the range of perspectives used from the management and social care literatures and the concern to ally conceptual and practical issues. The basis of the sample frame is established, including the reasoning behind the 12 cases drawn from four types of local authority. Attention is given to how the sample was constructed and balanced in relation to a mixture of dimensions. A rationale is offered of the sources of data, how they were collected and the safeguards employed in their processing. What is meant by the external management of children's homes is laid out, together with the justification for adopting a distinctive 'inclusive' view. The composite approach to evaluating external management adopted in the study is explained. The chapter also provides the opportunity to indicate the dominant themes in the overall profile of residential care which the sample produces.

The majority of the book is centred on what the study found to be the core processes in the external management of children's homes by local authorities. These are composed of: strategy and implementation (Chapter 4), the management of child placement (Chapter 5), line management (Chapter 6), managing and developing staff (Chapter 7), monitoring and control (Chapter 8), and the management of external residential placements (Chapter 9).

The full details of the study's data and findings are found in Chapters 4–9. Each has a similar shape. They contain: an inspection of both relevant official guidance and the current understandings of the particular aspects of management practice in question; a synthesis of appropriate management literature; a summary picture of the evidence relating to the practice from across the case authorities; an evaluation of the effectiveness of the approaches adopted to the particular aspect of the management in question; and a conclusion which includes a set of recommendations. It should be noted that data from the London 3 authority was not used in Chapters 5, 6 or 7 given that the authority has no in-house provision; it was selected in order to illustrate issues associated with managing relations with the independent sector.

The first set of findings appear in Chapter 4. It begins coverage of the key elements of the external management of children's homes by dealing with how strategies for children's services and residential care are created and implemented. It notes the enthusiasm in the sector for planning and strategy. What emerges is the variation in what informs departmental plans and who is involved. Implementation will be shown to be a major problem.

The management of child placement is the subject of Chapter 5 and develops our inclusive conception of the external management of residential care. The concern is how far social services departments are able to ensure that placements are planned, based on assessments of need and linked to precise statements of purpose and function for each home in their control. The structures and procedures for 'gate-keeping' resources are investigated and how far they maintain the specialisation of children's homes.

Chapter 6 covers those who have line management responsibility for children's homes. It establishes the character of line management relations in the public sector – practitioner autonomy, peer control and a 'custodial' view of management. The chapter explores the attempts to replace custodial with more managerialist orientations. It describes the variety of supervisory roles that exist and how the identity and style of residential supervisors influences their relations with residential staff.

Chapter 7 turns to the concerns of Warner (DH 1992) and others over the management and development of staff. The importance of training, development and career progression for residential care are widely recognised. Our research points to the contribution of SSDs and the extent to which they are restricted by the personnel policies of local authorities. The ability to redeploy and train residential staff is critical to achieving the specialisation and redesign of services described in earlier chapters.

Chapter 8 looks at management monitoring and control in the context of the new regulatory framework of the 1990s. The aim of the chapter is to discover how far increased regulation of children's homes has led to effective management information systems. Regulation 22 visits and arms-length inspections, in particular, are reviewed. The way the implementation of new regulations has been negotiated between professionals and their supervisors is highlighted.

Given the increased role for the mixed economy in residential care, Chapter 9 is devoted to the management of external placements. It addresses the questions: have management practices altered and has a more sophisticated apparatus for making external placements in children's residential care grown up? In the absence of any established research on the subject, the intention will be to construct how the market for children's residential care has developed, including the ambiguity that exists at the policy level.

The objective of the conclusion is two-fold: to summarise the research findings and to offer a set of recommendations to those who have interests in residential care and its management. The findings will relate not only to the pattern of experience across the sample authorities but also the implications of the results for the current understandings of management that operate in the sector will, in turn, be considered.

2
Understanding the External Management of Children's Homes

Introduction

In this chapter the aim is to develop a framework for understanding the external management of children's residential care as an inclusive process. That is, a process which involves not only the direct line management and inspection of children's homes, but also the strategic co-ordination of services between different functions and professional groups. To achieve this objective, the chapter is divided into four main sections. The first outlines the historical evolution of children's homes, the role of management and the major problems that have arisen. The second section offers a general definition of management as a generic process. In the third, we concentrate on what this implies for children's residential services and how, given the goals of these services, the effectiveness of management could be evaluated. In the fourth section, drawing on contingency theory, an attempt is made to develop a realistic understanding of the organisational context in which social services managers operate. This identifies certain constraints on management action, which, it is argued, are important to consider when seeking to establish better practice in this area.

2.1 The management of children's homes by local authorities

Before 1948, child care outside the family was conducted almost exclusively by unpaid carers who helped to 'rescue the unfortunate poor' on a largely individual and uncoordinated basis (Fisher *et al.* 1986; Collshed 1990). Following the *Children Act 1948*, the welfare state began to absorb philanthropic activities within a legislative framework that gave the possibility for coercive intervention by social workers (Clarke 1988). The local authority children's departments that were created in 1948 had, however, no power to assist families unless severe problems became apparent. In effect, the social workers within children's departments provided a compromise between the liberal vision of unhindered private philanthropy and the socialist vision of the all-encompassing state.

Until the end of the 1960s, as part of this compromise, residential children's homes in the United Kingdom were either run independently or maintained by voluntary and charitable organisations. A key change to this pattern occurred in 1971 when, following the *Seebohm Report 1968* and the *Local Authority Social Services Act 1970*, local authorities were required to establish social services departments (SSDs). The intention was to amalgamate and improve the co-ordination of services that had previously been provided by separate children's welfare and mental health departments. A key feature of the new SSDs was that they became responsible for the management of children's homes within their geographical area.

Although practice varied, most SSDs adopted similar arrangements for the management of children's residential care. First was the creation of a rigid division of labour between the professional functions of field social work and those of providing resources, including children's homes (Challis 1990) (see Chapter 5 for more detail on the nature and consequences of this division). Second, within each resource division, emphasis was placed on the decentralisation of children's home provision to allow high degrees of autonomy to the unit managers (UMs). Brown and Payne (1990: 167) have suggested that the new SSDs lacked personnel with the management skills necessary to supervise the UMs. Inside SSDs, specialist line managers of children's homes were not employed widely until the mid-1970s. This development followed Seebohm's (1968: para 524) conclusion that:

> there ought to be someone, at both headquarters and area team level, with a particular responsibility for helping with the problems of residential institutions.

Gradually, some superintendents and masters of the old style residential establishments were appointed as external 'homes advisors' to manage groups of smaller and often more specialised homes (RCA 1982: 11). Slowly, the advisors came to be seen as significant within a process of line management in which they were expected to help 'maintain' practice standards. Within this limited approach to the line management of children's homes, UMs maintained considerable discretion and control over service provision (Bills *et al.* 1980).

There was a considerable expansion in the number of children's homes during the 1970s and '80s. During this period, however, the belief in the value of institutional treatment declined as it was viewed increasingly as unethical and intrusive by liberals, and expensive and ineffective by traditionalists (Kahan 1974). Studies by Fisher *et al.* (1986), Millham *et al.* (1986), Packman *et al.* (1986) and Vernon and Fruin (1986) all showed that field social workers (FSWs), and sometimes residential workers, came to associate the provision of residential care for children with failure. This view was rooted in the influential research of Rowe and Lambert (1973) which stressed the supremacy of the family as the basis for alternative public care of children. Previously, residential care had been seen as the solution for many young children; it was now considered as part of the problem (Waterhouse 1988: 96).

These concerns emerged at the same time as many local authorities had started to reduce their own residential provision. In 1979, for example, 29,000 young people were placed in local authority run children's homes in England and Wales, representing 31 per cent of all those in care. By 1992, however, this number had shrunk to only 8700 residents (Sinclair and Gibbs 1996: 2–3). This rapid decline in the use of residential care (also matched by the trend in home closures (see Berridge and Brodie 1997)) was driven in large part by the growing emphasis on family placement services.

By the mid-1980s, there was increasing government unease with the economic performance of the social services sector (Foster and Wilding 2000). There was also a shift in fundamental values relating to the relationship between the state and the 'natural' family, and how far the law should intervene to mediate and to transfer parental rights (Harding 1994). Professionally, social work was increasingly criticised for being overly bureaucratic, remote and inefficient. Questions were raised about the very '*raison d'être* of the profession, its philosophy and methods'. With regard to practice within children's homes, these concerns were amplified by research pointing to the lack of planning and a failure to match needs with services (DH 1991c; Waterhouse 1988). Also important were successive disclosures of malpractice in homes (Shaw 1995). It was shown that some SSDs had been unable to control practices within their own establishments. Berridge and Brodie's (1996: 184) analysis, for example, of reports into the well-publicised scandals in Staffordshire, Gwent and Leicestershire reveals a common theme: 'the ineffective or non-existent line management of children's homes'. In each case, it was found that local authority managers had minimal, if any, direct contact with the units and so were in no position 'to observe malpractice, assuming of course that they would have recognised it'. Following the Pindown revelations in Staffordshire, the Government sponsored, and later endorsed the recommendation of, a number of initiatives relating to policy and practice in residential child care. Table 2.1 lists the key reports and summarises their major areas of concern (see also Chapter 10, Section 10.2).

Several of the initiatives include elements that relate to the management and organisation of children's homes by SSDs. The *Children Act Guidance and Regulations 1991* (DH 1991b), for example, provides a comprehensive framework for the management and operation of children's homes within the context of the *Children Act 1989*. A key feature of this Act was the requirement for local authorities to produce a statement of purpose and function for each home. The intention was that this would help tackle the unfocussed approach of much residential care and the 'dumping ground' mentality that had led to the inappropriate placement of children into residential care. It was hoped that advantages would derive from making explicit what each home could be expected to achieve. The *Guidance* also covered record keeping, staffing, training and supervision, the physical environment and aspects of daily care. In addition, reviews in 1991 of residential care in England and Wales also addressed issues pertinent to the management of children's homes, including the report by Utting (DH 1991a), which identified the training of residential staff as a major area of concern.

Besides enhancing the regulation of children's homes, the *Children Act 1989* (Part III) directed local authorities to 'diminish the need to receive children into or keep them in care'. As part of this approach, local authorities are required to provide a continuum of services incorporating at one extreme, services for children looked after and, at the other, services for children supported at home (Packman and Hall 1996; Dartington Social Research Unit 1997b: 27). This notion of a continuum also incorporates provision from a host of agencies including health, social services and education. Although the numbers of children accommodated in children's homes fell to about 7000 by 1996 (DH 1998a), residential care continued to serve important functions within the continuum of available services. Residential care for children was said to be especially relevant for children who

> have decided that they do not wish to be fostered; have had bad experiences of foster care; have been so abused within the family that another family placement is inappropriate; are from the same family and otherwise cannot be kept together; or who require expert, multidisciplinary help with social and personal problems. (DH 1991a: 8)

Table 2.1 Initiatives in Residential Child Care

1991	*Children Act 1989 Guidance and Regulations – Volume 4 Residential Care* (DH 1991b). Detailed policy and practice guidance on residential child care in the context of the new legislation.
1991	National review of residential child care in England leading to the report *Children in the Public Care* (Utting 1991).
1991	Similar exercise undertaken in Wales – *Accommodating Children: A Review of Children's Homes in Wales* (SSI Wales and Social Information Systems 1991).
1992	Committee chaired by Norman Warner, in response to events in Leicestershire, on selection and recruitment of staff in residential child care, *Choosing with Care* (DH 1992).
1992	*The Quality of Care* (Local Government Management Board 1992). A wide-ranging review that had the specific effect of improving residential staff salaries.
1992	Efforts to enhance the inclusion of residential child care in social work qualifying training, resulting in setting *Quality Standards for Residential Care* (Central Council for Education and Training in Social Work [CCETSW] and Department of Health Expert Group 1992).
1992	*Residential Child Care Initiative* aimed to increase the number of senior staff in children's homeswho are professionally qualified.
1992	Setting up of *ARCC* (Advancement of Residential Child Care).
1993	*Guidance on Permissible Forms of Control in Children's Residential Care* (DH 1993).
1993	Establishment of the *Department of Health Support Force for Children's Residential Care*, with a brief to offer advice to individual local authorities on issues associated with quality of care and management.
1993	Development of national project at the National Children's Bureau to identify, develop and disseminate good practice in residential child care.
1993	National Social Services Inspectorate inspection of children's homes (SSI, Department of Health 1993).
1993	Funding by the Department of Health of major research programme on residential child care.
1994	*Growing Up in Groups* (Kahan 1994). A multi-disciplinary project highlighting good practice in child care across education, health and social service boundaries.
1994	*Seen But Not Heard* (Audit Commission 1994). Stresses importance of local, inter-agency planning of services based upon improved information systems and needs assessment.
1995	*Managing For Care: The External Management of Children's Homes* (SSI 1995a) following seminar and workshop series.
1996	*Matching Needs and Services* (Dartington Social Research Unit 1996b). Methodology designed to help assess local needs and design appropriate services.
1997	*People Like Us: The Review of the Safeguards for Children Living Away From Home* (Utting 1997). Calls for government action to 'drive up standards all round' through improved planning and systems.

Source: Developed from Berridge and Brodie (1996: 188).

Despite the structural reorganisations outlined above, reports such as Utting (DH 1991a) and Warner (DH 1992) suggest that many social services departments (SSDs) still lacked the necessary information systems and planning skills to introduce the major principles contained within the *Children Act 1989*. Guidance for SSDs was required, according to the reports, in three key areas. The Support Force for Children's Residential Care (1995) was set up to provide practical advice in order to help SSDs implement the recommendations of the various reports from the Department of Health.

All these developments occurred against a wider backdrop in which SSDs faced intense demands from central government to engage in radical restructuring and the adoption of new management practices imported from the private sector (Langan and Clarke 1994). The most notable changes have, of course, been those which followed the implementation of the *NHS and Community Care Act 1990*. As has been widely discussed elsewhere, this major reform has led to the development of care management and purchaser/provider splits (Wistow *et al.* 1996). To-date, however, much of the impact of these changes has been primarily in SSD services for adults. There is evidence, for example, of some delegation of budgets to care managers, of systematic assessment procedures being set up which limit professional autonomy and the development of central information systems to support the strategic planning of needs and services (Lewis and Glennerster 1996; Means and Smith 1998). These changes may imply some departure from the notion of professional bureaucracy described below. In particular, there has been some reduction in professional autonomy and the creation of far more intrusive top down management systems designed to control and standardise decision making (Harris 1998).

To-date, this model of management has not been applied in any significant way to SSD services for children and families. While some SSDs have attempted to implement purchaser/provider splits for all client groups (SSI 1996b) there is some evidence to suggest that most have done so in a rather cosmetic fashion and with some negative results in terms of even greater fragmentation between field social work and residential staffs (Jones and Bilton 1994; Kirkpatrick *et al.* 1999). Most SSDs have avoided much radical change linked to care management in children's services and many have moved towards a client split (see Chapter 3). This is not to suggest that major restructuring has not occurred. There is evidence that SSDs have continued to experiment with new structures and that this trend has intensified in the context of local government reorganisation (Hall 1997; Craig and Manthorpe 1998).

However, the key point is that while there may have been some limited departure from the professional-led structures in adult services this does not seem to have occurred in any significant way to children's services. As such, the trend is one in which children's services have moved towards a 'divergent model' of organisation (Clarke 1995: 52) (also see Chapter 9).

2.2 What is management?

It is beyond the scope of this chapter to summarise the variety of definitions of management that exist in the literature (see Reed (1996) for a discussion of these issues). Instead we differentiate two broad approaches towards management that have been most influential. The first, and possibly a most widely shared view, is that management refers to a technical *activity* or *process* which occurs in any organisation where some attempt is made to achieve specific goals through collaborative action. Fayol (1949), an early exponent of this view, described management as a process of planning, organising, co-ordinating, commanding and control. In short, he argued that 'to govern an undertaking is to conduct it towards its objective by trying to make the best possible use of the resources at its disposal'. A feature of this definition is that it assumes that management is something that occurs in any organisation, be it public or private, profit or non-profit. The idea is that management skills are somehow portable and universally applicable to different settings even though actors may pursue markedly different goals (Hood 1991). The idea implies that whilst management may be a discrete function, it is also a process which involves staff who may not occupy positions with the job title of manager.

A second way of understanding management derives from economics and the sociological literature. Some see management in terms of an elite grouping enjoying certain kinds of social power. The emphasis is therefore not on management as a generic activity, but as consisting of a distinct class or occupational group with specific interests and shared values. From this perspective 'managers' are also those who promote a particular ideology or set of beliefs relating to the purpose and goals of an organisation (Pollitt 1993). Clarke and Newman (1997: IX), for example, refer to 'managerialism' in the public sector as a 'cultural formation and a distinctive set of ideologies and practices ...' that prioritise goals of efficiency and the control of resources. In the context of social services, some have adopted this approach to describe the emergence of a new management cadre with interests and priorities in opposition to those of rank and file professional staffs (Pahl 1994).

For the purpose of this study, while the second view is recognised as having some relevance, the concept of management as a generic process is considered to be more useful. In other words, there is a need to achieve some degree of control and co-ordination to meet goals in any organisation and this in turn requires *management* whether or not it is given such a label. Of course, in any hierarchical organisation, management also refers to a group of workers who devote a large proportion of their time to this task of control and co-ordination. For us, however, the main point is to regard management as a wider process involving these groups and others, concerned primarily with the attainment of an organisation's goals in the most effective way possible within existing resources.

2.3   Management goals in children's residential care

If management is defined as a technical process of achieving organisational goals in the most effective way possible, what does this mean in the context of children's residential care? The first point to make is that it requires some degree of clarity over what the goals or objectives of the service are. In other words, how should management effectiveness be judged?

A key feature of most organisations is that there may be many competing sub-goals, for example, between those of different professionals, between managers and practitioners or managers and politicians (Perrow 1986). This fact has led some writers simply to describe professional services as 'negotiated orders' in which collective goals involve some bargaining and compromise between different groups (Strauss *et al.* 1973). In the context of local authority children's services, this idea rings true as it is possible to articulate many, possibly competing goals or outcomes. Parker *et al.* (1991: 20), for example, identify 'at least five kinds of outcomes in child care that reflect different perspectives and interests'. These include public, service, professional, family and child outcomes.

Despite this appearance of confusion over goals, it is also the case that the 'over-arching' goals (Brown and Payne 1990) of these services are fairly clear and are set out in legislation, notably in the *Children Act 1989*. This legislation imposes two interrelated requirements on SSDs with regard to children's residential care. First, the goal of management must be to ensure that effective supervision and control is exercised over children's homes in line with existing regulations and in the interests of their residents (DH 1991a). Politicians and managers need to be able to ensure that adequate safeguards are in place to guarantee the safety of children in the public care (DH 1997). This means that adequate management information systems must be in place, systems that communicate information effectively through a hierarchy and allow for the speedy identification and rectification of any malpractice.

A second, far wider goal which management must pursue is with regard to the quality and effectiveness of residential services. Whilst there are many ways of understanding 'effective' outcomes of children's residential care (see Sinclair and Gibbs 1996 for a discussion) the broadest criteria on which these services will be judged is the extent to which they are matched with, and then meet, the assessed needs of clients. This wider goal is clearly set out in legislation (DH 1991b) and in almost all subsequent guidance and research (Dartington 1995; SFCRC 1996). One aspect of this is the increased specialisation of children's homes and the development of clear statements of purpose and function (DH 1992). This corroborates the findings of a variety of investigations that identify links between specialisation, clarity of purpose and effective outcomes at the level of the home (Sinclair and Gibbs 1996; Berridge and Brodie 1997). These goals go beyond the design of residential services and have implications for the wider strategy and the links between different professional groupings. What is required is a high degree of strategic integration of these (increasingly high cost) services so that they may most effectively achieve wider goals. As the first Utting report (1991: 45) suggested, the effectiveness of residential care ultimately rests on the existence of a 'coherent policy framework' and that 'directors of social services should verify that their arrangements for managing residential care within an overall strategy for children's services are effective'.

To summarise, we argue that in general terms the goals which management pursue in the context of children's residential care are two fold: both to ensure effective controls and safeguards and to strive towards the maximum quality and effectiveness of these services by seeking to achieve a greater matching between assessed needs and available resources. Given this broad definition of management goals, a second related concern is to identify who in the organisation is actually involved in this management process.

Much previous research has tended to concentrate on the children's home in isolation and has considered management only in terms of relationships between unit managers and supervisors (Kahan 1994; Whittaker *et al.* 1996; Berridge and Brodie 1997). While these relations are important, especially in terms of understanding the issues around the effective control and regulation of children's homes (see Chapter 8), attention to them alone would not enable us to comment on the wider goals of management to improve the quality and effectiveness of services. This latter concern requires that a wider *inclusive* perspective on external management is taken (see also Chapter 3). Put briefly, our understanding of the external management of children's homes is that it represents a multifaceted activity, involving other professional groups (including field social work teams and registration and inspection units) and different levels of the organisation's hierarchy (senior managers, planning staffs and politicians). To understand how far management goals of improving the effectiveness of services are attained one must look at the wider development of strategy (see Chapter 4), at staff training and development (Chapter 7) and at the management of placement decision making (Chapter 5). An inclusive approach to external management, therefore, addresses a wider set of activities that are part of a management process of achieving the goals of residential care services.

2.4   A contingency approach to the management of children's homes

So far a broad definition of management as a generic process has been offered together with what this might mean in the context of children's residential care. However, in order to understand what this form of management involves in practice and the difficulties of achieving operational goals, it is necessary to return briefly to the literature on organisations. The aim is to gain a clearer view of the context of social service departments as the organisations within which this type of management operates.

In the management and organisation literature there are important differences between what might be described as normative and contingency approaches. The former refers to a wide variety of ideas propounded by management gurus through 'how to do it' text books. What these writers share is a belief that it is possible to identify universal prescriptions for management practice. The classic example of this was Taylor who over 80 years ago popularised notions of scientific management. More recent examples include the literature on changing corporate culture (Deal and Kennedy 1982; Peters and Waterman 1982), total quality management or business process re-engineering (Hammer and Champy 1993). All these approaches have one thing in common: they suggest universal blue-prints for how to manage effectively in any context. Such an approach, if followed blindly, could by implication involve crude attempts to transfer specific concepts and practices from one context to another, such as, a simple imposition of practices relevant to the private sector to professional public services.

By contrast to these normative approaches, there exist what are known as contingency theories of management and organisation (Burns and Stalker 1962; Child 1985). From this perspective, the activity of management (co-ordination and control to achieve goals) is understood differently depending on the particular tasks, power relations and environmental conditions of organisations. According to Buchanan and Huczynski (1997: 445), 'Whilst contingency writers do not offer ready-made answers, they do have a set of questions and provide a way of thinking which can help managers analyse their organisations within their particular situation to enable them to make an informed choice about the organisational structure that is most appropriate for their specific enterprise.'

Contingency approaches have certain benefits over normative views of management. The obvious advantage is that they ensure a greater sensitivity towards the different contexts in which management is enacted. This may be especially important when considering the development of management within public sector professional services. These, as has already been noted, pursue different goals to private organisations and operate different ways of organising and delivering services. A contingency approach which recognises these differences may be helpful not only in terms of developing more realistic solutions to problems, but might avoid some of the crude excesses of new public management and the importation of alien ideas and concepts from the private to public sectors (Pollitt 1993).

2.5   Social service departments as professional bureaucracies

Adopting a contingency approach means recognising some key differences between organisations within which management activity occurs. In the context of this study, it specifically requires that we outline some key differences between SSDs and other types of organisation.

A useful starting point for achieving this goal is the typology of five basic organisational forms developed by Mintzberg (1993). These organisational forms represent different ways of achieving the task of control and co-ordination in an organisation and are suitable in different contexts depending on the complexity of services and on environmental conditions. The best known form is what Mintzberg describes as a 'machine bureaucracy'. This, he argues, exists in any organisation where the main task is to mass produce relatively simple, standardised goods or services. To achieve this goal, organisations require extensive formal rules to control work, a clear division of labour with fixed job descriptions and a hierarchy to ensure that top management decisions are implemented by operational staffs. In the private sector, examples of this would include most large manufacturing firms, banks and insurance companies. In the public sector, large bureaucracies involved in the delivery of fairly standardised services such as the Department of Social Security would be examples. According to Mintzberg, the extreme opposite to the machine bureaucracy would be the adhocracy or 'organic firm' (Burns and Stalker 1962). These organisations produce highly complex services under conditions of extreme uncertainty and continuous change and innovation. In such organisations, for example media firms, management consultancies and some high-tech manufacturing, there may be few written rules, job descriptions and relatively flat hierarchies.

Social services departments have many of the features of Mintzberg's machine bureaucracy. Not only are they hierarchical, but there are also well-established (in most cases) functional divisions of labour between resources and field work and extensive formal rules (many originating through legislation) that govern the delivery of services. SSDs tend, however, to bear a far closer resemblance to Mintzberg's third organisational form, the professional bureaucracy. By contrast to a machine bureaucracy, the professional variant exists in organisations where the main goal is to provide services that are standardised, but also complex. The complexity of services means that while some rules are necessary to achieve basic co-ordination, there is also a heavy reliance on the discretion of expert professional workers who may have been trained and socialised outside the organisation (Raelin 1992). Rather than rely exclusively on rules to achieve standardisation, the professional bureaucracy relies on the shared education, skill and competency of its professional staffs and their ability to make appropriate decisions within general guidelines (a process described by Mintzberg as 'pigeon holing').

A key difference between machine and professional bureaucracies is that operational staffs in the latter may exercise considerable autonomy and discretion in their work. Such autonomy is necessary because the production of complex services requires the exercise of discretion. In addition, however, autonomy may also be justified by professional staffs themselves as being necessary to promote the interests of the client; this is linked to what has often been described as the strong service ethos of professionals (Raelin 1992). The latter may lead to some conflict between professional demands for autonomy of action and organisational demands for effective control over the delivery of services in order to ensure standardisation. The existence of such conflicts is a well-known feature of work in SSDs and has been widely reported (Webb and Wistow 1987; Pithouse 1989; Pahl 1994).

These characteristics of the professional bureaucracy ensure that management action is subject to constraints that are far less pronounced in organisations closer to the machine bureaucracy form. Three main types of constraint can be identified. First, those in management positions are less able to exercise direct control over the work of rank and file staffs. Like other organisations SSDs are hierarchical, normally with a clear management structure and chain of command through director, assistant director (AD) and resource manager (Challis 1990). While this hierarchy exists, relationships between superiors and subordinates are not exactly similar to those found in other organisations. A key difference is that senior managers in professional bureaucracies are themselves almost entirely recruited from the ranks of the profession (Lawler and Hearn 1997). There is also a blurring of management/practitioner roles. This has a number of implications. One is that managers share many of the same values and beliefs of junior professionals (Ackroyd *et al.* 1989) and may be unwilling or unable to exert greater control or interfere with the autonomy of junior staffs. They may share the assumption that professional autonomy is sacred and that professionals should regulate their own practice. This also has implications for the supervision process (discussed in Chapters 6 and 8) where the supervisor may be seen as first amongst equals or as a 'coach' (Scott 1965). The implication is that managers are unable to exert anything like the same degree of control over work as they might in a machine bureaucracy. They may need to rely extensively on influence or persuasion rather than direct orders. Indeed, attempts to be directive may be counter-productive as professionals have considerable ability to undermine decision making.

A further constraint on management action arises from the fact that professional bureaucracies (SSDs being no exception) are often what Weick (1976) describes as 'loosely-coupled' organisations. This refers to a situation in which internal departments or divisions are: 'somehow attached, but that each retains some identity and separateness and that this attachment may be circumscribed, infrequent, weak in its mutual effects and/or slow to respond' (op cit.: 3). A key reason for this loose coupling in SSDs is that divisions of labour are also constructed along professional lines (e.g. mental health workers, psychiatrists, social workers, and residential workers). These different groups may have subgoals based not only on immediate task interests, but also on wider professional training, values and socialisation (Iles and Auluck 1993). One of the best examples of this (which will be discussed in greater detail later) is the history of rivalry and poor communication between field social work and residential staffs (Challis 1990). These poor lateral communications based on occupational subcultures tend to exaggerate an already difficult management task of achieving effective co-ordination between different parts of the organisation.

A final constraint on management in professional bureaucracies relates to the problem of implementing top-down change. This point has been widely acknowledged in the literature focusing on professional organisations in many different contexts (Hinings *et al.* 1991; Mintzberg 1993; Denis *et al.* 1999). Ackroyd *et al.* (1989), for example, describe professional bureaucracies as systems that tend to maintenance of the *status quo*, where change, if it occurs at all, is likely to be practitioner-driven and incremental. More generally, Greenwood and Hinings (1988: 310) argue that change in professional contexts is often 'convergent', or shaped by the 'contoured mould of existing design orientations'.

This problem of change in professional bureaucracies stems in large part from the internal characteristics that have already been described. Implementing a new strategy or policy is difficult in a context where management is often unable to exert its authority and where co-ordination between professional groups is poor. Innovations do occur but often in a diffuse and bottom-up way as practitioners themselves take initiatives or work through committees or project teams (Mintzberg 1993). This means that management groups will be required to negotiate with front line staffs over both the process and content of any change strategy. Consequently, the 'solutions chosen' (such as new management structures and procedures) are most likely to be 'captured by some of the same dynamics that caused the problems they were intended to solve' (Denis *et al.* 1999: 108).

A further characteristic of professional bureaucracy that may prevent radical change (especially in the context of public services) is the location of these organisations within larger institutions, or supra-organisational structures. SSDs, for example, are governed not only by national policy frameworks, but also by the bureaucratic structures of the local state (Harris 1998). As such they remain 'semi anonymised organisations' in which management functions and powers are dispersed (Hood 1995). One consequence of this is that management decision making within SSDs is subject to various external controls, especially pronounced with regard to staff deployment and resource utilisation. Also important is the role played by local politics in terms of exaggerating ambiguity over policy goals and interfering with long term change strategies (Greenwood and Stewart 1986; Denis *et al.* 1999).

Together, these factors mean that management in SSDs, and other professional bureaucracies, operates within a set of constraints that are less evident both in the machine bureaucracies of the public sector and in private sector firms. In particular, the tasks of attaining control and co-ordination to achieve organisational goals are extremely difficult given the proliferation of interests and highly decentralised nature of much decision making. As a result, certain types of management changes and practice that may be effective elsewhere are likely to be less effective in the SSD context. As noted earlier, it is essential to understand the nature of these constraints prior to exploring contemporary management practices.

Conclusion

The description of SSDs as professional bureaucracies suggests that external management of residential care will operate within certain structural constraints. In addition, during the 1990s, most SSDs were also required to implement change in a context of growing pressure on resources (Means and Smith 1998: 104). According to Huntington (1999: 242) this has led to 'increasingly chaotic working environments within underfunded and over-burdened social services departments'. Even Utting (DH 1997: 175) acknowldeges that change may be difficult as local managers are faced with running a range of diverse services in a context of high public expectations and strained resources.

These facts, we argue, must be clearly understood when attempting to explore the effectiveness of management in terms of achieving the goals of these services, that is, of improved controls/safeguards and of higher quality services based on a clearer matching of needs and resources.

In terms of control, we have already hinted at how the structures of professional bureaucracy may act in a constraining fashion. A key issue is how far line managers, through supervisory meetings and other visits, can interfere with the autonomy of (often highly experienced) unit managers of children's homes. Whittaker *et al.* (1996), for example, note how the line manager is often in a difficult position of having to balance competing objectives: those of senior managers to whom they are accountable and of overworked residential staffs who line managers may wish to protect and offer support (also see Chapters 6 and 8). A further question relates to the resources available for effective control and supervision. Even if SSDs introduce guidelines and protocols for staff supervision or Regulation 22 inspections, how far is it the case that these tasks can be undertaken when overall staff resources are under pressure? Berridge and Brodie (1997) have noted how, despite the current emphasis on control, most children's homes have less contact with line managers than they did 15 years ago.

To an even greater extent, the structures of professional bureaucracy generate major constraints on the ability of management to achieve improved quality services. As we noted earlier, the goal of 'matching needs and services' can only be achieved through greater multifunctional collaboration and through the development and implementation of strategy. A key question here is how far is it possible to achieve this collaboration between different functions, and notably between residential staffs, and field-social work staffs, given the loosely-coupled nature of SSDs and the long history of rivalry and poor communication between these occupational groups. Another concern is how far SSDs can develop and implement clear strategies with regard to children's residential care which design specialised services around assessed needs (Audit Commission 1994).

Given the nature of management in SSDs, the role of politicians in decision making and resource constraints, the goal of redesigning services to meet needs through long-term strategies is likely to be extremely difficult. Such goals are, of course, further problematised by the trend to engage in constant, in some cases virtually annual, reorganisations of services (Jones and Bilton 1994).

The conclusion from this discussion is that the particular structures of SSDs are likely to place important limits on management action. In particular, this means that the goals of achieving greater control of developing services are likely to be extremely difficult to achieve. The reason for making these points is not to apologise for what might be slow progress in terms of implementing legislation and guidance, but to frame expectations of what is possible under the circumstances in which management operates. An understanding of the difficulties and structural constraints involved will lead to the development of more realistic appreciations of the external management of children's homes and their potential for change.

3
The Study

Introduction

Having outlined the problems associated with residential care for children and the particular form of management found in social services departments (SSDs), this chapter explains the nature of the study conducted into these areas. This includes coverage of the origins of the project and the aims of the project set by the Department of Health, the sponsor. The core purpose of the work was to understand the nature of the external management of children's homes and to devote separate attention to the subject for the first time. The following sections outline the attempt made in the study to blend perspectives from the fields of child care, organisational studies and management as a means to shedding fresh light on the problem of external management.

The basis of the choice of a comparative-intensive design is presented while the chapter explains the relevance of the qualitative method and attendant techniques employed and the safeguards constructed. Care is taken to make clear the character of the data sources, the range of respondents, the form of observation conducted and the types of documentary information collected.

It will also be necessary to show how the project's orientation to the external management of children's homes rests on an 'inclusive' approach, embracing not only the immediate home and line manager. Coverage extends to those in service and resource functions, fieldworkers, senior managers, allied professionals, and the inspection and regulation fields at the local and the national level.

Understanding the sample of 12 local authorities covering four main authority types across England and Wales is approached with extra care. The sample not only provides a bridge with previous work on residential care, it also uses the previously unexplored categories such as the London and Unitary authorities. The types of regional and population characteristics that the sample contains are also made clear. The intention of the sample design is to ensure that common national themes may emerge whilst at the same time allowing comparisons across the four types to be made. Although mindful of the limitations of the framework, early findings pointed to certain shared aspects of residential care across the sample. These features of placement decision making and the demand and supply of residential provision are reported in the last section of this chapter.

The chapter concludes by reminding the reader of the main aims of the project in order to reveal how the findings are reported in a way which addresses those intentions, as well as structuring the book. In short, the six main elements of external management found in the sample SSDs are shown to be the basis for the subsequent Chapters 4–9.

3.1 Project outline

The study arose from the Department of Health's Research Initiative on Residential Care (DH 1998a). The Department 's concern with the external management of children's homes emerged from a set of anxieties. These included the inability of some authorities to detect serious misconduct, together with the inappropriate emphases in the management of homes highlighted by a series of inquiries (see Section 2.1). The research brief had one main thrust: the need for research to explain the external management process, with particular regard to the relationship between the home and line management.

A three year study resulted, between 1996–99, covering England and Wales and based on a comparative-intensive design which recognised different types of local authorities and contrasting approaches to the external management of homes. The project was carried out by a team of researchers. The members of the team brought together expertise in both the study of management and organisations in the private and public sectors as well as direct experience of working in health and social care. None of the team had conducted research into residential care before.

The main aims of the project were:

1. to provide an understanding of the models of management which inform the conduct of SSDs and how they impact on the external management of children's homes by local authorities in England and Wales;

2. to evaluate the appropriateness of the models of management being used and to suggest forms of management which might help to solve the key problems in the external management relationship;
3. to discover how far techniques of monitoring performance and of remedial intervention have been developed;
4. to develop a framework for the external management of children's homes which builds upon the specific context of the public sector, the needs of those involved and the factors which facilitate effective practice.

Subsidiary objectives included the need to extend existing research, link with other experts on residential care, and provide feedback to interested parties during the research process.

Perspectives

The project was developed by considering the contexts in which the problem had arisen, including the nature of child care institutions, developments in local authority SSDs and the wider upheavals in the public sector. The intention was to link such contexts to contemporary models of management, to recognise the potential for the nature of SSDs to shape the management of children's homes, to appreciate the subtleties of managerial processes, including their unintended consequences, and to employ a composite approach to performance evaluation (Whipp 1992).

The early phase of the research brought together a collection of specialist writing. These included: official reports (DH 1991a) and the technical accounts of child care (Morgan and Righton 1994), the general treatments of the public sector (including the formulation known as the 'New Public Management' (Hood 1991), and the established field of management and organisation (see e.g., Mintzberg 1993). This combination has produced a number of benefits.

The first was the confirmation of the gap in the literature on child care. Systematic research on the management of child care and especially residential care, is conspicuously absent. The subject of management is mentioned either at a very general level in relation to public services as a whole (James 1994), or obliquely via attempts to describe innovations in social work (Smale 1996).

The second advantage has been the opportunity to combine hitherto separate traditions of academic research with the intention of using fresh concepts and crafting an enhanced language to describe SSDs and residential care. The turbulence in such departments, for example, can be understood by employing frameworks from the management process literature. Child care professionals are concerned at the way radical upheavals dominate their departments (feedback from SSI workshops March 1997). The 'incremental' (Quinn 1980) or 'punctuated equilibrium' (Gersick 1991) models of innovation offer alternative ways for practitioners to frame the problem.

The third benefit to arise from combining different specialisms is a composite notion of evaluation. This meant assessing the models and practices of external management in terms of how far they help to deliver the goals specified by legislation, the Department of Health, and relevant professional bodies. There was also an opportunity to assess the actions of managers against established measures in the academic literature. This resulted in a set of evaluation criteria composed of the following:

i. management and organisational measures from the relevant literatures
ii. legislation and legal requirements (principally the *Children Act 1989*) in prevention and protection.
iii. Department of Health policies and guidelines which elaborate and extend the themes within the *Children Act 1989*, including the reports of the Support Force (1995), the Looking after Children programme, and *Matching Needs and Services* (1997).

The three groups of criteria produced a way of evaluating management practices against both recognised academic indicators and the specific requirements of the child care service seen in, for example, the need for service planning, service integration, inspection and placement planning. These criteria are used throughout the following chapters which examine such management practices in detail.

3.2   Method

The research method employed in the study was largely qualitative in character, as befits the first exploration of the subject in this form. It was not possible to use a quantitative approach since no prior work existed on which to build meaningful hypotheses. The aim instead was to help construct such propositions. The emphasis was on intensive, comparative examination of a relatively small number of local authorities thereby building knowledge of the management process from the ground up. Similar bases from the research tradition on child care settings have been successfully used by Packham and Hall (1996) or Whittaker *et al.* (1996). The method involved structured comparisons between similar organisational settings that would uncover differences in managerial outcomes related to residential care. It was recognised that detailed insights into a hitherto neglected area would be achieved, to a certain extent, at the expense of full generalisability. To this end, appropriate safeguards were employed in both the data collection techniques and sample rationale.

Data collection

The types of published, secondary sources consulted from the management and child care literatures have to an extent been outlined in the previous section and Chapters 1 and 2. Separate attention was devoted to the extensive body of reports, guidelines and published statistics which have grown up around the social services sector, examples of which will be found throughout this chapter. Documentary and archival material was sought in each case, including internal communications, reports and accounts. Insights were drawn as much from official departmental documents (produced for formal inquiries by the SSI for example) as from the working notes of individuals. The chapters that follow, however, have only been able to make limited reference to such material in order to protect the anonymity agreed with the local authorities that co-operated in the study.

Observational work took place both in the offices of the SSDs, residential homes and various types of local care and support centres. The aim was to witness the operation of the SSDs and residential homes concerned and to compare practice with official procedures and national guidelines. Observations occurred on an agreed basis, usually as part of an extended period of fieldwork that combined interview, desk work and observation of internal meetings. Around a quarter of the interviews and meetings took place inside residential units, often with children present in the home. Each researcher's working relationship with a case authority was both extensive and intensive. Intensive during the first year of study in order to assemble material and develop the necessary links; extensive in that data collection and feedback occurred over the three years of the project.

The intensive character of the study emphasised the triangulation of sources (interviews, observation, archival and secondary data) and their mutual testing (Denzin and Lincoln 1994). This was pursued by two means. The first was sought by the collection of the different data sources in parallel. The tensions that appeared between the results that arose from these sources were a major spur to the next stage of the cycle of questioning and interpretation in each case. As will be seen in the chapters dealing with the core aspects of external management, such divergences often pointed up serious differences of approach among those involved with the residential care of children. The second way of achieving triangulation was via the research team. Two people were assigned to each case: one as the lead researcher, the other to ensure that their colleague did not develop a partial or native view. The second member of the pair was also able to convey alternative or confirmatory results from their work on other cases in the sample. Each pair was obliged to report findings periodically to the team and to justify emerging interpretations. As broader results covering the whole project were developed, 'ownership' of each completed case was ceded by the pair concerned as each researcher explored and wrote up an overall theme which, by definition, ranged across the 12 cases.

'Exclusive' emphasis on the relationship between the children's home and the immediate line manager alone would be restrictive, given the project's aims. The study has sought, therefore, to take an 'inclusive' approach to the problem of external management (see Chapter 2). The approach forms the basis of our initial response to the project's fourth

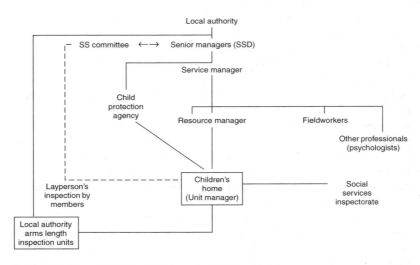

Figure 3.1 The external management of children's homes

main aim of constructing a framework for understanding the external management of children's homes (see Figure 3.1). This framework encompasses not only the home and line manager but also residential staff, service and resource managers, fieldworkers, senior managers, support staff, other professionals (from health and education, for example), those responsible for inspection, and members of social services committees. (The outcome of the 'inclusive' approach has been to work with the people represented in Appendices 1 and 2.) The result is an interview base of 261 transcripts.

In year 1 of the study the emphasis was on the larger users of residential care (both as providers of in-house care and/or contractors for out-of-authority placements). The assumption was that these high activity levels should provide the richest research settings for studying external management. Year 1 revealed the separate but related management issues when dealing with independent providers. The aim in years 2 and 3 was to give attention as well to the management models in private and voluntary suppliers (see especially London 3 case). Discussions with Department of Health staff, service professionals and those attending SSI regional workshops pointed to possible high levels of innovation or at least alternative modes of external management. This aim was reinforced by the discussions following the Burgner review (1996). This led to the collection of additional data including: interviews with two extra London boroughs responsible for new working arrangements with the private and voluntary sector; meetings with co-ordinators of regional databases (for London [Carebase], the north-west [NWASSA] and the west-midlands [Social Care Association]); and sessions with the co-ordinators of ADSS regional consortia. This additional data is reported in Chapter 9.

The study sought to maximise the contribution of organisations and individuals who are central to the social services and child care constituencies. The aim has sometimes been practical – as when informing the ADSS of our research – or, more specific, when drawing on the knowledge of an expert (e.g. Adrianne Jones). Organisations consulted included: SSI (at various levels and in different regions), the Support Force, NCB, NAIRC, BASW, ARCC and Children in Wales. Key individuals, such as Tim Brown, Jane Partington, Mike Simm or Keith Bilton, have been interviewed because of the relevance of their experience to a precise area of our study (e.g. Mike Simm in relation to his current advisory role for unitary authorities and their planning). Conventional exchanges have been made with relevant academics, sometimes through SSI or events organised by the Department of Health.

The research teams at York, Dartington and Luton have been extremely helpful.

The study's approach to the problem of external management, the issues contained in the *pro forma* document (see Appendix 1) and the rationale behind the sample frame were all scrutinised by the project's advisory group, made up of a mixture of policy experts from the Department of Health, leading academic authorities on child care, a member of the SSI and a director of social services not directly involved in the sample frame.

Presentations of emerging findings were made, for example, to four regional SSI events on residential care in 1997 and 1998. Team members have also participated in the Department of Health seminar chaired by Daniel Lambert on organisational structures and the workshop for residential care managers in Wales, organised by the Welsh Office. Interim feedback has been provided to the case authorities via planning and training events. The chance to check findings and discuss our interpretations with such audiences was essential for the construction of the results laid out below in Chapters 4–9. Presentations have been given to national consultation meetings for practitioners organised by, for example, Dartington, the ADSS in 1998 and the Children's Society in 2000.

3.3 Sample

The original sample frame reflected the comparative-intensive nature of the study. The first version was composed of the metropolitan, shire and London authority types, with three studies of each category, making a total of nine. The essence of that frame was retained but also expanded in the light of fieldwork. The main addition has been the unitary authority type to make a total of 12 (see Table 3.1).

The cases have been chosen so that they represent a spread of characteristics. The aim is to facilitate comparisons and provide an

Table 3.1 Sample frame

No. of pilot authorities	Authority type	Case studies		
3	Metropolitan	1	2	3
7	Shire	1	2	3
3	London	1	2	3
1	Unitary	1	2	3

appropriate test of findings. The main features of the sample are as follows:

Pilot work

The pilot work indicated in column 1 of Table 3.1 was necessary in the light of the research team's limited previous experience of residential child care settings. There was an enthusiastic response to a note summarising the research that appeared in the ADSS newsletter. Social services departments from across England and Wales were anxious to discuss the project in the light of their experience. The additional effort was exceptionally useful in piloting the *pro forma*, testing questions and confirming the inclusive approach discussed in the previous section.

Types of local authority

The use of the metropolitan and shire categories follows the pattern of earlier residential and child care studies. London boroughs are included due to the capital's unusual circumstances, seen, for example, in the extent of contracting, the political profile and the presence of specific problems such as refugee children. The additional time cost for the project was counter-balanced by the relatively small size of the London boroughs and their operations. A unitary authority category was added as a result of the first year's work and the major impact of local government reform in 1996/97. It appeared that although the reduced scale and resources of the new unitaries was a real concern, at the same time the potential for innovative approaches (in, for example, cross-departmental working) could be high.

The sample contained a mixed pattern in terms of political control with all three main political parties represented and two cases where there was no single party in an overall majority.

Regions

We were anxious to go beyond the limitations of previous work by including examples of local authorities from north and south. Most regions are represented – the north west (Shire 2 and Metro 3); the north east (Metro 2 and Unitary 3); the midlands (Shire 1 and Metro 1); London (3 cases); the south (Shire 3 and Unitary 1); and Wales (Unitary 2).

The 12 cases represent a mixture of urban and rural settings, varieties of economic well being, ethnic mix as well as large and small populations (see Table 3.2). There are also contrasts between authorities which cover large areas with dispersed populations, as in the shire counties and

Table 3.2   Population and children looked after rates in case authorities

Authority	1996			
	Total population	Population under 18	Population under 18 %	Children looked after rate per 10,000 under 18
Metropolitan districts				
Metro 1	1,017,500	260,480	25.6	56
Metro 2	725,000	163,125	22.5	71
Metro 3	221,800	53,232	24.0	51
Shire counties				
Shire 1	1,056,400	239,803	22.7	37
Shire 2	1,426,000	333,684	23.4	52
Shire 3	1,577,500	353,360	22.4	38
London boroughs				
London 1	204,000	48,144	23.6	54
London 2	175,200	36,792	21.0	98
London 3	293,400	61,614	21.0	38
Unitary authorities				
Unitary 1	180,000	51,000	28.3	47
Unitary 2	239,600	58,942	24.60	46
Unitary 3	142,800	34,558	24.20	46
Total England	48,903,600	12,030,286	24.60	44
Total Wales	2,916,800	717,533	24.60	42

Sources: Personal Social Services Statistics (CIPFA 1996; 1997) Children looked after by local authorities year ending 31 March 1996, England, Department of Health.

those with smaller, more concentrated settings, such as some of the unitary and London cases.

Reputation and looked after rates

The authorities studied encompass contrasting records of managing residential care, including those with high reputations (such as Metro 2 and Shire 3) and those who have experienced difficulties (Shire 1 and London 2, for example).

The sample authorities provide a variable profile in terms of looked after rates. Two shires and one London borough are below the looked after rate per 10,000 children under 18 for England and Wales. The rest exceed that level, in two instances by a large margin. It should be noted, therefore, that London 3 does not appear in the chapters on Line Management or Managing Staff since the authority was chosen in order to illustrate the issues associated with its reliance on the independent sector for residential care.

Leaving aside the recently created unitary authorities, the metropolitan, shire and London cases are representative of the broad trends in the use of residential care. All but one metropolitan authority and one London borough show declines in the percentage of looked after young people in residential care between 1991 and 1996 (see Table 3.3). The reduction was between 21 and 55 percent, a trend which broadly matches the change recorded in England for the same period (see *Children Looked After by Local Authorities Year Ending 31 March 1993, 1994, 1995 and 1996*, England tables).

Scale

The 12 authorities offer contrasting examples of the scale of operations in residential care to be managed. The difference is not simply between shire/metropolitan and London/unitary authorities. As Table 3.3 shows, there are marked contrasts within the metro and shire categories, in terms of number of children in residential care and the number of homes to be externally managed. The reasons for the divergent choices and how the resulting systems are managed lie at the heart of Chapters 4–9.

Structures

The sample has also provided the opportunity to examine the varying types of organisational structures within the SSDs. Using the framework developed by Challis (1990), Table 3.4 summarises the number of staff in children's services in each SSD and the structures in which they work. The basis of the table is that all SSDs can be classified using three dimensions of geography (division into zones, regions or area teams), function (FSW or resources) and client (adults or children). SSD structures are then classified by examining the character of the divisions created (i.e. functional, geographical or client-based) which exist at each level of the their hierarchies. The scheme begins by examining the level immediately below the director (AD) and works down *two* levels of the hierarchy.

Following this model it can be seen that, with the exception of two cases (Metros 1 and 2), all the SSDs had established client based structures. In doing so they were part of a more general trend that began in the 1980s, but was accelerated by the Children Act 1989 (Hall 1997). Table 3.4 also gives an indication of how the SSDs were organised below this level. It can be seen, for example, that, of the nine cases with a client

Table 3.3 Trends in the use of children's residential care by case authorities

Authority	1991			1996			Actual change in % in residential care 1991–96	Number of children's homes (1997)
	Total no. looked after	Number in residential care	% in residential care	Total number looked after	Number in residential care	% in residential care		
Metro 1	1,758	466	26.5	1,456	275	18.9	−28.7	26
Metro 2	1,284	368	28.7	1,151	153	13.3	−53.6	21
Metro 3	383	91	23.8	272	29	10.7	−55.1	6
Shire 1	1,166	180	15.4	896	172	19.2	24.4	8
Shire 2	2,135	648	30.4	1,722	400	23.2	−23.5	39*
Shire 3	1,330	139	10.5	1,344	110	8.2	−21.7	10
London 1	275	61	22.2	261	45	17.2	−22.3	4
London 2	N/A	N/A	N/A	373	94	25.2	29.7	8
London 3	217	68	31.3	232	44	19.0	−39.5	—
Unitary 1			Not	Applicable				
Unitary 2			Not	Applicable				4
Unitary 3			Not	Applicable				5

Note: * Not including homes for children with disabilities.
Source: Children in Care of Local Authorities Year ending March 1991–96. England, Department of Health.

Table 3.4 The organisational structures of 12 case SSDs

Authority	First level sub-division	Second level	Management structure of residential services	Levels between UM and SS director	Total staff in children's services 1995*
Metro 1	*Functional* [Resources/ FSW]	*Client* [Within 'Resources' division]	*Fragmented* [2 zones]	5	1,428
Metro 2	*Functional* [Resources/ FSW]	*Client* [Within 'Resources' division]	*Unified*	5	981
Metro 3	*Client* [Child/ Adult]	*Functional* [Within 'Child' division]	*Unified*	4	342
Shire 1	*Client* [Child/ Adult]	*Functional* [Within division] 'Child'	*Fragmented* [4 Areas]	5	860
Shire 2	*Client* [Child/ Adult]	*Geographic* [Within 'Child' division]	*Fragmented* [9 sub regions]	5	1,465
Shire 3	*Client* [Child/ Adult]	*Functional* [Within 'Child' division]	*Unified*	5	867
London 1	*Client* [Child/ Adult]	*Functional* [Within 'Child' division]	*Unified*	3	229
London 2	*Client* [Child/ Adult]	*Functional* [Within 'Child' division]	*Unified*	4	265
London 3	*Client* [Child Adult]	N/A	N/A	N/A	102
Unitary 1	*Client* [Child/ Adult]	*Functional* [Within 'Child' division]	*Unified*	3	200
Unitary 2	*Client* [Child/	*Geographic* [Within	*Unified*	3	254

Table 3.4   Continued

Authority	First level sub-division	Second level	Management structure of residential services	Levels between UM and SS director	Total staff in children's services 1995*
	Adult]	'Child' division]			
Unitary 3	*Client* [Child/ Adult]	*Functional* [Within 'Child' division]	*Unified*	4	256

* *Source*: *Personal Social Services Statistics (CIPFA, 1996).*

structure (excluding London 3), seven had further subdivided opera-tions along functional lines (a spilt between resources and FSW). The remaining SSDs were sub-divided along geographical lines (with a tier of regional or area managers responsible for both FSW and resources).

A final point to make about Table 3.4 is with regard to the organisa-tional structures for children's residential care (also see chapter 6). In the third column it can be seen that eight SSDs adopted *unified* structures, with all homes (and other resources) managed as part of a single divi-sion. By contrast, three cases had *fragmented* structures, indicating that children's homes fell under the responsibility of different, region-based, managers. A key advantage of this arrangement was that local managers were given freedom to 'consume their own smoke' (Shire 2). The down-side, however, was a lack of 'corporacy' (Director: Shire 3) and problems associated with the co-ordination of services.

3.4   Supply and demand for residential care

The early comparisons made of the case authorities selected also provide insights into the character of residential care across England and Wales. This general profile highlights key elements of the general context in which those responsible for managing residential care operate; it also offers a first sense of some of the core issues and findings to be discussed in subsequent chapters. The main features which stand out across the authorities relate to the nature of placement decision making and the demand and supply of residential provision.

Table 3.5 Unplanned admissions to residential care and occupancy levels in case SSDs

Authority	% Estimates of proportion of unplanned' admissions to non-disabilities residential care (own provision) 1996/97*	Average % occupancy levels in own residential provision 1996+
Metro 1	80	58
Metro 2	60	89
Metro 3	—	Not available
Shire 1	—	99
Shire 2	37	80
Shire 3	73	82
London 1	—	85
London 2	80	85
Unitary 1	—	Not available
Unitary 2	50	80
Unitary 3	—	69

* Based on estimates provided by line managers and placement officers.
+ *Source*: *Personal Social Services Statistics, 1995/96* (CIPFA: 1995/96).

Unplanned and emergency admissions

The first point to make is that, to a greater or lesser extent, all eleven cases were unable to conform fully with expectations (DH 1991b) that placements will be planned and 'appropriate' given assessed needs. A significant proportion of admissions to in-house children's homes were made on an emergency or unplanned basis. The estimates presented in Table 3.5 give some indication of the seriousness of this problem. The proportion of unplanned placements is over 30 per cent in all cases. This picture is largely consistent with other studies which have estimated the proportion of unplanned admissions as ranging between 50 per cent (Sinclair and Gibbs 1996) and 80 per cent (SFCRC 1996).

In addition, we noted a trend in which the SSDs were 'shoe-horning children into vacancies in unsuitable establishments' (DH 1997: 22). While this practice was most pronounced in those SSDs with fewer in-house resources (see Table 3.6), it also applied to the larger providers. As the Director of Shire 2 admitted: 'At the end of the day no authority is likely to have at its fingertips ... the whole spectrum of resources and facilities that will meet every need ... So, almost inevitably, you might have to learn to describe needs in a different way so that they fit your statement of purpose ... that's the harsh reality.'

Table 3.6 Levels of specialisation in own residential care in case SSDs

	Number of children's homes	Categories of home	Organisation of residential services	Date of last re-structuring of residential	Basis for specialisation
Metro 1	31	2 CHEs, 9 Group 1, 14 Group 2, 6 Disability	Functional	1991	Historical
Metro 2	21	2 Resource centres; 3 Leaving care; 1 Secure; 2 'Therapeutic'; 2 Respite/long term; 4 Short term	Functional	1994	Survey of users' perceptions of current need
Metro 3	6	2 Resource centres; 4 Respite/disability	Functional	1996	Management Blueprint
Shire 1	8	2 Long term; 4 Short term (multi-purpose); 2 Respite/disability	Functional (Homes aim to serve local needs)	1996	Management Blueprint
Shire 2	39*	2 CHEs; 9 Resource centres; 28 Community homes (mix of long, short term and leaving care)	Geographic (9 districts/3 regions)	1993	Partly historical, partly linked to management blueprint

Shire 3	10	2 Leaving care; 1 Short-term emergency (younger ages); 5 Disability	Functional	1996	Survey of users' perceptions of current need
London 1	4	2 Resource centres; 2 Long-term	Functional	1994	Management Blueprint
London 2	8	3 Short-stay emergency; 3 Long-stay; 2 Respite/Disability	Functional	1994	Historical
Unitary 1	3	2 Respite/Disability; 1 Short-term	Functional	1997 (LGR)	Historical
Unitary 2	4	1 Emergency/short-term 3 'Multi-purpose,	Functional	1996 (LGR)	Historical
Unitary 3	5	1 'Challenging behaviour'; 2 Short-term; 1 Respite/disability; 1 Resource centre	Functional	1997 (LGR)	Survey of users' perceptions of current need

Note: * Does not include disability/respite homes which are managed separately.

Reduction of supply

A variety of factors seemed to have contributed to this situation. There was a general decline in the supply of residential beds in all the case SSDs (see Chapter 1). Many followed the trend of Metro 1, where it was reported that since 1991, 'the Department's internal provision of residential care has reduced by 30% and the provision of family based care has increased slightly ...' (Strategic Plan 1997). Only in one case (Metro 2) were there any concrete plans to expand in-house residential provision and that was part of a refurbishment strategy.

Specialisation

Linked to this reduction in supply was the inability of SSDs to differentiate internal provision in order to expand choice (see Chapter 4). Generally, two broad approaches to 'specialisation' had been pursued. First, were those SSDs (Shire 1 and Metro 3) which had designated their children's homes as primarily 'multi-purpose' establishments geared to taking referrals from the local community. As the director of Shire 1 explained, these homes were 'just good, honest to goodness, bog standard children's homes'. The remaining authorities, to a greater or lesser extent had attempted to develop specialisation by function as authority-wide resources (with the exception of Shire 2). In the smaller SSDs, this functional specialisation was extremely limited, at best involving some split between short term intake units and long stay establishments which were generally undifferentiated (Unitary 2) or 'all over the place' (Unitary 1).

It was, therefore, only in the larger SSDs, in effect Metros 1 and 2 and Shires 2 and 3, that any serious attempt had been made to specialise. Moreover, of these four, it was only in Shire 3 and Metro 2 that the specialisation of units had been informed by any kind of survey of local needs. In Metro 1, statement's of purpose and function had been determined 'bottom-up'. In Shire 2, a strategy of creating local resource centres and supporting units had been imposed centrally. Interestingly, the largest provider in this sub group, Shire 2 (with 39 children's homes) had been the least successful in terms of differentiating its resources. As one unit manager explained:

> We have got a massive residential base but its very limited and inflexible in the fact that you have got maybe your 3 strands of care. You have got your secure, structured CHEs. You have got your short term structured resource centres and you have got your long term, far less structured and less staffed children's homes ... Three pigeonholes.

The general picture was that with the possible exception of Metro 2 and Shire 3, the level of specialisation in the eleven SSDs was limited. Such a profile is entirely consistent with the observations made by other studies (Berridge and Brodie 1997: 91). Sinclair and Gibbs (1996: 64–5), for example, note how most statements of purpose are vague and best described as 'general purpose' or 'all things to all people'.

High occupancy levels

A further contributory factor to the high number of inappropriate and unplanned admissions were the high levels of occupancy in most children's homes (see Table 3.5). When questioned about this and the possibilities of maintaining some slack or a "vacancy factor" (SFCRC 1996), most senior managers replied that political demands to maximise the utilisation of expensive residential resources ruled out such a policy. According to the director of Unitary 1, for example,

> Utting said, you need to keep a certain number of placements vacant in order to give you some flexibility. If you keep places vacant in a children's home, the unit costs then start to go up and the district auditor comes in and says 'Why are you running children's homes that are costing you £1,200 a week when you could run for £800?'

Other factors which seemed to contribute to very high occupancy rates in homes were practices such as 'bed blocking' (e.g. in Metro 1) whereby unit managers retained a high degree of control over vacancies by assigning names to beds. Also evident were the problems of children in long term residential care being 'unassigned' for long periods due to work loads. This reduced throughput in some children's homes almost to a snail's pace (especially in Shire 2).

Demand

As mentioned earlier, the perception of many informants was that the demand for residential care had continued to outstrip supply. However, as Packman and Hall (1996) explain, demand for residential care is a complex matter, related to a number of factors including socio-economic conditions, operational contingencies and the 'working philosophies' of social work teams. In the case of the SSDs, a similar complexity was evident when trying to compare demand. A particular issue was that many placements were not as a consequence of a positive choice based on a clear assessment. Reflecting a much wider trend (Millham *et al.* 1986; DH 1991c), the strategy of seeking family placement as a first option for all young people was either implicit or part of a stated policy. In some SSDs this had been taken to extreme lengths with clear strategies for avoiding longer term residential placements at all costs. At Metro 3, for example, one line manager explained that,

> Residential care should be the very last resort. That has angered some people because they are saying that residential care should be seen as a positive option, which we agree with. I don't think that the residential care that we are providing is bad, but I think that we could do better elsewhere. ... I don't dislike residential care, I just don't think its the best thing for kids and I don't think children should be living in residential care all their lives.

Although not all field social workers shared this negative view of residential care the dominant practice overall was to pursue other options in the 'looked after' system first. Partly as a consequence of this a significant proportion of residential placements were made on an emergency or unplanned basis. Because residential care was often used as a last report, the demand for placements only came after a breakdown had occurred elsewhere in the system and no alternatives were left (DH 1997).

A further point to note is that, in many cases, demand for residential care was essentially supply driven. As one fieldwork manager in Metro 1 argued, 'You don't get a "we need this many homes for kids" – you get a response "we've got this many places – go and get some kids in" '. In all cases, fieldwork staffs remarked on how they were increasingly managing unacceptable levels of risk and that the existence of residential beds was always regarded as a potential means of reducing this pressure – a fallback position. In at least two SSDs (Unitary 1 and London 1), this view had begun to inform management strategies aimed at reducing demand by cutting supply. As a fieldwork manager in London 1 explained for example:

> I think what we've found that as long as there is a unit open, people will fill it whereas once you close it, then people do look more for family placements. Its quite interesting. When we closed the unit, out of the 6 young people that were there, only one went to residential. One went home, 2 went to grandparents, and the other 3 went to other family placements. I think that kind of bears out what we were saying. The strategy does focus on reducing demand and that's partly because of budgetary considerations.

Refocussing

By contrast, in other SSDs more positive approaches towards reducing demand – which involved preserving some in-house residential provision – had been adopted. A key way in which this had occurred was through the development of various refocussing initiatives and attempts to prevent young people from entering the looked after system. At Metros 1, 2 and 3 and Shire 2, for example, a number of family support teams or resource centres had been established. They offered a range of outreach services targeted towards adolescent youths and their families. The effectiveness of these services was variable. In cases such as Metro 1, they were resented by professional social workers. The clearest example of a successful team was in Metro 3 where, between 1995 and 1996, the intake of adolescent youths into the looked-after system had been reduced by 92 per cent (Annual Report 1997). According to the director, this initiative had a key impact in terms of creating a degree of slack within other parts of the looked-after system, including the residential:

> That has been important for our strategy because I think it has allowed us to see the wood through the trees really. It has allowed us to move from a reactive mode and simply grappling with all cases coming through. Clearly we are still under pressure from demand but, in the main, we were able then to think 'OK, we have steadied the ship quite considerably'. We have probably got the youngsters coming in to public care who, by and large, will definitely need to be ... It gave us a chance to reflect and do some more quality work.

Conclusion

This chapter has sought to explain the character of the project and the origins of the study. The aims of the project were set by the Department of Health. In trying to understand the nature of the external management of children's homes, the study has sought to break new ground by attempting to link the fields of child care, organisational studies and management. The researchers did so with some caution since the topic had not been the subject of a separate study before. The choice of a comparative-intensive design was also governed largely by the absence of previous empirical attention or conceptual development on the subject. The chapter has also sought to explain the basis of the qualitative method and specific techniques employed. The character of the data sources used and their means of collection should by now be clear, including the range of respondents from the case authorities, the form of observation used and types of documentary information acquired. Particular attention was given to the safeguards constructed in order to convey how the process of triangulation of data and interpretation worked in practice together with the obligations of the research team.

The previous pages have also shown how in order to understand the external management of children's homes the study adopted an 'inclusive' approach to the problem. This orientation embraces the immediate home and line manager but also extends to those represented in Figure 3.1. The list ranges from residential staff, service and resource managers through to fieldworkers, senior managers, support and allied professionals and those responsible for inspection and regulation at local and national level. As will become apparent, this inclusive schema not only provided the map which guided data collection in each case, it also addresses the project's fourth main aim of creating a framework for understanding the external management of children's homes.

A separate inspection was made of the balanced sample of 12 local authorities covering four main authority types. The sample frame contains a mixture of features. It both provides a potential link with previous work (in the Shire and Metropolitan categories) but also seeks to include new categories and dimensions; these include the London and Unitary authorities and the bringing together of regional and population characteristics. Such a framework is designed to ensure that recurrent national themes may be grasped as well as offering a platform for comparisons and contrasts across the four types. Any findings that emerge should do so from an appropriately searching test. Whilst the study acknowledges the limits to yielding fully generalisable outcomes, even in the first phases of the project it was clear that certain general characteristics of residential care were shared across the sample. These features of placement decision making and the demand and supply of residential provision (such as high occupancy levels and an apparent lack of specialisation, for example) supplied many key questions and starting points for the fieldwork in each of the cases.

The main aims of the project centre on understanding and evaluating the models of management in the external management of children's homes (see Section 3.1) and suggesting solutions to some of the key problems of management. The findings of the project are reported accordingly so as to address those intentions in the following way. Six areas of activity stand out as central in their importance to the form of external management found in the sample SSDs. Each is dealt with in a separate chapter as follows:

- Chapter 4 strategic management
- Chapter 5 the management of child placement
- Chapter 6 line management
- Chapter 7 the management of staff
- Chapter 8 monitoring and control
- Chapter 9 the management of external placements.

It is by examining each of these in turn in the following chapters that one is able to respond to the first aim of the project and to see the main components of the model of management, what informs it and how it operates at the level of practice and in the context described in this and the previous chapter.

Chapters 4–9 all share a common structure in order to satisfy the second broad aim of evaluating the elements of this model of external management (Section 4 of each chapter) and pointing to alternative means of improvement (Section 5 of each chapter). The individual chapters, therefore, contain the following sections in common:

1. A summary of the official requirements and guidance relevant to the management area concerned;
2. An outline of appropriate parts of the management literature which relate to the management activity in question;
3. An account of the experiences of the aspect of external management in the sample cases;
4. An evaluation of the management practices seen in the 12 authorities; and
5. A set of practical recommendations.

In responding to the second project aim, of evaluating the appropriateness of the models of management being used, a combined method was adopted. The three criteria were derived from recognised indicators from the management literature (Section 2 of each chapter), the obligations arising from relevant legislation and lastly the standards set by evolving good practice norms (Section 1 of each chapter) within the child care sector (seen in, for instance, service integration, and placement planning).

The third and specific project aim of discovering how far monitoring performance and the means of remedial intervention have been developed is primarily tackled in Chapter 8.

In the conclusion chapter, we return to the fourth aim of the study and the inclusive framework for grasping the external management of children's homes which was initiated earlier in this chapter. The construct is reassessed in the light of the findings in the core chapters. In addition, the implications of both for the most recent reforms in the residential care field and the wider body of knowledge on the public sector and management are addressed.

4
Strategy and Implementation

Introduction

The emphasis in Chapters 4 to 9 will be on the key processes involved in the external management of children's homes. In this chapter, attention is given to the activity that has the potential to link such processes – the development of strategic thinking and planning in relation to children's services and residential care.

Outside social services, the use of the word 'strategy' and its adjective 'strategic' has become pervasive. In practice, their adoption is often motivated by a desire to enhance the status of a project or department within an organisation (Lyles 1990). At the same time, an extensive body of academic research devoted to the issue of business strategy developed during the 1980s. It is unsurprising therefore, that both the Department of Health (DH) and social services departments (SSDs) turned to notions of strategy as they wrestled with the problems associated with the provision of children's services described in previous chapters.

As this chapter will show, the results have not been straightforward. The aim of the following sections is, therefore, to examine the way the concept of strategy has been applied in this sector, and more particularly, to report on how a strategic approach to children's services and residential care has been attempted in the case authorities. In subsequent chapters, a picture will emerge of the content of the strategies adopted by the sample SSDs, including the core elements of specialisation, needs analysis and placement. This chapter is more concerned with how given strategies are created and, above all, implemented.

In order to accomplish its task, the chapter moves through four main phases. Section 4.1 gives an outline of the local government sector and

Table 4.1 Strategy and related meetings during one year in the children's division of an SSD

Strategy meetings/discussions	= 285 per annum
Child protection conferences	
– ICC	= 84 per annum
– Reviews	= 108 per annum
Number of children looked after	= 151 per annum
Foster carer reviews	= 71 per annum
Regulation 22 reports	= 60 per annum
Number of children out of county placements	= 6 per annum
Secure accommodation reviews	= 2 per annum (approx.)
Support force check list	= 2/3 per annum (approx.)
Adoption reviews	= 5/6 per annum (approx.)

Source: Internal document Unitary 1.

the child care area and how both have been affected by the more general enthusiasm for strategic thinking. The time taken up by such activity is illustrated by Unitary 1 in our sample, and its list of meetings per year devoted to strategy and related children's services' issues (see Table 4.1). Planning is an accepted activity within local authorities but to what extent it supports a more strategic approach to conducting local services is questionable. In the children and residential care spheres, the injunctions to adopt a strategic orientation are many, not least from Department of Health inquiries and reports. Whilst the message is unequivocal, the technical advice, especially in relation to implementation, is more limited.

Section 4.2 of the chapter is devoted to the specialist research on strategy and planning. Its purpose is to act as a reminder that the subject is contentious. Competing understandings exist which take different positions on the extent to which planning can be fully rational. An awareness of the subjective dimension of strategic activity may prove useful in understanding the mixed record of SSDs in constructing appropriate plans for children and families divisions and then putting them into practice.

Such observations prepare the reader for the findings from the study data. As in the other external management processes, the adoption of a strategic approach by SSDs to children's services is shown to be still at an early stage. This is the subject of Section 4.3. There is considerable variation in what research and local data informs departmental plans, as to who is involved and what structures facilitate their development. Interesting commonalties appear in what precipitates strategic plans. Section 4.4 deals separately with the process of implementation. It is clear that departments with often quite sophisticated analyses are unable to realise such goals due to weaknesses in translating plans into everyday use. The ability to recognise the implementation problem, to generate appropriate information, to involve residential staff and manage resistance are critical to the operationalisation of new plans. Without them, homes with statements of purpose appropriate to patterns of local need, specialised units, or alternative forms of placement often fail to materialise.

4.1 Strategy and residential care in social services departments

Strategic approaches to residential care

Those responsible for planning in the area of children and residential care have received extra attention from the Department of Health. Advice on a strategic approach in particular has been forthcoming throughout the 1990s.

The *National Health Service and Community Care Act, 1990* gave SSDs the responsibility to manage the social care market. The onus was placed on departments to plan strategically with an emphasis on assessing the needs of the whole district (Hall 1997: 14). Meanwhile, with regard to residential care, *The Children Act* (Department of Health 1991b) emphasised the need for a strategic approach, a call that has been reinforced in subsequent reports.

The first Utting review (DH 1991a) pointed to the lack of a 'coherent policy framework' for residential care in local authorities with the residential element seldom part of a wider strategic plan for child care. His report recommended that managing residential care 'must be framed in terms of an overall policy for residential care which is not free-standing but forms part of a wider policy covering a whole range of child care policies and services' (DH 1991a: 46). The Audit Commission confirmed the undeveloped nature of planning in 1994. It drew particular attention to the paucity of systematic needs analysis for given populations and how few authorities used data on need to redesign services (Audit Commission 1994: 19). The report called for a 're-balancing' of resources in SSDs away from a reliance on residential care (op.cit.: 43) towards family support activities, thereby freeing resources for reinvestment (ibid.: 56).

The findings of the Support Force for Children's Residential Care sustained the call for enhanced forms of strategic thinking. It concluded that,

> For residential child care to succeed as a quality resource requires sustained attention at the policy making level. It requires a recognition by senior managers of the valuable role residential care can play in promoting the welfare of young people, a commitment to a strategic and managed approach to its planning and delivery. (SFCRC 1996: 4)

The Support Force also published strategic planning frameworks to help improve collaboration between agencies and also engaged with SSDs who took up its offer of consultation (SFCRC 1995a, 1995b).

In 1996, the Dartington Social Research Unit (1996b) issued its Matching Needs and Services methodology. The aim was to assist managers in identifying local needs and redesigning services accordingly. The starting point of the report was that existing services tend to be 'supply led' (op.cit.: 28) and that much planning in local authorities is based on short-term enthusiasm and 'ill conceived organisational change' (op.cit.: 46: see also Dartington 1996a: 49). The Looking After Children (LAC) materials developed by the same Unit, and promoted by the Department of Health, raise the prospect for SSDs of identifying systematically the needs of individual children and the action required. Aggregate data could be produced for the looked after population to be used in planning (Rowlands 1995: 150).

In spite of the range of reports and recommendations issued during this period since the *Children Act, 1989*, implementation has been a problem. The Dartington team (1996b: 15) found that dissemination and development of such guidance at local level was 'piecemeal'. Advisory work by the Social Sciences Inspectorate in Wales is informed by the same concerns (Social Services Inspectorate for Wales 1995). Interviews with inspectors and members of the groups set up to assist SSDs following the Support Force reinforce the problem of implementation. As one put it:

> most [children's services plans] were merely descriptive, or if there were strategic intentions, they weren't really in any way linked to any form of implementation programme. The difficulty was ... the failure to implement things, or the failure to know whether you've implemented.

Local authorities

The situation in SSDs bears the imprint of the problems faced by local authorities. Packham and Hall (1996: 153–4) speak of the 'chronic organisational turbulence'. The Local Government Management Board also found that SSDs are particularly vulnerable to unpredictability in service demand and political intervention (Leach 1997: 3).

It is widely recognised that the local government sector provides a challenging setting in which to develop strategic approaches to service delivery. A brief consideration of this environment may aid a more realistic appreciation of the circumstances in the children's divisions of SSDs. Three features are worth emphasising: the difficulties local authorities face in planning, the limitations of available data, and the emergence of a 'corporate model'.

The problems that confront local government's attempts to operate strategically are considerable. Strategic thinking has to encompass economic, social and demographic factors, to respond to the demands of different users, and to deploy scare resources over which they have limited control. The relationship between policy and planning is problematic (Worrall *et al.* 1996: 16). The assumptions behind strategic analysis differ from those that inform public policy creation. Policy does not necessarily rely on theory nor data and may be discontinuous, even inconsistent, for political reasons (Gregory 1989).

The lack of appropriate information, or the ability to mobilise it when making strategic decisions is a widespread difficulty. Recent studies of UK local government's response to financial constraints discovered that particular directions are chosen with very limited support information and 'on the basis of soundings and other informal know-how transfer generated through social and professional networks' (Bovaird and Davis 1997: 7). The Society of Information Technology Managers reports indicate that barely 50 per cent of local authorities have an information systems strategy (SOCITM 1994). Studies of service quality in local government find the use of formal indicators is, as yet, low (Davison and Grieves 1996). It is also apparent that authorities are subject to the rigidities of conventional approaches to financial information. Most use incremental budgeting (building on the previous year's budget) against a background of widely differing forms of priority setting. An awareness of such constraints will become relevant when considering the ability of the case authorities to create and implement a strategic approach to children and residential care.

In the light of these difficulties, it would be easy to build a picture of local authorities as comparatively weak in strategic management

(Bryson 1998: 42). Although this might be consistent with the low innovation potential of the professional bureaucracy outlined in Chapter 2, as a conclusion it is oversimplified. The strategic capabilities of authorities such as Cheshire County Council, Wrekin Council or Kirklees Metropolitan District Council are recognised as leading examples (Worrall *et al.* 1996: 16). Nutt and Backoff (1992) also point to instances of authorities which have used public needs to produce innovative strategic management (see also Leach 1997). Furthermore, the forces that have been labelled the 'New Public Management' have enhanced the role of managers and created new forms of organisation through which public services are delivered (Ashburner and Ferlie 1994). Local government has sought to break services down into smaller, more autonomous provider units that should deliver services to clients with specific needs. Meanwhile, the centre specialises in a 'strategic, co-ordinating and controlling role' (Kessler and Purcell 1996: 209). The notion of the 'enabling' authority (which links public services with private and voluntary agencies via a market relationship) is, after all, predicated on its ability to generate plans, use appropriate data on need and involve the user (Wistow *et al.* 1994: 17).

4.2   Strategy and planning

The body of academic research on strategy is extensive. Contrary to the impression given by some commentators, planning and strategic decision making may take many contrasting forms. Sharply differing frameworks exist for understanding strategic processes within organisations. It is not necessary to survey the field comprehensively (cf. Whipp 2002), yet even a brief summary raises important issues which could inform an understanding of the character of strategic activity in SSDs. What stands out is the danger of regarding planning in practice as a totally logical or objective exercise. As will be apparent later in Section 4.3, those SSDs that appreciate the limitations within the strategy process stand the greater chance of crafting more durable policies and programmes of care.

Approaches

There are a variety of approaches to strategic decision making. The oldest and most established is the planning perspective. Strategies are said to develop through an intentional process involving a logical view of an organisation. In this approach, clear objectives are set by senior management, information is rationally assessed and strategic options are judged against criteria which reflect strategic goals. Strategies are passed down through the organisation via specific plans and implemented by those below (Andrews 1971). In essence, strategy is seen as the 'determination of the basic long-term goals of an organisation, and the adoption of courses of action and the allocation of resources necessary for carrying out these goals' (Chandler 1962: 13). This view has enjoyed prominence since it emphasises rational assumptions about the future and the reduction of uncertainty.

Whilst practitioners, consultants and policy makers have adopted the planning perspective enthusiastically, it has often proved disappointing in use. The major problem lies in its failure to engage with the less objective aspects of an organisation. Social, political and cognitive dimensions are ignored. Building on the identification of management as a process in Chapter 2, it is possible to recognise strategy generation and implementation as not simply linear but a more demanding activity. Management research provides five main additional frameworks.

The first is the logical incremental perspective. Strategies are seen to be created in an intentional way but, contrary to the planning approach, strategies are reassessed and modified throughout their development and implementation (Quinn 1982). Options are continually experimented with, through partial implementation. In the second variant, the political perspective, strategies are viewed as emerging through the processes of bargaining and compromise between interest groups, each attempting to achieve their own ends. A commonly acceptable strategy is adopted because it meets the requirements of those who influence the decision processes and not solely because it satisfies objective criteria (Johnson 1987).

The third approach is labelled the interpretive since it maintains that strategies are the product of cognition rather than an objective response to a given context. It is important, therefore, to appreciate the shared mental models of organisational members which they use to interpret new situations and guide behaviour. Strategies develop in accord with such assumptions and accepted 'recipes' (Schwenk 1989). The fourth orientation to strategy is termed the visionary perspective. In this case, the strategy of an organisation comes from a vision – a desired future state – that is associated primarily with an individual or small group. This directs the organisation's strategy and the process by which its strategic decisions are made (Trice and Beyer 1986). The last type of approach is the ecological perspective. External constraints operate to prescribe strategic options and limit the discretion organisational members may play in their selection. The development of a strategy is akin to natural selection in biology rather than an openly rational choice (Aldrich 1971).

The strategy field within management studies therefore offers three important observations to those studying strategy in particular locations such as social services departments. First, that planning is but one element in the construction of strategic choices and programmes of action. Furthermore, the conventional association of planning only with logically ordered sequences of design and execution is misplaced. Second, that so many different types of strategic decision making have been discovered is a reminder of the complexity of such processes. Different variants of strategic decision making may occur within the same organisation. And, third, that the link between strategic choices and operational forms is inherently problematic. As will become clear, SSDs are not exceptions to such findings.

4.3   Creating strategic plans for children's services and residential care

The understanding of strategic decision making processes in general and in local authorities, presented in the previous sections, suggests a two-fold examination of our case SSDs. The first deals with the way departments construct their plans for residential and other forms of care. This includes: what informs their thinking? who makes the plans? and what organisational forms do they require? This allows separate attention to be given to how such plans are implemented in Section 4.

Major influences

In truth, the 12 SSDs have been subject to a wealth of influences as they have addressed the requirement to plan their residential and related provision. The dominant forces which have shaped their thinking come under the headings of: inheritance, specialisation, costs and catalysts.

1. Inherited assumptions: Although it takes on different forms, the prevailing orthodoxy and assumptions regarding residential care weighed heavily on the managers in four authorities. The influence was at its most potent in Shire 2. Staff at all levels 'believe very strongly, that there is a culture of just expecting accommodation when it is requested' (unit manager) and where 'residential care has been the only option' (youth justice manager). The result has been that the county remained one of the largest providers of in-house residential care in England. A similar atmosphere has been maintained in Metro 2 with its 'big establishments, big budgets, big structures' (development manager). The impact on senior staff from members can be restrictive. As the director of Metro 2 explains:

> There's no point in me walking into my committee and saying 'why don't we do it this way because Bradford, Manchester, Newcastle do it this way?'. ... So I can't use other people's work as examples of good practice, as a persuasive argument.

Strong local traditions of social services provision could also be more positive (as in Metro 1 and Unitary 2) when public support for residential care helped to ensure children's homes were a real part of SSD plans. *2. Specialisation:* Needs analysis and specialisation in residential care provision informed SSD plans to widely varying degrees. The strongest use of a matching needs and services approach leading to the re-designation of provision appears in Metro 2, Shire 3 and Unitary 3. It is noteworthy too, how all three departments also shared a general commitment to residential care that informed their determination to redesign it. Metro 2 reordered its 21 homes into functional areas including: secure unit, leaving care, family resource centres/short-term respite and emergency units, therapeutic units (long term) learning disabilities, long-term gender spilt, short-term rehabilitation, PACE beds.

Similarly, Shire 3's specialisation initiative involved a clear commitment to 'therapeutic services' in order to deal appropriately with especially damaged children. In the words of the AD:

> I do actually think that some young people need structured residential care. I actually believe some young people require it. I don't see it as a last resort ... but its got to be well managed. It can't be like a zoo for kids.

Consequently, the department carried out an audit of 14 children's homes in order to understand the management processes involved: how children were referred, what decision-making processes led to admittance, what were the general outcomes? The audit was published in 1994 with 34 recommendations on how to redesign the service. A 'child needs survey' was also conducted based on a 120 item questionnaire. The result was the reshaping of provision around the types of home, with an emergency unit to act as a vital buffer and the appointment of a placement resource manager to centralise resources. Unitary 3 has taken a similar course of analysis and action.

The attempts by Metros 1 and 3, Shire 2 and London 2 were more fragmented and incomplete. Metro 3 unbalanced its strategy of specialisation by emphasising its family support work at the expense of residential placements. Metro 1 found it more difficult to link analysis of need and implementation. Most importantly, it placed an overdue reliance on foster provision and the closure of residential units. It is interesting that those authorities which placed cost cutting as the highest short-term priority were also associated with the weakest examples of specialisation based on needs analysis (London 1 and 3).

3. *Catalysts* Whilst the inherited context of SSDs and the objective of specialisation are the dominant internal forces that shape strategic approaches to residential care, a third factor requires attention in order to complete the picture. All the case authorities' strategic thinking was affected by external catalysts. These took the form of official inquiries, the appointment of new directors of social services from outside, and local government reorganisation.

In the case of Metro 3, a SSI report in 1994 devastated the department and forced the management to rethink its entire residential policy. In the words of the assistant director responsible for children's services:

> It was shocking because the borough and the staff felt that they ran a blue ribbon service ... [in fact] we had burnt-out staff, no policies, some homes were dirty, no investment in it, no understanding of what work went on ... So, all sorts of difficulties, just actually saying: 'you don't know what you're doing in providing residential care.'

During our period of study, Shire 1 and London 2 were approaching residential care in the shadow of major scandals that had been investigated and reported on in the early 1990s. The senior management of London 2 used the results of four separate investigations as a platform for their combined policy of beginning to specialise provision, cut down out-of-borough placements and centralise control.

Five of the case authorities found that the arrival of a new director of social services had a dramatic impact on the department's orientation towards residential care (Shires 1, 2 and 3, London 1 and 2, and Metro 3 at AD level). Metro 3, Shire 1 and London 2 experienced the combined impact of a new director and the results of a critical inquiry. As in other sectors, the incoming appointment proved decisive in identifying and legitimating new types of thinking and challenging 'introverted' departmental cultures (Shire 1). In Metro 3, the new AD children was appointed in early 1994 and was able to use the negative SSI report as the entry point for her radical thinking. She was able therefore to sign up Metro 3 immediately as a LAC pilot authority and invited in the Support Force in August 1995. Conversely, the recent loss of the assistant director (children) at Shire 2 in 1997 had the opposite effect.

As one might expect, local government reform in England and Wales (which ran in parallel to the programme of this project) had an obvious effect on the three unitary authorities in the sample. On the whole, local government reform (LGR) proved beneficial in a number of ways. Senior managers found the change liberating to the extent that wholesale redesign was a necessity, established patterns were swept away overnight, and that reductions in the scale of operation forced all staff to think again – often from very different starting points. Unitary 3 used LGR to add impetus to its 're-focusing' strategy that had already begun by 1996. Unitary 2, meanwhile, found that previously 'tribal' relations were overturned by the imperative to co-operate with health and education or suffer the consequences. Less assured senior managers at Unitary 1 found the transition more difficult.

Who are the planners?

The manner in which the case SSDs prepare and develop their children's services plans, including the residential element, at first sight appears generally uniform. Most of the authorities have one or two 'planning officers', either working within the SSD or in a specialist function which covers the whole authority. The requirement to produce children's services plans from 1996 has been an obvious stimulant. Where the case SSDs differ is in the way they have conceived of the role of planners. The divergence does not relate to scale. Unitary 3 is as innovative in this respect as its larger Metro 2 counterpart.

Planning staff should be able to give separate attention to future projections and examine patterns of need and link them to in-house policies on provision. It is how such a resource is developed which appears to make a difference to the delivery of appropriate care. In Shire 2, information was fed into a strategic planning cycle (the child care work programme) with specialist task groups involved and links to the child care senior management team. Yet this work was often stymied by the entrenched views of members. As one area manager explained: 'until we get some flexibility, you can't ask people to be creative because they are hide bound by death-by-committee.' Metro 2 fares better with closer working ties between its members, planning staff (under the AD co-ordination), children's operations group and senior management team. Metros 1 and 3, Shire 3 and Unitaries 2 and 3 all operate through similar combinations.

The role of specialist staff is a sensitive one. A member of Metro 3's planning, commissioning and contracting unit puts it this way:

> Our responsibility is to support the strategy makers. Having said that I feel we have a legitimate voice to be heard and we have a high level of influence because we have direct conversations with members. But we are not developing the strategy of the department. We are there to enable them to develop.

The planning and development manager in Unitary 3 echoes these distinctions and emphasises the need for an educative approach if a more needs-led system is to result:

> Planning is a very new function in this department. It's probably only been in place for about three years. It's not something that's ever been thought about as being needed really ... My role has been to convince the division that they ought to set about children's service planning and to help devise the approach and help my staff work through the more senior staff in children's division to make that happen ... They now have in place a number of tools within the children's planning process that enable them to manage towards that. Previously, it was just a frenzy of different objectives going on.

Unitary 3 seems to be the most adept at the linking of formal planning data, community views and staff experience in the generation of strategies. For example:

> We always had planning officers who go away and they would do it [service plan] and we would respond to that. Whereas now what we are actually doing is taking bits of it away ourselves. (AD children and families)

At Unitary 2, in addition to using LAC material and statistical data, one of the planning officers organised a drama workshop where young people in residential care fed their views into the children's services plan.

Organisational forms

It is clear that the formulation of plans for children's services, which include residential care, cannot be left to planning specialists alone.

In order to produce strategic positions (which encompass the goals identified by various Department of Health inquiries mentioned in Section 4.2) requires thought about how specialists, members, staff and young people's needs can be integrated.

The organisational characteristic in the case SSDs that is associated with such integration is centralisation. This is not to argue that a centralised SSD produces more mature plans and strategic thinking. Clearly the abilities of managers and their choices make a critical contribution. What emerges is that the more creative forms of strategic thinking tend to flourish where older geographically based structures have been reworked – (see also Table 3.4 in Chapter 3). Above all, the reworking into a more centralised structure has been accompanied by key managerial co-ordinating positions linked to receptive planning apparatus. The need to work increasingly with other agencies on service plans reinforces the point. Producing specialised residential units, backed up by a range of emergency preventative resources and based on systematic needs analysis in Metro 2, Shire 3 and Unitary 3 (and the improvements in Shire 2, Metros 1 and 3, London 2 and Unitary 2) relied on such an integrated profile.

4.4   Implementation

Having created new strategic positions on children's services and residential care, the difficulties encountered by the case SSDs in converting them to operational form have been considerable. In some instances, the inability to translate plan into practice has been fateful: new initiatives have been stillborn. Overall, the ability to implement 're-focused' provision and specialisation among the departments studied is not strong. Even where SSDs had encountered new residential care plans built on best practice, their inability to handle the difficulties of implementation resulted in the dilution and even neutralising of such initiatives.

The earlier sections of the chapter outlined the complexities of the strategy process, including the difficulties surrounding the more subjective elements (as shown in the interpretive and political perspectives, see Section 4.2). In practice, the skills of implementation include the building of a receptive context for change. In short, the analytical, educational and political aspects of a change project require attention. The technical assessment has to be matched by an awareness of the development needs of staff in order to cope with new tasks, together with an appreciation of the vested interests that will be affected. Those responsible for implementing changes require a collection of specific abilities including: creating appropriate structures, identifying change managers, target-setting and rethinking communication and reward systems. (See Pettigrew and Whipp 1991: chapter 5.)

The general impression from the case authorities is that SSDs have a weak grasp of such skills. This absence becomes all the more vital when faced by the challenging nature of the policies they were attempting to introduce. All the SSDs involved in the study encountered difficulties in altering their residential provision. The main obstacles included field social worker resistance (Metros 1 and 3, London 2 and 3), friction between residential and fieldworkers (Metro 2, Shire 3), and opposition from the local areas where children's homes were to be closed (Shire 2). In other instances (London 2), lack of information left many categories of staff confused and demoralised. It is still premature to assess the fully operational forms of the changes begun in the new unitary authorities. At the time of the study, they appear to be benefiting from the advantages associated with LGR mentioned earlier.

The difficulties experienced by the case authorities are best summarised around three central problems: the recognition of the implementation task, the generation of suitable information, and the involvement of residential staff.

Recognising the implementation problem

Both Unitary 2 and 3 showed a clear recognition of the separate attention which the implementation of their specialisation plans required. Their strengths will be illustrated in the paragraphs below dealing with the involvement of staff. Metro 1 presents a mixed picture. As Chapter 3 showed, Metro 1 did not rely solely on the inherent logic of its first and second waves of strategic planning to expand foster care and release residential units from unintended placements. The department created a framework of linkages covering most levels of responsibility. As a result, exchanges took place between the: fortnightly children's division management team, the monthly unit managers meetings, the fortnightly south and north area team meetings. These were reinforced by the activities of the nine service improvement groups (established in April 1995) to develop and monitor standards. As a result, Metro 1 shifted its emphasis between the first and second waves of strategic planning. As the AD planning and management systems explained:

> [the first strategic plan] was a classic strategic planning model based on detailed plans and predictions, step by step ... I think that the

evidence of the experience of these five years showed that, that we were off course almost immediately – as you are when you do those sorts of things. LABC2 is more of a logical incrementalism type of approach.

Metro 1 was less successful in coping with the effect of political intervention, scale and management turnover.

Shires 2 and 3 especially had more sophisticated plans based on needs analysis but only belatedly gave the implementation problem the attention such plans required. Shire 2 relied on its tradition of strong local management to deliver service changes. The result was cumbersome decision making and increasingly inconsistent practices between the three county regions. Shire 3 achieved its earlier re-structuring of children's services into six divisions and its process of centralisation from 1996. Yet both were retarded by the department's poor ability to involve junior staff and hence the resistance shown to re-designating residential homes and the relocation/retraining of staff. London 2 suffered in a similar way as its attempts to revise the statements of purpose of homes, and deal with its out-of-borough placement costs, left staff uninformed. The lack of training given to field social workers in London 3 severely hampered its ability to manage contracts with the private sector (also see Chapter 9).

Generating suitable information

All the departments studied found that limitations in their information eroded their attempts to operationalise their plans. The finding broadly reflects the studies (mentioned in Section 4.1) showing the modest information capabilities of local government. Shire 1 was trying to develop locality profiles (linking need and demographic characteristics) as it was restructuring provision. Similarly, London 3, in spite of its radical use of out-of-area placements did so without detailed information. As a planning and development manager stated in relation to the department's children's services plan:

> It was the first time actually that we went and found how many children we were servicing. We never knew that. We just knew how many service units we were dishing out.

Unitary 2 had purchased the SID computer system designed for child care but had been unable to find the time and money to train staff to use all its features. Even with their resources, the larger metropolitan and shire SSDs experienced difficulties. Metro 1's plans to reorder provision in residential and foster care was impeded as late as 1996 by the way 'we lack some astounding basic information' (AD area services), notably in the lack of collation between referrals by area teams and unmet needs. The business information section of Shire 2 attempted its own statistical profiling of children's need in November 1993. Yet at the operational level FSW managers, for example, commented how they were:

> Not getting good quality feedback management information. People are saying that these things are working but I am not getting any evidence – such as the way teams are working. Really having the cases here and tracking them. We would have to do that. We haven't done it as yet.

Metro 2 lacked a central database of referral patterns or admissions to residential care. As we have seen, many of the SSDs have introduced LAC yet it is hard to find evidence of LAC information being aggregated and made available across a department.

Staff involvement

The involvement of residential and fieldwork staff in the process of implementation is uneven and emphasises the mixed abilities of the case authorities. The three unitary authorities stand out. All have taken the opportunity presented by LGR to draw staff into the formulation of new approaches. This also seems to have acted as a prompt to rethink the links between senior management and residential care. We have already noted the contribution to the children's services plan by staff in Unitary 3. In Unitary 2, the involvement of staff and young people in the plan ran in parallel. Here, as in London 1, the established network of meetings of service managers and unit heads has been strengthened by LGR. As a head of home in Unitary 2 explains:

> We're actually quite a powerful group when there's six of us together ... we are included on working parties. What I have found is that things that have been suggested, that I have suggested, have been actually taken on board and working parties have come from that and so [I have] quite a loud voice in that both as an individual and part of the unit managers' group.

One of the undoubted strengths of Shire 2's whole process of planning is its tradition of involving staff from different parts of the county. Indeed, task groups were responsible for a number of 'bottom up' innovations which became part of formal strategy. The sharpest example was the 1993 Childcare Review. The review was based on the innovative practices of one district, which was led by a regional manager, and led to a forum of resource managers being established to oversee implementation between 1994 and 1997. The weaker general implementation skills of Metro 2 or Shire 3 were reflected in their low use of junior and residential staff in their initiatives.

Conclusion

This chapter has brought together conceptions of strategy developed by management academics in order to understand the attempts of local authorities to manage in a more strategic way. The evidence from the case authorities suggests that SSDs are in the early stages of constructing a fully considered approach to strategic management. What is clear is that the implications for the external management of residential care are of immense importance. The first main aim of the research was to uncover the models of management which inform the conduct of SSDs and how they impact on the external management of children's homes (see Chapter 3). In the area of strategy and implementation it is a mixed picture: current thinking is somewhat narrow and restricted in some authorities but more creative in others.

The chapter has been at pains to establish that strategy is not a synonym for planning. Research has shown that there are very different forms of strategic decision making. Planning is only one element involved in the making of strategic choices and action. Nevertheless, policy makers, children's services specialists (such as the Support Force) and SSD staff have one thing in common: their inclination to equate strategy with planning. Their actions suggest a very limited appreciation of the alternative perspectives for thinking about strategy.

Section 4.1 helped to make sense of such limitations (to observers from outside the sector) by reference to the situation in local government. The relationship between policy and planning is fraught with difficulties, financial conventions are often entrenched and information systems immature. These constraints notwithstanding, it does appear that islands of innovation exist which have, in part, used the opportunities created by the New Public Management.

Within our sample, the authorities and SSDs concerned broadly reflect the picture presented in Section 4.1. It is worth emphasising, however, that no dominant approach to strategy emerges. Each authority presents its own mix of inherited values, new senior decision makers, patterns of

Table 4.2   Strategic planning capabilities in the 12 SSDs

Authority	Approach	Informed by	Specialist staff	Implementation
Metro 1	Planning/ incremental	Some specialisation	Planning officers	Use of special interest groups (SIGS)
Metro 2	Strategic	Specialisation	Separate department	Via 3 groups
Metro 3	Strategic	Specialisation	Business management division	Via business units
Shire 1	Reactive	Late needs analysis	Senior managers	Weak
Shire 2	Operational	Inflexible needs analysis	2 + Looked after(LA) team	Task group pilot projects
Shire 3	Strategic	Specialisation	Intelligence unit	Centralised
London 1	Director led	Some specialisation	Planning officer	Partial
London 2	Director/ AD led	Some specialisation	LA department	Centralised
London 3	Strategic	Some Specialisation	Planning department	Weak
Unitary 1	Reactive	Some specialisation	LA staff	Early
Unitary 2	Strategic	Some specialisation	2 in SSD	Co-ordinator
Unitary 3	Strategic	Specialisation	Secondee from LA	Co-ordinator

involvement and operational challenges (see Table 4.2). Even the circumstances brought about by LGR evoked differing responses within the three unitaries. Unitaries 2 and 3 share a strong strategic intent built on 're-focusing' and a commitment to residential care which informs their actions. Unitary 1 meanwhile (which was created a year later) has begun more cautiously.

The sample may be grouped according to three types of strategic thinking. The first contains those authorities that were anxious to construct a systematic view of children's services supported by an analysis of need and which would involve the redesign of those services accordingly. They aspired to a planned approach that also addressed both the future and operational constraints. Shire 3, Metros 1, 2, 3 and Unitaries 2 and 3 fall within this group. Yet each authority differs in the particular combination of strengths and limitations they exhibit.

The second group is made up of Shires 1 and 2, London 3 and Unitary 1. Whilst these authorities show an awareness of the need for a systematic view of children's services, each is more reactive. All four are in some way trying to catch-up with such practices following reactions to earlier residential scandals.

The third category involves those authorities which have taken a more extreme response to such problems and, albeit temporarily, have concentrated their strategic decision making within the office of the director and assistant director.

Reviewing the experience of the SSDs in the sample, one is able to appreciate how the capability to construct strategic decisions over children's services and implement them impacts on residential care. It could, therefore, supply one of the 'forms of management which help to solve the key problems in the external management relationship' which the projects set out to identify. This strategic and implementation capability may be indirect and often filtered by the action of third parties. The standards laid down by Utting and expanded by the Support Force cannot be developed in isolation. The LAC materials and the Matching Needs and Services method do not make sense if approached as separate projects. In order for appropriate placements to occur and statements of purpose to be respected, residential services have to be more specialised within a range of care offered by an SSD. Such arrangements rely on adequate knowledge of the needs of given populations and provision designed accordingly.

Those in the sample who had made progress towards these goals in residential care share the following features in both creating strategic plans and implementing them (see Figure 4.1). They developed a capacity to generate objective data on all aspects of children's needs and existing services. Managers were able to reflect on such findings, in a ground-breaking way if necessary and not be constrained by piecemeal, additive notions of planning. The most successful linked such analysis with the development of member support. All were able to exploit the impetus given to their thinking by using external reports and/or new directors as catalysts. The existence of specialist planning functions was not, of itself, decisive; how planning staff were used was. They could educate other staff on the potential of key data. The more adroit SSDs linked planners, members and SSD staff during the early stages of researching options for service plans thus making the carrying out of the plan more likely to happen as intended.

The implementation of new plans faced a variety of obstacles, not least from staff groups who lacked understanding of given changes and were anxious about the consequences. Implementation skills appear

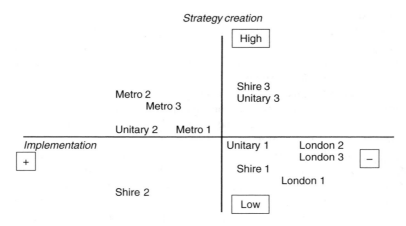

Figure 4.1 Creating and implementing strategic plans

underdeveloped in the sample authorities by comparison to the achievements in other sectors. Nonetheless, those SSDs that dealt with the challenges of translating plans into practice shared certain characteristics. New approaches to planning seemed to work better in more centralised structures that contained some form of co-ordinating roles for key aspects of residential care. Converting data collected centrally by planners and others into usable formats for staff was essential. The involvement of such staff, especially field and residential workers, cannot be overstated. The range of mechanisms used not only helped to bring staff into the initiatives concerned; in some cases (Shire 2 and Metro 2) these became the source of staff-led innovations. The sample also points to the dangers of supporting operational projects (such as Shire 2's children's review) at the expense of nurturing a strategic planning capability. New initiatives can emerge from staff groups for example, and yet wither due to the lack of an appropriate strategic decision-making process to take them forward.

The results of the case authorities, when taken together with the inquiries mentioned in the earlier sections of this chapter, lead to two overall conclusions. First, how local authorities approach strategic planning is of major importance to their ability to provide appropriate residential care within a thought-out range of children's services. Second, a basis exists for developing a set of strategic decision making and implementation skills that are specific to the sector yet draw on techniques from a much wider range of settings.

5
The Management of Child Placement

Introduction

One of the most damaging criticisms made of local authority-run children's residential care in recent years is that these services have largely failed to meet the needs of young people (DH 1991c; Dartington 1995; Support Force 1996). As we saw in Chapter 4, a key reason for this is that residential services have suffered from 'indifferent management and control' (Audit Commission 1994: 16) and from the lack of a 'coherent policy framework' (DH 1991a: 45). Also important has been the way in which the process of making admissions into children's homes has been managed. In many cases, placement decision making remains *ad hoc*, inconsistent and unplanned (DH 1997; Waterhouse, 1988: 108). Where homes had been designated specialist functions, all too often these are treated as 'negotiable' (Berridge 1985: 81). In many cases, residential staff groups have found themselves responding to a succession of unplanned admissions and therefore unable to specialise or improve services (Dartington 1996b; Sinclair and Gibbs 1996; Whittaker *et al.* 1996).

In recognition of these difficulties, from the early 1990s legislation and guidance has sought to promote a greater level of planning in the management of children's residential care. Considerable attention has been given, for example, to ensuring that young people admitted to residential homes have a care plan negotiated with staff groups (DH 1991b: 47–9). Social Service Departments (SSDs) are also required to ensure that the process of admission involves prior discussion between different stakeholders and that young people make introductory visits to homes (SFCRC 1995d: 121–4). The policy and guidance also calls for SSDs to move towards a greater 'matching' of assessed needs and services (Dartington 1995). The intention is that all placements should ' ... take careful account of the suitability of the home and its current staff and residents, to the needs of the child to be placed' (DH 1991b: 6).

Some of the ways in which SSDs are responding to these demands have already been discussed in Chapter 4 on strategy. In this chapter our aim is to focus on a more specific set of concerns relating to the *process* of placement decision making itself. Here our main concern is with the different ways in which SSDs organise this activity and with the identi-fication of structures and decision-making practices that are most likely to be effective.

In order to address these issues the chapter is divided into four main sections. First we define more carefully what is meant by placement decision making and examine the nature of the organisational struc-tures that frame this activity. Section 5.2 then looks at the more specific problems associated with placement decision making, notably those arising from lack of co-ordination between the professional groups involved. In Section 5.3 the decision-making structures and roles in 11 case SSDs are compared. Finally, in Section 5.4 we consider the effec-tiveness of these different management practices.

5.1   The organisation of placement decision making

Placement decision making is a process in which field social workers conduct a needs assessment, develop care plans and then make requests for services provided by residential children's homes (or other services). In most SSDs (including all within our sample) this activity takes place within a more general organisational structure based on a functional division of labour between fieldwork and resources (SSI 1996a). These divisions are 'long standing' in SSDs and date back to their formation following the Seebohm report (Challis 1990: 74). At that time choices were made about how to organise work, choices that tended to reinforce existing boundaries and divisions between professional specialisms. In SSDs, as in other public services, dominant professional groups were able to determine boundaries and 'co-ordinate a division of labour' (Friedson 1994: 65).

Despite the established nature of these structures in SSDs, there remains considerable ambiguity over how they should operate and what the nature of relationships between different functions and groups should be. This is especially problematic with regard to the issue of child placement decision making. Confusion arises over the division of responsibilities between resource and fieldwork staffs and the extent to which these should be formalised. To understand the problem it is useful to compare two ideal type models of placement decision making.

First is what we have loosely defined as the *negotiation* model. This refers to the situation that has existed in the great majority of SSDs (including those in our own sample) where access to residential beds is controlled by resource managers. In this model of working, Field Social Work (FSW) staffs can not simply demand resources but must negotiate access with resource managers who act as gatekeepers (perhaps involving a panel or placement officer). It is implied that placement decision making is the shared responsibility of both field social workers and resource professionals (Jones and Bilton 1994). As Waterhouse (1988: 109) suggests 'residential workers need to take part in decisions as to whether to admit children to care, and, if so, when and on what basis'.

A second model for organising child placement is more recent and is based on more formal *contractual* relationships. This model is linked to the structures that were established in adult services during the 1990s, following the implementation of care management and the purchaser/provider split (Department of Health 1991a; Lewis *et al.* 1996). Under these arrangements the emphasis is less on placement being a joint decision, and more on field social workers (or care managers) acting as proxy consumers of services which are then 'purchased' as in a market-place. As such, the role of providers becomes more passive, limited to delivering through a contract (or 'service level agreement' (DH 1992: 6)) whatever services are commissioned from them.

There has been some confusion in policy and guidance concerning the relative merits of contract and negotiation models for handling placement decision making (see Kirkpatrick *et al.* 1999 for a summary). While some have argued that a greater use of contractual relationships will be beneficial (DH 1991a) (also see Chapter 9), others contend that they will be problematic in a service where 'an ethos of co-operation and collaboration, not competition must prevail' (SFCRC 1996: 12). Looking at practice more generally, some SSDs have experimented with purchaser – provider splits for children's services (Hood 1997). However, the great majority have shied away from this kind of change and continue to manage placement decision making broadly along the lines of the negotiation model. Two main factors help to explain this continuity.

First is the ambiguous and complex nature of children's residential care. In the contract model it is assumed that the needs of young people can be easily specified in advance and that those who 'purchase' a service (social workers or care managers) always have clear objectives. Unfortunately neither of these assumptions sit well with the practice of decision making in children's residential care. To start with, these services are not easy to specify, but take the form of 'credence goods' where 'neither client nor contractor may be very clear about what is happening in complex and ill-understood technologies' (Walsh *et al.* 1997: 37). As one SSI (1996a: 3) report suggested:

> most work with children and families is highly complex, developmental, unstable … the outcomes of SSD intervention are not always easily anticipated, controlled or evaluated.

Added to this complexity is the way (noted in Chapter 3) that field social workers themselves are often unclear about why they are using residential care. In many cases, teams only request this service as a last resort and often without a care plan (DH 1991c). Under these conditions it is not surprising that few SSDs have been willing or able to implement a contract approach towards placement decision making. More appropriate is a system in which both resources managers and fieldwork staff are jointly involved in the decision-making process with regard to deciding both the need for placements and their nature.

The second difficulty with the contract model is that it is hard to reconcile with the broad context where demand for residential beds exceeds supply (DH 1997). As we saw in Chapter 3, all the case SSDs had undergone reductions in supply over the previous five years and only a minority had been able to differentiate their provision. Moreover, a large proportion of placements were being made on an emergency basis, partly because of the preferences of field social work teams to use residential care as a 'last resort' (Packman and Hall 1996). Under these conditions it is perhaps inevitable that resources staff will become actively engaged in some kind of gate-keeping or implicit (sometimes explicit) rationing of residential beds. This in turn largely negates the idea that providers should play a passive role simply responding to requests made to them to supply given services.

5.2   The 'problem' of placement decision making in SSDs

So far it has been argued that placement decision making is most likely to involve negotiation between field social workers who assess needs and resource providers. It has also been noted that such negotiation will, more often than not, involve some kind of gate-keeping or rationing of services. In this section we now turn to the problems faced by senior professionals in SSDs of managing this activity. Specifically, it will be argued that two main difficulties exist. First, those associated with achieving co-ordination between rival departments and professionals involved in decision making. Second are questions of how resource managers negotiate placements with their own residential care managers and staff groups.

Co-ordination

It has been argued that a placement decision not only requires negotiation between field social workers and resource managers but, to be effective, a genuine 'partnership' (Jones and Bilton 1994: 55). According to the Audit Commission (1994: 66): 'both the field social work and residential ... care worker ... need to feel responsible for the problems to be addressed in each case presented'. In practice, however, this level of 'partnership' is extremely difficult to achieve in SSDs.

One reason for these difficulties in SSDs, as in any other organisation, is that co-ordination is problematic when departments are highly differentiated and face competing demands. Field social work teams, for example, must deal with high levels of risk in managing cases in the community and require residential placements at short notice. By contrast, it is in the interest of resource managers to seek a more planned process of admission and, given resource constraints, to reject as many requests as possible. These different goals and priorities, in themselves, are likely to lead to 'considerable friction' at panels or other forums for decision making (Audit Commission 1994: 34).

There are also more general problems of co-ordination that arise from competing professional ideologies and values (Challis 1990: 74–7). In SSDs, as in other public services, the task of developing a high level of team-working between professional groups is one that is fraught with difficulties (Denis *et al.* 1999). According to Iles and Auluck (1993: 176) the problem stems from:

> Multiple disciplines of team members, with their different interests, priorities, perspectives and even languages, such as 'client' vs. 'patient', vs. 'resident' ... make co-operation problematic. Negative views may be held by many professionals, due to their socialisation and training, of the value of other professionals' contributions. There may be a lack of respect for other disciplines and differing rules about what counts as valid information.

In the context of social services this situation is made worse by power and status differences between field and residential social workers. As has been widely noted in the literature, the tendency has been to regard residential social work as an inferior, 'Cinderella' wing of the profession (Waterhouse 1988; Penna *et al.* 1995). Even in the 1990s it had been suggested that relations between these groups remain 'beset with differences in ideology and status' (Berridge and Brodie 1997: 126).

One implication for placement decision making of these intra-professional rivalries is that field social workers may resent having to negotiate for resources and may also question the role played by residential managers in gate-keeping these services. As a resource manager at one of the case SSDs (Metro 1) explained:

> Field social workers – when they are in conflict with us, as they quite often are – will say 'this is our professional assessment'. The implication is that they are being professional and we aren't.

These attitudes may exaggerate the conflict between groups in placement decision making. It is also possible, however that they could start to undermine the process more generally. This was the case in another SSD within our sample: Metro 2. In this authority field social workers questioned the right of the placement officer to prevent admissions and were using various tactics to manipulate or bypass the system (such as misrepresenting cases or making emergency admissions through the late hours duty team). According to an Area Manager: 'I'm not always convinced that we're actually going in the same direction! ... our success in obtaining a placement may be seen as their failure in not protecting their staff from the admission of this person.'

A key difficulty associated with the management of placements is therefore one of achieving co-operation between field social work teams and resources staff. When there is conflict between these different stakeholders it is more likely that child placements will be made in ways that are inconsistent, *ad hoc* and unplanned. In addition, conflicting interests and values also reduce the potential for joint working between resource and field social work staff which may, if allowed to develop, ensure more effective decision making and improved outcomes.

The resource management dimension

The second set of difficulties associated with placement decision making relates to the task of managing relationships between the centre and staff groups in children's homes (also see Chapter 6). A key problem faced by senior managers is that, given the problems of demand and supply for residential beds (see Chapter 3), it becomes hard (if not impossible) to avoid making some placements that are either 'inappro-priate' (given the specialist purpose of homes) or unplanned. As the Director at London 2 admitted:

> Quite often you get into a situation where, if you've only got one bed tonight and one child to place, that child goes into that bed irre-spective of whether their needs match the purpose and objectives of the home that the bed exists in.

In this situation a majority of resource managers find themselves having to make placements in a way that runs contrary to what is required in policy and guidance (DH 1991b). However, in practice this task is neither easy nor cost free.

In terms of the ease of decision making, resource managers may face a number of difficulties when seeking to make placements that are viewed as 'inappropriate'. Staff groups, for example, may try to contest admissions or slow down the process through protracted negotiations (Whittaker *et al.* 1996). This can be especially fraught when the imme-diate line manager also becomes involved (also see Chapter 6). In some cases staff groups also resist unwanted admissions by adopting tactics such as 'bed blocking', found at Metro 1, where managers and staff deliberately maintain high levels of occupancy in homes to limit the possibility of unwanted (emergency) admissions being imposed.

Making inappropriate placements is not only difficult but also poten-tially very costly, especially when imposed on staff. As Whittaker *et al.* (1996: 85) suggest, unplanned admissions can have a devastating effect on staff and may 'instantaneously plunge a Home into a bad patch' (see also Sinclair and Gibbs 1996). Beyond this are wider costs associated with declining staff morale, rising levels of stress (Balloch *et al.* 1998) and a growing 'siege mentality' (Simm 1995). Lastly there are the costs associated with rising staff cynicism with regard to management change strategies more generally (see Chapter 4). As one SSI report noted, there may be a tendency for local staff groups to get caught up in 'unhelpful attitudes, malaise or resistance to change' (SSI 1995a: 45).

These difficulties and costs associated with making inappropriate placements greatly increase the complexity of the task faced by resource managers. Unless these managers are prepared simply to impose admis-sions they must work hard at trying to persuade staff groups to com-promise and work outside their agreed statement of purpose and function. Resource managers need, therefore, to find ways to minimise the impact of unplanned admissions to homes, that is, by developing systems which ensure that at least some establishments are protected and allowed to specialise.

5.3 Approaches to child placement decision making in the 11 case SSDs

This section describes the management practices in 11 SSDs for child placement (summarised in Table 5.1). Comparisons are made along four main dimensions: decision making structures and roles; the process of decision making; unit manager involvement; and the provision for emergency placements.

Structures and roles

There were three distinct ways of organising child placement in the case SSDs. The first approach was to locate responsibility with a placement officer or placement team with the specific role of managing placements. This was the case in three authorities, Metros 1 and 2, and London 2. In the former, a placements team of four staff had been set up, while in Metro 2 and London 2 a single placement officer was the main point of access for all in-house residential beds.

A second approach was to make placement decisions through some kind of gatekeeping panel. In four cases, Metro 3, Shire 3 and Unitary 2 and 3, responsibility rested with a single, central panel, while in two others (Shires 1 and 2) a number of regional panels had been formed. Placement panels varied in their membership and composition. Some met weekly, others monthly and in one case, Metro 3, only when placements could not be agreed through a duty system. In most cases panels were attended by middle ranking resource managers and representatives from field social work. However, in Shire 3 and Unitary 1 more senior managers were involved. In the first, the panel had a 'very high profile within the department' (placement officer) and was attended by the AD as well as countywide resource and fieldwork managers.

The third approach was found in those authorities where no discrete post or panel existed. In these cases, decisions were made through direct negotiations between field social work staffs, line managers and the unit managers of children's homes.

In those SSDs which fell into the first or second category, panels or placement officers had become the main point of access for the majority of residential beds. In some cases, they were also the access point for other resources. In most SSDs family placement services could be

Table 5.1 Placement decision making

	Method of decision making	Membership of panels	Resources accessed by panels/placement offices	Involvement of unit managers	Degree of formalisation	Provision for emergency placements
Metro 1	Central placements team (4 staff)	N/A	In-house residential beds, some family placement and family support services.	Informal contacts between UM's and placement officers	FSW staff complete forms with basic information about clients prior to a referral	2 short-term intake units
Metro 2	Placement Officer	N/A	In-house residential, some family placement and family support services	Represented by line manager. PO attends some UM's meetings. 'Placements forum'	No clear system	Emergency beds in 2 resource centres and 1 short-term unit
Metro 3	Duty System and Panel	Line Managers (resources) FSW managers	In-house residential and some family support services.	Represented by line manager	No clear system	No system
Shire 1	4 regional access panels. FSW staff have allocated	Area managers (FSW), local youth justice, family placement and residential managers	In-house (local) residential beds and family placement resources	Attend regional access panels	No clear system	Emergencies go to 4 'multi purpose' children's homes

Table 5.1 Continued

	Method of decision making	Membership of panels	Resources accessed by panels/placement offices	Involvement of unit managers	Degree of formalisation	Provision for emergency placements
	beds in local children's homes					
Shire 2	9 district resource panels	Area managers (FSW) resource centre managers, line managers, family placements manager, parents	Local in-house residential beds, family support services, family placements	Represented by line manager and resource manager who attends local network meetings	General information required for panels	Emergency beds in 9 resource centres
Shire 3	Placement manager and panel	AD children, county resource manager, FSW managers, placement manager	In-house residential and external placements	Represented by line manager	FSW complete information pack prior to referral and discuss case with placement manager	1 short-term intake unit
London 1	FSW staff approach units directly.	N/A	N/A	Direct negotiation with FSW	No clear sysem	Emergency beds in 2 Resource

				staff making referrals		Centres
London 2	Placement officer	N/A	In-house residential beds, family placement co-ordinates external placements	Represented by line manager. Informal contacts with the PO	No clear system	3 short-term intake units
Unitary 1	FSW staff approach units directly.	N/A	N/A	Direct negotiations with FSW staff making referrals	No clear system	No system
Unitary 2	Panel linked to short-term intake unit	Resource manager, FSW area manager, unit managers	In-house residential beds	Attend panel meetings on a rota basis	Care plans requested at panel	1 short-term emergency unit
Unitary 3	Inter-agency resource panel linked to 'integrated child care facility'	Resource manager, FSW staff, family placement, family support, representatives from education and health	In-house residential, family placement, preventative services, resources funded by education and health	Represented by line manager	Care plans requested at panel	Family support team

accessed. In five cases, various preventative or family support services were also included on the menu of resources. The most ambitious version of this was found in Unitary 3. In this authority, plans had been set to develop an integrated child care facility and panel which would offer care packages which included residential care and inputs from other services.

What these findings indicate is a general trend towards developing clear systems for placement decision making, either through the appointment of a placement officer or the creation of panels. In five SSDs (Metros 2 and 3, Shire 3, London 2 and Unitary 2) these structures represented a distinct move towards greater central control and direction.

Decision-making procedures

While the basic procedure for making a placement was the same in all cases, there were important differences in the extent to which the process was formalised. Formalisation is taken to mean some explicit procedure whereby access to resources involved following certain rules. Such rules might stipulate that resources can only be accessed at certain times, that approval is required, or that social workers must present written information about care plans in advance of a decision being made.

In many cases no such formalisation was evident. Six SSDs (see Table 5.1 above) had no clear procedures and required no written information in advance of placements. In these cases, gate-keeping did occur, but the process was generally informal, relying on negotiations between field social workers and resource staffs. In London 2, for example, the placement officer described how, 'I want them [fieldworkers] to convince me. If I've got a bed, this young person may not be more important than the one that is going to ring me in half an hour's time.'

By contrast, in the remaining five SSDs, a greater degree of formalisation was evident. In these cases field social workers were required to offer some kind of advanced information about a child's needs prior to accessing resources. By far the most developed versions of this were found in Metro 1 and Shire 3. In the former, fieldwork staff were expected to 'phone in and answer a standard questionnaire about the child and the placement' prior to any resources being accessed. In Shire 3 a strict departmental policy of 'no paperwork, no placement' had also been imposed. This required fieldwork staff to complete a lengthy questionnaire about the child, the care plan and what alternative services had been considered at least four days before the panel meeting.

Involvement of unit managers in placement decision making

An additional scale along which it is useful to compare decision-making structures is the extent to which unit managers had some input (direct or indirect) in the process. The degree to which unit managers are involved might be crucial given the problems of low staff morale and isolation amongst many staff groups (Whittaker *et al.* 1996).

There were three (often over-lapping) ways in which unit managers were involved in decisions. The first and obvious was by unit managers directly negotiating with field social work staff about placements. This could be either through the mechanism of a panel or duty system (in Shires 1 and 2, Metro 3 and Unitary 2) or as referrals that were made straight to the home (for example in Unitary 1 and London 1).

A second mechanism for unit manager involvement was indirect, relying on line mangers and placements officers to exert influence on their behalf. A key factor here was the extent to which the latter possessed a good knowledge of in-house resources and of current developments in each home and used this to inform decisions.

A third way in which unit managers were included was via a dedicated system of consultation. This was evident in only two authorities (Shire 2 and Metro 2). In Shire 2, the most developed version, unit managers in each of the 9 districts attended monthly network meetings that were co-ordinated by the local resource manager. As one informant explained:

> As a network, as a district, we meet and I will go through all the youngsters we have got and I will say, possibly to Dave, from [X City] children's home, 'this one might be coming your way. It looks like it from what we have picked up so far, we have gleaned that it may be coming your way, so prepare for that.' Or I might say 'It looks highly likely that this youngster will move home.' Everyone is aware of the movement and equally, I want to know about Dave's youngsters, if they are likely to be moving home, to be going on to college, or going to get flats of their own, or whatever. That is the process. (Resource centre manager)

In Metro 2, a weekly placements forum meeting attended by unit managers city-wide had also been set up with a similar goal of planning movement between homes. A resource manager described the aim of this process as 'a meeting to look at the young people we are needing to move to try and get an agreed plan between managers about who we are going to offer placements to' (Resource manager, Metro 2).

Emergency placements

A final area where it is useful to draw comparisons between authorities is how each dealt with emergency or unplanned placements. As noted in Chapter 3, a large proportion of placements in all the case SSDs were described as emergency. This suggests that in very few cases were Department of Health guidelines for planning a placement followed (DH 1991b). However, while this was the general picture, there was also some variation between the case SSDs in the way these admissions were managed and, crucially, the extent to which all children's homes were exposed equally to such admissions.

The most striking differences were between authorities which had no obvious system and those which – as part of their attempts to specialise in in-house residential care – were operating with some notion of dealing separately with emergency admissions. In total, only three SSDs (Metro 3, Shire 1 and Unitary 1) fell into the former category. The remainder had some kind of system. In four SSDs (Metro 1, Shire 3, London 2 and Unitary 2) this centred on dedicated units which were designed to manage short-term crisis admission. In four others (Metro 2, Shire 2, London 1 and Unitary 3), emergency beds were located within resource centres. The function of these structures was, as one manager in Metro 1 explained, 'an intake facility which acts as a buffer zone which deals with the majority of admissions intake and stops them disrupting the [other] units'.

Looking across the sample it was clear that these systems did not always succeed in managing all unplanned admissions. One reason for this was that short-term units were not always successful in maintaining a steady throughput and turnover of cases in order to create new vacancies. In London 2, for example, a line manager complained that because the short-term units had time-limited placements for 72 hours, there was some overspill and young people 'tend to go where the vacancies are as opposed to where they ought to go, where might be considered best for them'. In some cases, this overspill was due to a lack of co-operation from field social work staffs. As one unit manager in Shire 3 explained, 'they [the young people] are not to be put here and left. We do require weekly visits at a minimum from social workers and that we are looking at their case constantly, virtually all the time … I must admit that some of the reactions we get with some social workers, its like "You have only got eight children there. We have got 50 on our case load." '

5.4   Comparing the effectiveness of different approaches to the management of child placement

In this section we turn to the question of how far the different structures and procedures described above either helped or hindered the process of placement decision making. This involves a return to the earlier discussion in Section 5.2 of the problems of managing child placement. Two main issues will be considered: first, structures and procedures that were helpful in terms of improving co-ordination between residential and field social workers in the process of gate-keeping; and second, the ways in which some SSDs had been successful in terms of minimising the impact of inappropriate admissions and in persuading staff groups to compromise.

The management of gate-keeping

Earlier it was noted how the process of gate-keeping resources for children's residential care was a difficult process to manage, primarily due to problems of inter-professional conflict and the pursuit of subgoals. However, in the sample it was also clear that these problems were more acute in some SSDs than in others. To understand why it is useful to point to three characteristics of placement decision making that were influential both in terms of reducing conflict and improving collaboration. First, is the centralisation of decision making. Second is how far decisions are formalised and governed by procedures. Third is the extent to which clear understandings had been achieved between stakeholders with regard to the nature and function of gate-keeping panels.

1. Centralisation   Unsurprisingly, problems associated with gate-keeping were less acute when decision making had been centralised. As Table 5.1 showed, in some SSDs residential beds could be accessed from a number of different points in the structure. A major weakness of this system is the increased likelihood that field social workers will be able to drive through placements. This, in turn, can mean a lack of control or consistency in the way resources are allocated, almost on a 'first-come, first-served' basis. At Unitary 3, for example, a unit manager explained how under a previously decentralised model:

> If we had a bed we took the young person ... it was wherever there was a vacancy regardless of mix of youngsters, difficulties in any of the behaviour that was going on here.

By contrast, when decision making had been centralised, the gate-keeping system was harder to manipulate and more likely to produce 'consistency of practice' (placement officer, Shire 3). This was especially so in those SSDs, such as Shire 3, where senior managers were also involved in central panels and actively monitored practice.

2. *Formalisation*   A high degree of formalisation of decision making was also important in minimising conflict and the opportunities to manipulate the system. At Shire 3, for example, a checklist of questions about the client had to be completed before a central panel, attended by senior managers, could make a final decision about the placement. According to the department's own procedure manual, the aim of this system was to 'ensure that children looked after have a clearly defined care plan' and also to 'maximise the prudent management of the Department's in-County residential resources'. As the placement manager also explained:

> What we are trying to do, in a relatively short hand, is to make sure that people have made a needs-led assessment for a youngster and that they have thought through all the alternatives and what they are seeking to present is in the best interests of that child. I would say that I believe it is gate-keeping on good practice.

This kind of advanced information meant that management in this case (and to a lesser extent at Metro 1) were able to get close to the goal of using residential services in a more targeted fashion to meet assessed needs.

In stark contrast to this more 'rational' allocation of resources were the difficulties experienced by those SSDs that had not yet formalised procedures (see Table 5.1). In these cases, the lack of clarity regarding the criteria for admission to residential care made the system far easier to bypass, especially with regard to emergencies. It also meant a greater chance that placements would be made in an *ad hoc* and unplanned way. As a development manager at Metro 2 put it:

> Often I think that children who have managed by the luck of the draw to get a place in children's homes are no different from the children who were refused. It is just often whether they ring at 9 in the morning or 11 in the morning.

These observations suggest, therefore, that some of the difficulties associated with managing placements can be minimised by the creation of 'explicit terms of reference for gate-keeping panels' (Audit Commission 1994: 66). However, it should be recognised that these moves towards a greater proceduralism will have wider implications for how services are managed. Above all, they imply a shift towards the kind of explicit rationing of resources that is now common place in adult services (Lewis and Glennerster 1996; Means and Smith 1998).

3. Clear terms of reference for gate-keeping panels   The final point to make in this section is that certain structures and practices did help to facilitate greater partnership between field social work and resource staffs. The most important development in this respect was the gate-keeping panels that had been established in Shire 3, Shire 2 and Unitary 3. In all three cases, panels were being used to access a full range of resources other than residential care – for example, foster care and family support services – (see Figure 5.1). More importantly, in these SSDs a high degree of consensus also existed between field work and resources staffs with regard to the nature and function of panels. A formally stated objective was that gate-keeping panels were not simply mechanisms for *allocating* resources, but also as forums in which to discuss individual cases and, if possible, develop more effective 'care packages'. As a fieldwork manager at Shire 3 explained:

> There is a danger of teams saying 'I have done the assessment. I am telling you I need a placement.' There needs to be an open dialogue, not to test each other's work to destruction, but to see what creative solutions can be found.

While practices varied between these SSDs, there was some evidence that gate-keeping panels were being used in a more positive way, to pool expertise and ideas. According to a unit manager at Shire 2, for example:

> I think quite of few of them [fieldwork staffs] are still locked into 'they are the professionals and they have got to come to panel to tell us what they want' and by the time they come to panel what they want is a residential bed, so we ought to provide it for them. Which isn't utilising outreach at all ... But I would say that over the last 12 months that way of thinking is being reduced. I think initially field social workers were coming to us and asking us to baby-sit kids during the day. Kids they were having problems with educating, or problems with their parents. So we did it, because it was all we were being asked to do. And then from that they started to move on to

well, 'OK they have done quite a good job with that, we will try a bit more.' We sold ourselves to the practice teams and told them that we can do things ... I think it is starting to build our reputation for doing proper outreach as opposed to the child-minding side of it, or let's use it to get the kid into residential ...

An even more ambitious example of this was found in Unitary 3. In this case, the central panel was linked to an 'integrated child care facility' the aim of which was to develop 'packages' of services which combined residential care with specialist foster care, family support teams and resources from other agencies (such as health and education).

The management of resources

Earlier it was noted that a key problem faced by resource managers was the tendency for staff groups to resist inappropriate admissions and the wider costs associated with such placements when they were imposed on staff. Turning to the case SSDs we noted two general ways in which these difficulties had been minimised in some instances. First were structures and procedures adopted in a minority of cases that reduced the number of emergency placements. Second were more general policies aimed at communicating with staff groups and, in the process, increasing their willingness to tolerate a small number of unplanned and inappropriate admissions.

1. Reducing the number of emergency placements In the case SSDs various ways of reducing the number of emergency placements were observed although two general strategies were most prominent. The first has already been discussed in some detail above and relates to the creation of short-term units designed to absorb the majority of unplanned admissions. As we saw, four authorities, Shires 2 and 3 and Metros 1 and 2 (all large in-house providers), had achieved some success in this area. In these cases the use of short-term units meant that other children's homes received greater protection. While all homes might still receive some unplanned admissions – especially when short-term units were full – the longer-term units were more able to operate closely to their agreed statement of purpose and function. As the Placements Officer of Shire 3 explained:

The majority of children in our long term units are there as a consequence of an agreed planning process, not through an emergency and, whilst there is no such thing as 'never never', it is avoided as much as possible.

A second way in which the impact of emergency placements was reduced was the practice, in four SSDs, of 'volunteering' beds. This involved giving unit managers of children's homes advanced information about young people (often in emergency units) awaiting a second (or third) placement. The aim was for these managers to then pre-empt an emergency placement by 'volunteering' to admit a young person whose needs they perceived could be met by staff working in their establishment. In its most developed form – Shire 2 and Metro 2 – the process of volunteering was conducted through regular placement forums and local networks.

A key advantage of this 'volunteering' system was that it helped to ensure that, with the exception of short-term units, a majority of placements in children's homes were 'planned'. In this respect the volunteer system further contributed to a situation in which a majority of homes were protected and more able to concentrate on developing specialised skills. At the same time though, it was also clear that the volunteer system carried certain risks. A key problem was that these policies were also driven by senior management goals of maximising occupancy levels in homes (see Chapter 3). For example, at Metro 2 the Assistant Director Resources admitted that one aim of the system was to train unit managers to:

> Realise that the sensible way for a home to operate is to operate smoothly and efficiently, but swift in terms of when somebody moves on, having somebody new move in …

While in itself this might be a reasonable objective (given the cost of residential care) an obvious risk was that raising occupancy levels became an end in itself. As a unit manager at Shire 2 explained:

> … people are always looking towards occupancy level, about closures. If you are only running at 50% occupancy, then you are likely to be closed down when the next wave of cuts come along. So there is a little bit of an element, if you like, of 'grabbing them off the streets'.

2. Minimising staff resistance to emergency placements   As noted earlier a major problem facing resource managers was how to persuade staff groups to accept some 'inappropriate' admissions and, in the process, avoid wider costs such as growing cynicism and declining morale. In the majority of the case SSDs (especially those with small in-house resources) this goal was hard, if not impossible to achieve. In three cases, however, – Shire 3, Metro 2 and Unitary 3 – there were signs that management had been partially successful in terms of persuading staff groups to co-operate.

In these cases, a greater staff willingness to tolerate *some* emergency placements followed the introduction of new consultation policies (also see Chapter 6). An explicit objective of these policies was not simply to offer support and improve top-down communication, but also to develop a greater sense of collective responsibility amongst unit managers. As a resource manager at Metro 2 put it:

> What we are trying to achieve is the idea of corporate mentalities, the idea of a corporate perspective. Making them [unit managers] feel that they're part of the whole and not just a part of something that they don't want to be part of.

In all three SSDs informants claimed that these consultation policies had helped to reduce the resistance of staff groups to placements that were 'inappropriate'. As a resource manager at Shire 3 explained:

> I would rather work with them [the unit managers] to accept it [emergency placement] than have 15 members of staff saying 'over my dead body', because they have still got a service to run for the other young people that are in there. The politics is very much about finite budgets, high level of bombardment and the need to respond to vulnerable young people, who have got nowhere else to go. Corporately, we are all in that ... I have noticed a change – 9 months ago, the response was always 'no way. We are a long-term unit' (or whatever it might be). I think there is much more recognition that whilst they may well have a particular statement of purpose and function, they also may be exceptions.

At Unitary 3, informants also described how unplanned admissions were often made, but within a context of open communication, where it was understood that management's ultimate aim was to protect, as far as possible statements of purpose and function. As one fieldwork manager suggested: 'at the end of the day I think it is about a holistic approach, everyone talks to everybody else. If you have got good communication then you know any concern should be able to quite quickly resolve any issues.'

Conclusion

The findings from this chapter have direct relevance to the first two aims of the research in uncovering and evaluating the main forms of management being used in the external management of children's homes and suggesting techniques which help to solve key problems. Drawing conclusions about the nature and effectiveness of child placement management in the case SSDs requires three issues to be addressed. The first concerns the broad pattern of management in the case SSDs. Second, the issue of the appropriateness of different approaches to placement decision making is considered. Finally, based on this discussion we outline a number of implications for practitioners.

When seeking to generalise about management practices for child placements across our sample, a number of observations can be made. What comes across most forcefully are the variations in practice between SSDs (see Table 5.1). There were marked contrasts, for example, between SSDs that had centralised placement decision making through panels or management posts and those that had not. Differences were also noted between cases where formal procedures had been introduced and those that relied on more informal practices. What these findings suggest is a gradual and uneven shift towards more centralised management control and direction of the child placement process.

Generally speaking there was little evidence of any relationship between the approach towards placement management in the case SSDs and other factors such as geographical location or authority type (i.e., London borough, metropolitan borough or shire). Only the size of the SSD, in terms of the in-house provision of residential care (see Chapter 3) seemed to be important. In particular, the larger providers (Metros 1 and 2 and Shires 2 and 3) were those which had introduced greater central control in the management of child placement. As was noted in Chapter 4, these also tended to be the SSDs where management had expressed a clear commitment to the future development of in-house services and where most progress had been made in terms of specialisation.

The second issue which needs to be considered here relates to the appropriateness of the different ways of managing child placement. At the beginning of this chapter it was argued that SSDs are likely to face a number of difficulties in managing this process. First are those associated with gate keeping and the co-ordination of decision making between field social work teams and resources. Second were problems associated with making placements in children's homes, especially when these were unplanned or contrary to the agreed statement of purpose and function of an establishment.

In the case SSDs it was apparent that certain management practices tended to either exaggerate or minimise these difficulties. The worst outcomes tended to occur in those SSDs where decision making was decentralised, where there was no attempt to develop joint-working between fieldwork and resources staffs and where there were no formal procedures for making decisions about the use of services. In these situations placement decision making was likely to be characterised by conflict and the pursuit of short term, sectional goals.

By contrast, in a minority of SSDs, new structures and management policies had been agreed to that tended to alleviate (if not remove) problems of placement decision making. Generally speaking, SSDs did better when they had centralised decision making, established some formal procedure for allocating resources and used gate-keeping panels as forums for developing greater partnership between resources and social work staffs. Problems associated with the implementation of placements in children's homes had also been addressed in some cases with structures and procedures designed to reduce emergency admissions and, more generally, improved communications with staff groups. Examples of these practices were found across the sample, although it was only in one SSD (Shire 3) where they had all been combined to maximum effect.

Our third concern is with the implications of these findings for practitioners. From the above discussion, the logical conclusion would be that those forms of placement management that are 'appropriate', are also those that other SSDs should seek to develop. Generally this would mean a move towards more centralised, tightly controlled gate-keeping of resources based on partnership between different staff groups (Audit Commission 1994). Such a change would, however, involve more than simply a restructuring of existing roles and procedures. It would also require a change in the whole approach towards managing residential care resources. There are two main aspects involved.

The first issue is that any future shift towards greater formalisation and centralisation will also necessitate a more explicit policy of gate-keeping and rationing of resources. The implication is that residential resources which, as has been noted elsewhere (Sinclair and Gibbs 1996; Knapp and Lowin 1997), are amongst the most expensive for SSDs to provide, should be used in a far more considered way. SSDs may therefore need to limit access to these services to clients who have been properly identified as having certain needs. The main advantage of this strategy is that, in the long term, it could help to change the way in which the service is used. As field social work teams are required to justify their requests for services this, in turn, could lead to more focussed care plans and a reduced tendency simply to use residential care as a last resort service.

Against these advantages of greater formalisation are a number of costs associated with such change. The main problem is the increased administration and paper work. This is especially so in a context where the overall burden of bureaucratic procedures on professional social workers has grown dramatically over the past decade, following the implementation of new legislation (Lewis and Glennerster 1996; Means and Langan 1996; Rushton and Nathan 1996). The demand for yet more administrative procedure is unlikely to go down well with front-line staffs who resent ' "haggling", "form filling" and "clerking" ' (Syrett *et al.* 1997: 160). In addition, there are risks that decision making gets bogged down in red tape and that an inordinate amount of resources, that could be used to provide services, are devoted to panel meetings.

The second issue has already been discussed (see also Chapter 4). This relates to the fact that new placement management practices need to be grounded within a more general strategy towards residential care. Of particular importance is the existence of a clear commitment amongst senior managers and politicians to the future development of residential care and a willingness to invest in it. Even more crucial are policies aimed at increasing specialisation and focusing services more closely around local needs. In the long term, placement management can only be improved if also underpinned by these wider changes.

6

Line Management

Introduction

During the last decade, increasing concern has been expressed about the ways in which children's homes are managed by the first line of external supervisors within SSDs (SSI 1993, 1995a; Kahan 1994; Berridge and Brodie 1996). Interest in these arrangements mounted against a background of rising costs and disclosures of malpractice within certain homes (ADSS 1997). In short, trust had waned in the capacity of professional supervisors to regulate the quality of children's homes and act entirely with competence and good faith. As a result SSDs have faced growing demands to reform line management (DH 1992; Green 1995). Central to recent policy and guidance is the goal of moving away from professionally led or 'custodial' modes of supervision towards practices similar to those found in other sectors.

The aim of this chapter is to examine the nature and process of line management within SSDs and assess how far change has occurred. In doing so we address the first and second key aims of the project (see Chapter 3). That is: to provide an understanding of the models of management which inform the conduct of social services departments and how they impact on the external management of children's homes; and to evaluate the appropriateness of current models of management being used.

To meet these objectives, this chapter contains five main sections. Section 6.1 explains how a distinctive set of features combined to produce a 'custodial' (Ackroyd *et al.* 1989) mode of line management in SSDs. Section 6.2 explains how new public management (NPM) ideas were influential in this context and describes the recent policy and guidance calling for new structures and practices of supervision. Section 6.3

draws upon our study data to describe and compare the general characteristics of line management within the case SSDs. In Section 6.4, attention turns to an evaluation of the practice of supervision and to other aspects of line management such as providing support and maintaining effective communication. The final section concludes by assessing the nature and extent of change and the prospects for future management reform.

6.1   The 'custodial' pattern of line management in children's services

Prior to examining line management arrangements in children's residential care it is useful to return briefly to the concept of professional bureaucracy introduced in Chapter 2 (Mintzberg 1993). The term refers to a loosely-coupled, decentralised form of organising in which front-line staffs exercise considerable autonomy. These structures produce managerial relationships that are distinct from those found in a pure bureaucracy. While there normally exists some kind of formal hierarchy (with senior and operational ranking professionals) this rarely amounts to a ' "command and control" mode of working' (Ferlie *et al.* 1996: 11). Professional managers are more likely to rely on the authority of 'presumed expertise' rather than of 'position'. These 'managers' are also usually drawn from the ranks of the profession itself and tend to share 'an exaggerated respect for practitioner autonomy' (Ackroyd *et al.* 1989: 612). This leads to management practices that are essentially 'custodial', geared to maintaining the status quo and avoiding direct interference with the work of practitioners. As Whittington *et al.* (1995: 835) suggest: 'line management functions (even if they were actually recognised as such)' are 'essentially about professionals co-ordinating the work of fellow professionals'.

These characteristics of line management in a professional bureaucracy do have certain advantages. By maintaining a 'fiction' of collegial equality they ensure that relationships remain informal and that conflict between levels is minimised (Friedson 1994: 140). The system may also contribute towards the self-esteem, job satisfaction and the service ethos of lower level professionals. However, at the same time, the system creates problems for those responsible for co-ordinating practice and for the wider performance of an agency. A key problem is that modes of supervision are focussed primarily on maintaining practitioner autonomy and not with monitoring and control. 'Management' in this context is likely to be passive and ineffective, at worst simply overseeing independent practice and defending the status quo (Ackroyd *et al.* 1989).

Line management and supervision in the context of children's residential care

It has been argued that SSDs represent an extreme 'managed' version of professional bureaucracy (Webb and Wistow 1987). As in Scott's (1965: 67) 'heteronomous' form, 'professional employees are clearly subordinated to an administrative framework, and the amount of autonomy granted is relatively small'. This 'managed' context for professional work has been especially evident in children's residential care services. As we saw in Chapter 2, for example, in most SSDs, a formal hierarchy was established with heads of homes being directly accountable to external managers, or 'homes advisors' (RCA 1982: 11; Challis 1990). In many respects, children's homes were 'outposts of bureaucracy', with key decisions regarding staffing, budgets, building maintenance, purchasing and child placements taken at higher levels (Burton 1993: 133).

Social services organisations in the United Kingdom therefore have been (and remain) examples of what Webb and Wistow (1987) describe as 'managed professional services'. However, at the same time, it should be noted that 'bureau–professional hierarchies were as much a basis for the power exercised *by* social workers as also the basis for the exercise of power *over* social workers' (Harris 1998: 844). A key indicator was the emergence of custodial patterns of line management similar to those described in the previous section. In children's residential care services, for example, a majority of the 'homes advisor' posts were dominated by professionals, often with past experience. This reflected a general trend in which the 'successful social worker' became 'an administrator of social services' (Younghusband 1978: 311). In addition, while many aspects of home administration (such as budgets and staffing issues) were externally controlled, few SSDs had developed formal procedures governing the practice of residential care work itself. Fewer still set out protocols determining the roles and responsibilities of line managers (Parsloe 1981; Berridge 1985; DHSS 1985). Consequently, many aspects of social work practice in SSDs regarded as ' "professional" territory' were 'not precisely defined' and 'frequently left in organisational limbo land' (Bills *et al.* 1980: 126). As Lewis and Glennerster (1996: 71) suggest, 'much was carried around in social workers' heads rather than being made explicit'.

These aspects of SSD organisation led to a particular style of line management in which the homes advisor offered general support for staffs and the co-ordination of services (Bills *et al.* 1980). While these managers could, in theory, have exercised authority of position and become more involved in directing operations, many declined to do so. As a result, the system led to heads of homes having considerable '*de facto* autonomy' and independence especially with regard to operational or 'professional' issues (Clare 1988; Brown and Payne 1990).

6.2 Towards the reform of line management in children's residential care

From the late 1980s, these management practices in SSDs were strongly criticised by policy makers and by many professionals themselves. In this section we first describe the nature of this critique and then consider what new management reforms were proposed.

The critique of line management

Three main problems were identified with the 'custodial' model of line management in children's residential care. First, it was argued that these arrangements were ineffective as a mechanism for ensuring proper control and accountability. As we saw, the tendency was for external managers not to interfere with or seek to direct the work of junior colleagues. Many preferred to 'submerge inappropriate practices within the occupational shibboleth of collegial care and support' (Pithouse 1989: 47). As a result, not only was it hard to co-ordinate or manage services, but local practice in homes remained 'invisible' or beyond the disciplinary gaze of senior professionals. All this was seen as contributing directly to a situation in which malpractice within homes might go undetected by senior managers and local politicians (Berridge and Brodie 1996: 184).

Second, custodial patterns of line management were criticised for their failure to provide adequate support for residential staff groups. This was especially the case when supervisors visited homes infrequently, leaving front line staffs feeling isolated or neglected (DHSS 1976; ARCC 1985). According to Berridge (1985: 57), 'a noticeable feature of the heads of homes was their isolation' with many staff receiving 'minimal management support, apart from those rare occasions when they experienced major control problems or were faced with difficult decisions about children in their charge'.

Finally, criticisms emerged about the way in which supervision itself was conducted. Under custodial management supervision tended to be infrequent, unstructured and concerned primarily with maintaining relationships. As Morrison (1997: 1) suggests 'the reality is that … supervision within agencies varies considerably both as to quality and availability … '. Few SSDs had developed effective systems for staff appraisal and development (SSI 1995a; DH 1992). Supervisory meetings tended to focus overwhelmingly on operational issues with little or no attention given to assessing professional development or training needs of unit managers and staffs (Rushton and Nathan 1996; Balloch *et al.* 1998).

Towards the reform of line management

In the 1990s these criticisms helped fuel more general calls for the reform of line management in UK social services. An idea promoted by the Audit Commission (1994) and, increasingly, the SSI and other groups, has been that SSDs should develop a model of performance management (Langan and Clarke 1994; Waine 2000). According to Hood (1995: 107) this implies 'the idea (or ideology) of homeostatic control', or the 'clarification of goals and missions in advance, and then building the accountability systems in relation to those present goals'. In particular, performance management envisages a situation in which organisations have clear strategies and that from these, more specific objectives will be derived that define the 'core business' and priorities of professional work (Clarke and Newman 1997).

This broad approach to management reform has specific implications for line management. First it suggests that external managers should become more focussed on control, direction and monitoring (Causor and Exworthy 1999: 85). Increasingly, senior professionals will be required to stress the 'inquisitorial' aspects of supervision which, in the past, had been downplayed or ignored (Rushton and Nathan 1996: 359). A further change is towards a more structured approach towards supervision, through the development of formal systems of performance appraisal. Increasingly, supervision should be concerned not solely with operational concerns, but also on the training and development needs of individual professionals (DH 1992). As Townley (1997: 266) argues, a 'developmental' model of performance appraisal is 'designed to identify individual strengths and weaknesses and develop skills and abilities'.

These arguments suggest that SSDs will need to introduce radical changes to their line management practice. However, it is also clear from much of the policy and guidance that older patterns of custodial management are not to be completely abandoned. One indicator is the growing emphasis on line managers providing support and advice to staff in children's homes (SFCRC 1995c). According to the SSI (1993: 4), line managers should 'collect relevant information for senior managers …' but also 'provide appropriate support to homes' managers'. A further indicator of continuity is the objective of enhancing the management autonomy and self-reliance of heads of home (DH 1992). While it is acknowledged that 'greater external management control' (Green 1995: 15) may be necessary in some contexts, the overall message is that the capacity of unit managers to control themselves should be enhanced (Sinclair and Gibbs 1996; Berridge and Brodie 1997). As Wagner (1988: 69) argues, the aim of external management should be to 'provide a framework within which positive practice can flourish and which encourages rather than stifles initiative'.

Specific proposals for change

Obviously the changes described above will take time to achieve and are likely to involve major transformations in attitudes and working practices. Much will depend, for example, on how far SSDs are able to develop a coherent strategy for residential care and, thereby, agree to clear goal or statements of purpose and function for individual establishments (see Chapter 4). As Green (1995: 15) suggests:

> To facilitate sound management of homes operational purposes and aims are needed which are firmly set within the overall departmental policy. Local management needs a strategy for assessing the staff's capacity to deliver the desired service and to monitor how this is achieved.

In addition to these broader strategic changes, more specific proposals were outlined in the early 1990s. To summarise, SSD managers were encouraged to pursue three sets of changes relating to: organisational structures, formal policies and procedures and staff training and development.

1. New structures Starting with organisational structures, policy and guidance has proposed two main changes. First, SSDs are encouraged to reorganise tasks so that line external managers are able to specialise exclusively in the management and supervision of children's residential care (DH 1992). The rationale involved is that it will allow managers to focus more fully on the special needs and demands of children's homes and therefore avoid 'conflicts of interest' that arise when these managers are also responsible for other functions (DH 1992). Furthermore, the unification of management structures will 'help to overcome problems of isolation of staff in smaller homes ... as managers can ensure frequent contact between groups of staff' (DH 1992: 91).

A second change in organisational structures is the demand for greater decentralisation of management responsibilities to unit managers (DH 1992; Wagner 1988). According to Utting (DH 1991a: 47), SSDs would benefit from a 'maximum delegation of management responsibility, including budgetary responsibility down the line', and more specifically, 'all heads of home should be responsible for managing all the resources of the home, and should be equipped to do so by appropriate training, experience and supervision'.

2. Policies   Since the early 1980s SSDs were criticised for the lack of clear procedures regarding different aspects of management. More recently, the SSI (1997: 8) commented on how many SSDs lacked 'written guidance which clarifies the purposes and expectations of supervision'. To rectify this problem SSDs have been encouraged to develop explicit policies and procedures with regard to external management and supervision (see Berridge and Brodie (1996: 188) for an outline).

One objective of these policies is to formalise requirements governing the *frequency* of supervision. Hence, Warner (DH 1992) proposes that all SSDs make guarantees that the formal supervision of unit managers will take place every two weeks. In addition, it is expected that new policies will be more explicit about the *process* of supervision. A favoured model is one based on formal staff appraisal. This implies that supervision meetings have a clear structure and that individual staff are given 'personal development contracts' (DH 1992: 126) (also see Chapter 7). Finally, these policies should seek to remove ambiguity over the *purpose* of supervision. There should be greater clarity regarding the role of the supervisor not only as a source of support for staff, but also as responsible for ensuring control (the inquisitorial function) and for personnel development (Green 1995: 11).

3. Staff skills and competencies   A final set of changes proposed by the guidance and policy in children's residential care relate to the skills and training of external managers. As we saw earlier, the tendency was for 'homes advisors' to be drawn almost exclusively from the ranks of the profession, often from residential care itself. Since the early 1990s, however, it has increasingly been argued that more emphasis should be placed on management competencies and qualifications (SFCRC 1995c; DH 1997; SSI 1994; Green 1995). According to Warner (DH 1992: 64):

Experience of residential child care is desirable whenever possible. However, there is no doubt in our minds that the line managers of heads of homes should be recruited primarily for their management competence.

The guidance and policy stresses, therefore, the need for SSDs to invest in management training, an area that has largely been 'neglected' in the past (SSI 1997: 49).

6.3 The general characteristics of line management in the case SSDs

This section turns to the data collected in 11 case SSDs (for obvious reasons, London 3 is excluded from the analysis). The objective is to provide an overview of the formal structures, policies and staffing arrangements with regard to line management. This will also give an indication of how far elements of the policies described above had been implemented.

Structures

From Table 6.1 it can be seen that line management was organised differently in the 11 case SSDs, although three main approaches were

Table 6.1 Line management structures in case authorities

Local authority	Total children's services staff*	No. of homes 1997	Specialist (S) or multi-functional (MF) line managers	No. of line managers	Average span of control for homes and other resources[+]
Metro 1	1,428	26	S	7	5
Metro 2	981	21	Mixed	3	7
Metro 3	342	6	MF	1	10
Shire 1	860	8	S	1	8
Shire 2	1,465	39	MF	9	6
Shire 3	867	10	S	1	10
London 1	229	4	MF	2	5
London 2	265	8	MF	2	6
Unitary 1	200	3	S	1	4
Unitary 2	Not available	4	Mixed	4	3
Unitary 3	256	5	S	1	5

Note: [+] 'Other resources' includes all or some of the following: family placement teams; day care services; family resource centres (or teams) and field social work area teams.

Source: * Personal Social Services Statistics (CIPFA 1996).

evident. First, five SSDs adopted a 'specialist' structure in which individual line managers were responsible only for groups of children's residential care establishments. Second, four SSDs line managers were classified as multifunctional. This meant that, in addition to children's homes, these managers were responsible for other professional activities, including family placement, day care services, family support teams and (in London 1) field social work teams. Third, there were two SSDs that adopted a 'mixed' structure in which some line managers specialised in residential care and others followed the mutifunctional model.

A further point to note from Table 6.1 regards the span of control of line managers. It can be seen how in half the case SSDs line managers were responsible for about five or more residential establishments or 'other resources'. Also apparent are the much larger spans of control in authorities such as Metros 2 and 3 and Shires 1 and 3. In these cases line management responsibilities had been extended in recent years, the result of more general organisational restructuring and de-layering initiatives. As we shall see, these widening spans of control did have consequences for work intensification and may have undermined the ability of line managers to conduct supervision and offer general support (also see Berridge and Brodie 1997: 52).

At first glance Table 6.1 reveals the same kind of variety of management arrangements in SSDs that has been noted elsewhere in the literature (for example, see Challis 1990). However, our analysis also revealed a pattern of convergence towards the specialist line management model. One indicator of this was the fact that three SSDs (Shire 3 and Unitarys 1 and 2) had only recently moved towards this approach, while a further two (Shire 2 and London 2) were planning to reorganise along these lines in future. At Shire 2, for example, a Development Officer explained how, under a forthcoming reorganisation the plan was to make line management 'more specialised' in order to 'free up their obvious potential and expertise in being product champions and people who can develop the quality of residential provision'.

Most informants agreed that moves towards a more 'specialist' model of line management for children's residential care were generally positive. Typical of this were the remarks of a unit manager at unitary 1:

I have to be honest, when I first came into this particular job, I wondered where the management was in the old county. Now, because we are smaller, there are people taking an interest in what is happening in your particular home, the problems you are having. Nobody was ever interested before. It was too big. The main office was in the county town. When you phoned the person who was supposed to be your manager, because he was a field social worker he was always involved in child protection work. Nobody else would know me from Adam. That is the difference now. I have a line manager who is interested and dedicated to children's homes. She is close-by and I can get hold of her quickly.

Of course, it was acknowledged that a multifunctional model did have some benefits, notably in resolving 'conflicts or disputes with the field social workers' (Line Manager: London 1). However, most felt that this arrangement made supervision more difficult, especially in those SSDs – such as in Metro 3 and London 2 (see Table 6.1) where line managers also had to deal with large spans of control.

A further issue to consider with regard to structures is the extent to which line managers were responsible for various decisions regarding the administration of children's homes. Our research revealed that, on the whole, line managers still played a considerable role in this area. Most continued to be involved in the administration of budgets (especially relating to overtime and staffing) and also in matters such as staff training, recruitment and selection. However, at the same time, we also noted a general trend was towards greater decentralisation. In most cases, for example, a decision had been taken to extend the responsibility of unit managers for a range of human resource issues including staff deployment, training and recruitment and selection (also see Chapter 7). Even more significant was the decentralisation of budgets. Most SSDs had moved away from past practice in which budgets were administered exclusively by the line manager. Many SSDs had also introduced greater flexibility in the use of resources, allowing unit managers to vire between different budgets (say between 'food and provisions', 'clothing' and 'equipment' budgets) without seeking approval. As a line manager at Shire 3 explained:

Say they [the unit manager] wanted to buy a new 3-piece suite and there was insufficient money in the furniture and fittings budget (which is where the department would say that spend should come from) and there was a bit of unspent money in another budget ... The homes manager can make the decision to vire some money from one budget to the other. They have got the authority to do that within financial constraints.

While there remained clear limits on how far administrative functions had been devolved, the general trend was clearly away from older arrangements where the tendency was to retain tight central control over such decisions.

Many informants welcomed these changes and some even viewed them as 'tremendously empowering for the staff and the young people' (unit manager: Metro 2). Yet while a majority of unit managers supported moves towards decentralisation, some did express reservations. According to an informant at Shire 2, for example:

> I didn't want budgetary responsibilities, I didn't come into this job to do that, but we're landed with it … It involves you having an allocation and you work within that allocation, whether its clothing, anything that you buy. There is such a lot of paperwork now.

A unit manager at Metro 1 also complained about how:

> Along with the responsibility came all the extra work. And I said, 'I didn't come into this work to be an accountant'. Did we get help? No we didn't.

Given these accounts it is important to recognise, as Whittaker *et al.* (1996) also suggest, that many staff had mixed feelings about the decentralisation of administrative duties. Such change might be 'empowering', but also implied greater accountability and, given a lack of clerical support, greater work intensification (Balloch *et al.* 1998).

Policies

A mixed picture emerged with regard to policies relating to line management and supervision. Approximately half of the case SSDs had not yet established formal written statements or policies. In these cases, senior managers (at AD and above) were able to articulate expectations regarding the frequency and purpose of supervision, but often only in very general terms. As a senior manager at Shire 1 explained, while it is necessary to 'ensure that the managers of the children's homes have regular supervision', the department itself did not 'actually lay down the content of … [that] supervision'.

In the remaining SSDs there was evidence of greater formalisation of policy, largely consistent with the expectation of central government policy goals (as stated earlier). In three cases (Metro 1, Metro 3 and Shire 3) departmental policies had existed for some time. For example, at Shire 3 a Resource manager explained how

> There is a departmental policy which lays down the standards of supervision and the expectations of supervision in terms of regularity and content and supervision contracts ... And I must say, they are pretty well embedded actually, even in residential which traditionally has not had as much structured supervision ... as elsewhere.

At Metro 1,there had also been moves to 'codify management practice and expectations' and to set out guidance that is 'necessarily prescriptive, particularly where there is an assumption of minimum expectations' (Internal Report 1989: 2). These SSDs, as well as Metro 2 and Shire 2, had also recently engaged in attempts to develop new procedures governing supervision in line with Investors in People (IIP) accreditation.

A common feature of these policy statements was an attempt to ensure greater standardisation with regard to the frequency of visits to homes and formal record keeping. The new procedures were also explicit about the process and goals of supervision. Most policy statements, for example, insisted that supervision take on a more structured character along the lines of a formal staff appraisal aimed at development (DH 1992). At Metro 1 it was claimed:

> We have a supervision procedure which we follow, which is the same as the field workers where we look at development. During supervision, the line manager will say, we know that these are the areas that need to be developed within your professional development plan, how best can we help? (Assistant Director, Children)

In most cases, these new policy statements not only emphasised the importance of staff development, but also the role of supervision as a 'judgmental system', concerned with control and monitoring of practice (Townely 1997). As the Assistant Director Resources at Metro 2 put it: 'I believe the [Line Managers] are inspectors ... They are not just there in a nice way, to support the workers, the managers, in the children's homes. They are also there to be very objective, and to inspect what's going on.'

Background and training of line managers

The third and final issue concerns the skills and competencies of line managers. Table 6.2 provides general information relating to the backgrounds of managers in the case SSDs. From this it can be seen that the

Table 6.2   Background of children's homes' line managers

Local authority	Number of line managers with responsibility for children's homes	Background of children's homes line managers
Metro 1	7	7 residential
Metro 2	3	2 residential; 1 field social work
Metro 3	1	1 nursing
Shire 1	1	1 residential
Shire 2	9	3 residential; 6 field social work
Shire 3	1	1 field social work
London 1	2	1 field social work; 1 day centre
London 2	2	2 field social work
London 3	Not applicable	not applicable
Unitary 1	1	1 field social work
Unitary 2	4	2 residential; 2 field social work
Unitary 3	3	1 residential; 2 field social work

vast majority were social work trained. It is also notable that approximately half had previous residential care experience. The overall picture, therefore, seems to be one of continuity with past practice in SSDs, with management positions still dominated by professionals and ex-practitioners. As elsewhere in social services, it would appear that a background in 'social services work' continues to represent an important 'rite of passage' for those entering management posts (Lawler and Hearn 1997: 209).

This continuity with past practice does not ignore the fact that some changes had occurred. Many senior professionals were raising questions about the criteria used to select line managers and how far these might need to be altered in future. According to the Director at London 1, for example:

I think experience is useful but I don't think its essential by any means. I think there are so many core management functions in terms of looking after and developing staff, supervision, appraisal systems, training, budget management, goal setting, planning, there are some very generic important things as [sic] common to all management tasks. Unfortunately, the type of people that come into residential work don't always have these skills.

A further indication of change had been moves in all the case SSDs towards increased investment in management training for professional staffs involved in supervision. At Metro 2 for example:

> We have had a strategy in the last year and a half which has been very much around focusing on middle managers requiring a lot of training in management skills – financial management, personnel management, equal opportunities ... So they have a lot of input through training. (Director)

Of course, training policies varied between the case SSDs, with some relying more than others on externally accredited courses (such as Certificates and Diplomas of Management Studies). Nevertheless, the overall trend was towards more investment in this area (SSI 1997: 49).

6.4 Management Practice

In this section attention turns from the structures and policies adopted in the case SSDs, to the practice of line management itself. Two core issues stand out – the practice of supervision, looking at frequency and process. The second concerns what Rushton and Nathan (1996: 359) describe as the 'emphatic containing', or 'support' function of line management.

Supervision

Two main issues dominate the practice of supervision. The first relates to the question of how frequently it occurs. The second concern relates to the process and content of supervision. These topics will be discussed separately. More general questions about how far (if at all) supervisory practices have changed will also be raised.

1. Frequency   As was seen earlier, policy guidance points to the need for 'structured individual supervision throughout the establishment, including for the unit manager' (Green 1995: 15). Although hard to assess, it did seem that a majority of unit managers in our sample were receiving some kind of supervision. However, it was also clear that visits were rarely as frequent as suggested by Warner (DH 1992) and others (i.e. every two weeks). Marked variations were noted between SSDs in the quantity and regularity of supervision. At one extreme were SSDs, such as Shire 3, where it was claimed that all managers were supervised monthly:

> We have just been doing some audits because of the SSI coming and I have been very impressed actually that supervision does take place.

> It does take place on a regular basis, it is recorded, there are super-
> vision contracts between supervisory staff and staff in the homes and
> it is pretty well embedded in the philosophy of Shire 3. (Resource
> manager)

At the opposite end of the continuum were a number of SSDs, for
example, Shire 2 and Metro 1, where it was evident that supervision did
not always take place. At Metro 1, a unit manager also remarked: 'all the
people I supervise sign and read their supervision notes. I haven't signed
or seen my supervision notes for two years'.

A key factor that seemed to explain these variations in the frequency
of supervision were growing resource pressures and competing demands
faced by line managers (Balloch *et al.* 1998: 334–7). Many informants
explained about how the line management role had been greatly
expanded in recent years, to include staff supervision and growing work
demands linked to widening spans of control (see Table 6.1). As the line
manager at Shire 3 (an authority where the span of control had recently
been extended to ten homes) explained: 'I used to see unit managers
twice a month with supervision and now I can only meet once a month.'

2. The process of supervision As well as specifying the need for more frequent supervision, current policy and guidance also suggests changes in
process and content. A key goal is to move from a custodial model, in
which emphasis has been on maintaining relationships and discussing
operational matters, to one based more on staff development and
management control.

Viewing the data collected in the 11 case SSDs leads to the conclusion
that key aspects of this 'custodial' model remained deeply embedded.
The vast majority of unit managers described their supervisory meetings
as essentially 'task orientated and problem orientated' (Unit Manager
Metro 2), or dominated by 'an element of problem-led response' (Line
Manager Metro 1). While accounts varied, most described their supervisory meetings as being primarily concerned with the discussion of current operational matters, such as reviewing cases of young people in the
home, staffing issues, budgets and general administration. Informants
also referred to how supervisory meetings often took on a very informal
and unstructured character. According to a line manager at Shire 1, for
example:

> Because I have worked with most of the unit managers for years, what
> tends to happen is that I go to the units for the supervision and you

get ensconced with the manager. You know, you put the world to rights, catch up on gossip and say who you've seen recently. That is historical and it keeps everybody happy. My manager is happy that I've done the supervision, I'm happy that I've been to the home and the unit manager is happy that I've called in. ... Its done in that way.

In a similar vein, a unit manager at London 2 remarked on how, supervision meetings were essentially 'an informal get together although it's obviously recorded and written up'.

These and other accounts therefore suggest considerable continuity with the past practice of custodial management. This gives rise to the question of just how much, if anything, has changed in recent years? The issue can be addressed by examining how far processes of staff supervision in the case SSDs had become more managerial and concerned with issues of staff development and formal monitoring and control.

Developmental focus

A key aim of recent policy and guidance was to formalise the process of supervision as a system of staff appraisal that would address the training and career development needs of individual unit managers. In order to reach this goal just under half the case SSDs had introduced formal policies, often linked to wider initiatives, such as Investors in People.

Turning to the question of how far practices had changed there was only limited evidence to suggest that supervision was now more directed to staff development. In two cases, Metro 1 and Metro 3, a proportion of supervisory meetings (perhaps two each year) had been formally designated as 'protected time' in which the focus was exclusively on professional development. However, in these authorities it was found that only a fraction of these staff appraisal supervision meetings were being held. Moreover, even when they did take place the process was deemed by participants to be highly unsatisfactory. For example, a unit manager at Metro 2 remarked on how 'most of the supervision I've had ... is an insult to call it supervision'. A council member at Metro 1 also suggested: 'there are various people in blocks up and down the hierarchy' who 'wouldn't understand a good supervision session if they fell over it'. In the remaining SSDs developmental concerns were either not raised at all (the majority) or included as part of a more general and wide-ranging supervisory meeting.

Control

A key aim of recent guidance is to encourage more directive forms of leadership with more emphasis in supervision on the formal monitoring of practice and on evaluation of performance against departmental goals. In the case SSDs there was some evidence of change in this direction. Most important was the introduction of monthly 'regulation 22' inspection visits (a policy described in greater detail in Chapter 8). In five SSDs, contrary to guidance, the decision had been taken to make line managers responsible for these visits and integrate them with supervision (see Table 8.1). While these visits were often infrequent and performed in a ceremonial fashion, they nevertheless did imply a more 'inquisitorial' element to supervisory sessions. According to a regional manager at Shire 2:

> People need to appreciate that you are going to be inspected as well as supervised. Because supervision is not just 'patting someone on the head'. Its trying to make progress.

A unit manager at London 1 also explained how: 'Since Pindown and the rest of it, managers are now breathing down your neck all the time. They want total control and want to keep checking up on us ... They dictate and control things.'

Beyond this, the only other signs of a shift towards more directive supervision were in Metro 3. In this case attempts were being made to use formal staff appraisal meetings in a more formal way to evaluate 'performance'. According to one unit manager, supervision was:

> actually done in quite a formalised way compared to what we have been used to and it does identify the gaps that are in your performance. There is always then a 'need to do', a 'need to pick up', a 'need to do this', 'a need to do that', which next time will be followed up.

In this case, individual homes had also been redefined as 'business units', with unit managers given wide-ranging responsibilities for the allocation of budgets, staffing and planning of services.

These observations do point to a limited change in the direction of a more judgmental approach to supervision. However, it is important not to exaggerate this movement. In the great majority of SSDs (even those that had implemented the reg. 22 procedures) supervision continued to be dominated by a custodial pattern with line managers not questioning practice or exercising their positional authority. In general, three main reasons for this can be identified.

First, directive supervision was made difficult because of continued role ambiguity of line managers. Despite moves in some of the case SSDs to formalise job descriptions and expectations most informants echoed the views of a line manager at Metro 1 who suggested that 'the job is in many ways what you make it'. As a result much confusion remained over the 'position authority' of the line manager and over how far he or she should try to direct operations or cast judgement on local practice. All too often line managers found themselves 'caught in the middle', between the priorities of the agency and those of staff groups (also see Whittaker *et al.* 1996).

This role ambiguity did not, in itself, prevent some line managers from becoming more inquisitorial. It did however make such practice increasingly difficult, especially given the expectation that managers should also be the primary focus for staff support and assistance (see later). Under these circumstances it is perhaps inevitable that some managers would get 'sucked in to unhelpful attitudes, malaise or resistance to change' (SSI 1995c: 45) (also see Chapter 5).

A second obstacle to a more interventionist form of supervision was an asymmetry of knowledge and experience between professional staffs and their external managers. In reality, it is very difficult for line managers to pass judgement or significantly interfere with the autonomy of practitioners when they themselves lack detailed knowledge or understanding. A unit manager at Shire 2 admitted:

> I'm not an expert on everything. Some of them are far better than me in running budgets and rotas and things like that. I let them get on with it. I delegate it. If they can do it better than me, let them do it!

This knowledge-gap exaggerated the tendency for line managers to adopt a 'hands off' approach towards supervision and to rely heavily on the goodwill of unit managers. Of course this dependency was less apparent when line managers also had past residential experience (see Table 6.1). However, even in these cases it was difficult to interfere or direct simply because 'professional experience, unexercised, is a decaying asset' (Pollitt 1990: 438).

Finally, it is important to note how changes in management practice were limited by the lack of clear goals against which staff 'performance' could be assessed. Even where more general goals had been agreed, for example, with the new statements or purpose and function for individual homes (see Chapter 4), these could not be used to assess 'performance and conduct in a much more legally binding way ...' (DH 1992: 107). As we saw in Chapter 5, resource constraints and placement politics make it hard, if not impossible, for a majority of unit managers to operate within agreed statements of purpose and function. Quite often the line managers themselves were the main external agency forcing staff groups to deviate from their formal goals, especially when there was a requirement to make placements that were unplanned or inappropriate.

Support

Policy and guidance has placed more emphasis on this support activity and, more generally, on the role of line managers in 'facilitating effective channels of communication' (Green 1995: 15). Increasingly, the expectation is that line managers will visit homes frequently, provide advice and assistance and, if necessary, become directly involved in local operational concerns.

The results show that a majority of line managers were taking this support role seriously. Many, for example, talked at length about the importance of building strong relationships with staff groups, of visiting frequently (beyond what was required for formal supervision) and being prepared to offer help and advice when required. As a line manager at London 2 explained

I do go to children's homes and see staff or usually the manager for other issues, if there are neighbours complaints or local issues that maybe I need to be involved in. In terms of informal supervision then homes managers and staff ... know my contact numbers both for the office, the mobile and my home number. Whilst I would not be keen to be phoned every night and every weekend to have a 'general chat' the message with that is 'please contact me if you want to make contact with me'. Homes managers will frequently use the phone to check out, sound out, problems and issues. The proverbial 'Can I just run this past you?' kind of conversation.

There were also numerous examples from across our sample of managers providing more direct assistance or 'back up' to residential staff groups in crisis situations. In some cases these practices were strongly prescribed by senior managers and local politicians. According to the Director at Metro 2, for example: 'I hope we have developed a general attitude amongst our residential child care staffs that if they've got problems, we are going to be there. It's not, "well I'm off duty, wait till the morning", it's "we'll be there and we'll support you" '.

Not surprisingly many informants regarded past experience in residential care as being central to the support role. According to a line manager at Metro 2:

> The children in the homes know me because I visit them. The staff in the homes know me. I have been around forever and a day. I have known colleagues for a very long time. Most of the managers I have managed elsewhere before their present posts ... So really, in every aspect of the children's homes I have a kind of finger in the pie and a management role ... I can judge a unit based on my experience, what they're doing. I can feel it in the gut. You walk through the door and your gut tells you what the unit's up to. You can feel the atmosphere, it feels good, it feels bad. You've got to understand the concept of residential. I believe its so unique ... There's no substitute for having that experience around you ... The AD does not have residential experience. I don't know if she's ever been up at 3 o'clock in the morning facing a kid of 16 with a knife who wants to slash his wrists ... That's the uniqueness of residential care. There's very few environments where you face that, but the staff face that day in and day out. Its knowing the feelings associated with that, the guts, how everything churns, how you feel before, how you feel afterwards. How you cope with it. Its all those. Because it is unique, it is different.

Across the sample many other informants articulated a similar view. A unit manager at Metro 2 argued: 'if you haven't had that experience and you're trying to support and guide and manage people who are in those posts, you don't necessarily understand'.

Despite these often strongly held views, it was also acknowledged that, under some circumstances, external managers who lacked residential experience could provide effective support. Such people could also offer different kinds of 'support' to staff groups. According to a line manager at London 1:

> I feel as if I have got a whole different set of skills which enable me, in the forums that I come into, that I can represent people's interests ... I know my way around the organisation. I have got a different range of contacts within social services to the people here.

In the recent literature focusing on residential care it has been suggested that levels of external management involvement in homes have decreased and that, consequently, staff groups have become more isolated (Whittaker *et al.* 1996; Berridge and Brodie 1997: 182). What seems clear from our data is that the extent to which line managers were able to perform this role was variable both within and between SSDs. Much of this variation could be explained by the same resource pressures that were making it hard for line managers to conduct regular supervision (as stated earlier).

Partly because of the growing pressures faced by line managers questions had been raised in some of the case SSDs about the continued viability of traditional methods of providing 'support'. Not only were these practices time consuming, but also potentially counter-productive. According to the Director at Metro 3, for example:

> One way of solving isolation is to have the line manager often popping in and being almost 'part of the establishment'. I feel there are enormous dangers in that, as well as a loss of use of that line manager's real potential, if they do that.

To counter these difficulties some SSDs had tried to develop alternative mechanisms for providing support to staff groups. One example of this was the practice (in all SSDs) of inviting unit managers to various external meetings, workshops and training sessions. The purpose of these meetings was partly to communicate policy (see Chapter 4) and develop a shared sense of responsibility for managing services (see Chapter 5).

A quite different approach was the establishment of alternative mechanisms for providing support outside the framework of line management (DH 1992). This idea was discussed in a number of SSDs, although only in Shire 3 had concrete measures been taken. In this case a 'therapeutic co-ordinator' was appointed to focus on the 'practice' and general support elements of supervision (also see Syrett *et al.* (1996)). A further initiative was the creation of an independent team of psychiatrists and psychologists, headed by a consultant child psychiatrist. According to the resource manager, the objective of this team was to 'absorb some of that "real toxic muck" that supervisors have to manage' and to 'provide a proper therapeutic service to children looked after and for the carers.'

Conclusion

This chapter set out to examine the structures and practices of external line management in SSDs. To this end time was devoted to a description of the pattern of 'custodial management' that emerged in SSDs from the early 1970s. More recent attempts by policy makers to promote a 'managerial mode of co-ordination' in SSDs (Clarke and Newman 1997) were also covered. In this section, now that the main findings have been described, our aim is to develop some general conclusions. In particular, two main issues will be addressed: the question of how far line management practices have changed, and the extent to which change is likely in future and the implications for practitioners.

With regard to the first issue, the study revealed that SSDs in England and Wales were attempting to restructure line management. In keeping with policy and guidance (DH 1991a) many had started to create more specialist line manager posts (allowing the incumbents to concentrate on developments within children's homes). A further change was the increased decentralisation of administrative responsibilities (especially for budgets) to unit managers. Approximately half of our sample had created policies aimed at formalising expectations with regard to the frequency and content of staff supervision. Finally, reflecting broader initiatives across social services (Lawler and Hearn 1997; SSI 1997), all had begun to invest more in management training and development.

These observations show that change has occurred and that new management practices are slowly being adopted. However, it is necessary to exercise caution for two main reasons. First, while management restructuring is clearly under way, the pattern of change is uneven. Many SSDs, have not yet moved towards a specialist model of line management, and fewer still have developed clear policies and procedures governing supervision. In fact, looking at the sample as a whole, progress towards management reform seems to have been remarkably slow. This is especially so when compared to developments elsewhere in UK public services, such as health or central government (Redman *et al.* 2000; Waine 2000; Foster and Hoggett 1999). In many respects our findings lend support to Ackroyd's (1995: 32) view that 'the personal social services ... have showed the weakest development in terms of the introduction of new management'.

A second reason for not overstating change is that the *practice* of supervision itself remains dominated by a 'custodial' approach. It was noted, for example, that supervision was infrequent in many cases. Also, while some attempts had been made to introduce developmental appraisals, supervisory sessions continued to be unstructured and operationally driven. Beyond this, there were few signs that line management had become more effective as a mechanism for control and monitoring practice. Many of the obstacles to this kind of management – goal ambiguity, conflicting demands and asymmetries in knowledge and experience between supervisors and staff – seemed to be as pronounced now as they have ever been. Taken together these observations point towards the existence of a mode of supervision almost identical to the custodial approach described in the literature. The emphasis continues to be on providing support for staff and on minimising aspects of management that might be perceived as being overly judgmental or directive (also see SSI 1998).

In seeking to explain this limited progress of management reform a number of points can be made. First, many of the problems encountered in the case SSDs are similar to those that might arise in any professional bureaucracy. As we saw in Chapter 2, radical change in these contexts is often difficult given conflicting goals, ambiguous authority relationships and the custodial orientations of senior managers (Ackroyd *et al.* 1989; Mintzberg 1993). In addition, the slow pace of change can be explained by the fact that reforms were introduced in a 'climate of financial retrenchment' (Lewis and Glennerster 1996: 70). In the case SSDs, rising spans of control and other demands on line managers had made it more difficult to ensure frequent supervision or to provide effective support. In this respect our SSDs reflect a wider trend throughout UK social services (Thomas *et al.* 2000; Balloch 1998). According to Thompson *et al.* (1996: 659) professional managers have themselves been forced to respond to competing demands and unable to find time to conduct supervision.

The second issue to be discussed relates to the wider implications of our findings. A key question is how far SSDs will be able to reform management arrangements in future? Given the problems identified above, is further change in management structures and practices likely? It is beyond the scope of this chapter to fully answer these questions. However, it is useful to identify *three* main factors that may influence future change.

The first concerns resources. Given the points made above, one way in which line management practices could change in future is if SSDs were prepared to spend more on line management. Extra resources might help in a number of ways, for example, by reducing spans of control through the appointment of new managers or by creating slack to conduct supervision and reduce workloads (Audit Commission 1994). In practice, however, such investment will be hard to make in SSDs. Partly this is due to overall resource constraints mentioned earlier (Means and Smith 1998). Also important is the fact that not all practitioners accept the necessity for extra spending on management. Even now many would regard management as an unnecessary overhead (Pahl 1994) and might question the assumption that 'Effective supervision will improve the quality of services' (SFCRC 1995c).

A second issue relates to different models of line management. In current policy and guidance (see Table 6.2) the emphasis has been on developing specialist line managers, able to perform a range of functions including supervision, monitoring and general support. However, as we saw in the case SSDs, many line managers (especially those lacking past residential experience) found it hard to combine all these different tasks. Given this constraint, it might be argued that, in future, change would only occur if SSDs were able to find ways of minimising these difficulties. To do so may mean looking at alternative models of line management to those outlined in the guidance. One option, for example, is the model of formally separating 'practice' and 'management' aspects of supervision (Syrett *et al.* 1997; Heyes 1996). Another possibility is to develop alternative support functions (such as those created in Shire 3) that are able to take on many of the tasks currently performed by line managers.

The final point highlights the link between line management reform and wider policies relating to children's residential care. In future, a key issue will be how far SSDs are able to define clear objectives for homes (statements of purpose and function) and ensure that staff are able to work according to them (see Chapters 4 and 5). Unless these changes occur it seems unlikely that more judgemental modes of supervision will emerge. Even assuming that line managers are willing, their ability to engage in practices of performance appraisal will ultimately be limited by the lack of clarity over objectives. It seems therefore that further change in line management practice will depend on the success of more general strategies and policies aimed at reorganising and specialising children's homes.

7
Managing and Developing Staff

Introduction

This chapter is concerned with the way staff are managed and its relevance to the external management of children's homes. This requires the use of two main bodies of work to inform an examination of the structures and processes involved. First, specialised findings in Wagner, Warner, the Support Force and ARCC, for example, have addressed specific issues relating to the nature of employment in the children's residential sector. Their reports and recommendations centre on recruitment, training and development, the creation of appropriate skill bases within homes, status and the use of agency staff.

Second, research on employment in the public sector reveals the context in which child care staff and managers have attempted to address the issues raised by the official inquiries of the last decade. Studies provide important clues on the restrictions staff in residential care face from the way their local authority approaches the management of people. Local authorities are generally seen as 'corporatist', dominated by central bargaining and contractual constraints. Managers have no common training or self-image yet ironically, outbreaks of enthusiastic managerialism occur. Personnel departments appear to fall into two broad types: centralised, rule-based or advisory facilitators; as will become clear, these characteristics have important influences on the way those responsible for residential care deal with the problems of staff recruitiment, deployment and training.

This chapter deals with information on both fronts by considering the personnel regimes of SSDs within local authority settings, and their impact on residential staff and their managers. Yet there is an important specific theme which runs through the sections which follow: how far does the character of personnel policies regarding contracts, redeployment and retraining, enable key decisions over service design, specialisation and their associated changes to be implemented? Managing staff could be seen as a component of the implementation process, which was covered in Chapter 4. The problem is given separate attention here in the light of its prominence in recent inquiries and commentary.

The chapter opens with a summary of the recommendations which have emanated from official reports and research. The major problems of the qualifications of staff, the need for an inclusive orientation from senior managers and the lack of training at all levels are explored. A discussion of personnel management and the form that it has taken in the public sector appears in Section 7.2. The intention is to understand the context in which SSDs operate when dealing with staff. Approaches to people management differ markedly across the sector. The status of the personnel function is by no means uniform when different local authorities are compared. It will then be possible in Section 7.3 to observe the contrasting experience between the case authorities of managing staff and the implications for the external management of residential care.

7.1 Managing staff and residential care

Research on the personnel management regimes of social services departments (SSDs) has been slight. The same cannot be said of the problems surrounding the issue of staff in residential care. Department of Health and related work has been extensive over the past 16 years.

The report by Wagner in 1988, advocated residential care as a positive choice. She saw that the importance of staffing and training was central, as the following recommendations show. Care staff should be graded as officer or professional equivalent. All senior posts were to be filled by qualified social workers by 1993. A staff training plan must be prepared for each establishment. Unqualified staff who move into residential work should receive conversion training. Wagner also emphasised an holistic view of staffing (Wagner 1988: 85) and the need for a higher status for residential workers (op.cit.: 75). The first Utting review of residential care (DH 1991a) confirmed and extended these conclusions. He highlighted the need for not only professional training (55) but also retention plans to stop the flow of professionally qualified staff into field social work. Most important of all, the report recommended:

the need for a more managerially-led staffing policy throughout child care services generally ... such an approach would powerfully assist the integration of residential care within social work generally. (55–6)

The *Report of the Committee of Enquiry into the Selection, Development and Management of Staff in Children's Homes*, chaired by Warner, was published in 1992. It reinforced the prevailing notions of residential care as problematic, emphasising the declining number of homes which were expected to cope with a more complex set of demands from adolescents. The neglect of children's homes by some SSDs, their poor management, deficient employment practices and the underdevelopment of professional-training and knowledge were pinpointed. Many of the recommendations of Warner have been explored in Chapter 6's account of line management. In respect of staff, Warner argued for: systematic recruitment and selection procedures, formal supervision of unit managers to occur every two weeks, a national programme based on in-house training (with New Vocational Qualification (NVQ) accreditation) for junior staff and a new professional qualification in residential care for management (123–6). The report bemoaned the lack of policy and planning frameworks for children's homes (see Chapter 4).

Subsequent work on staffing issues has elaborated on these themes. The Support Force in 1995 endorsed the use of assessment centres in selection, a code of employment practice (40) and using a diversity of routes to professional qualification (18). The ARCC (1995) has underlined the difficulties involved in the Warner proposals, including the residential element of the DipSW.

The Tavistock Institute's assessment (1997) of the Department of Health's Residential Child Care Initiative found that DipSW did not provide sufficient management training (134). The assessment also concluded that an SSD's orientation to 'human resource policies' had a key impact on the way such training could be exploited within a residential unit (135). In the same year, the work of Lawler and Hearn (1997) pointed to the low levels of preparation for managerial positions, the lack of common training and the uneasy self-images of managers in social services (196–207). At unit level, Sinclair and Gibbs (1996) found that the high morale of residential staff was more likely if they, *inter alia*, received regular supervision, had clear job descriptions and had induction training (212). Berridge and Brodie (1997) could find no positive relationship, however, between staff qualifications/training and the quality of residential care (166). Whilst many of the findings of these reports have been consistent, hardly any addressed the impact of local authority personnel policies on the staff and practices in residential care.

7.2 Personnel management and the public sector

A note of caution should be struck when dealing with the subject of managing people, especially in the UK economy. The development of people management has been late, incomplete and often problematic. At the time of the Wagner report in 1988, a cross-industry survey in the UK showed that although a majority of companies claimed to have an overall policy for the management of people, less than half had put that policy in writing (Sisson 1989). The record of the public sector should be viewed accordingly.

Poor performance by western organisations in the early 1980s led to renewed emphasis on the management of human resources. A new approach to the management of people emerged called 'human resource management' (HRM). The main objective of HRM is to integrate human resource planning and strategic management. It aims to foster commitment from individuals to the success of an organisation through a quality orientation in the performance of individuals and departments. HRM seeks to maximise the knowledge and skills within an organisation in order for it to compete.

Previously, personnel management emphasised a reactive posture, with a concern for consistency and regulation. HRM specialists saw themselves as positive, developmental and seeking to link human resource levers to competitive requirements. Line managers, it was argued, under personnel management would expect personnel specialists to be responsible for staff issues (such as training and development). In an HRM organisation the line manager takes active ownership of such problems. Just as personnel management practices were adopted in a limited way down to the 1980s, so the spread of HRM has been uneven and faced opposition from managers and employees alike. The strategic elements of HRM have not sat easily with the ingrained short-termism and pragmatism of many British organisations.

The growth of personnel and human resource management in the public sector has been equally patchy and especially in local government. People management in the public services has its own traditions. Collectivist institutions of industrial relations evolved from the political reforms of the twentieth century. The main characteristics included: a centralised administrative personnel style, standardised employment practices, paternalist management and the belief that state employers should be model employers (Farnham and Horton 1996: 43). The public services also differ from other sectors with respect to broader social duties. Staff cannot readily be regarded only as a resource since they are also seen as agents who provide essential services, often guided by professional values (op.cit.: 32. See also Chapter 2).

The emergence of the new public management (see Chapter 6) has challenged the conventional approach to managing people in public services. During the 1980s and early 1990s, governments re-shaped public services with a view to controlling public expenditure via the increase of private provision. The introduction of competitive forces was accompanied by the arrival of financial and management techniques from the private sector. Some associated aspects of human resource management have made inroads as part of this initiative (Kessler and Purcell 1996: 215). Two results stand out – decentralisation and fragmentation.

In local government especially, the traditional, centralised model of people management had by the late 1990s been challenged. Through decentralisation local authorities have attempted to devolve personnel decisions to line managers, including decisions over staffing levels, selection and appraisal. This development was strongly supported by the Audit Commission and mirrored a trend seen across the public sector. Meanwhile, personnel departments changed shape and function (Bach 1999). A more fragmented picture emerged following the extension of competitive tendering to white collar staff in 1992. Some personnel functions were contracted out while others assumed a more client-based relationship with service departments (White and Hutchinson 1996: 194–7).

The result is a mixed picture made up of sometimes opposing features. Social services staff moving from one local authority to another may encounter personnel managers in one authority who facilitate and advise line managers in problem solving and, in another, those who remain in a more corporate role given the political control exercised by some councils. Both positive and negative implications are apparent. Client-centred approaches, for example, may be attractive but the decentralisation which they depend on could further weaken the strategic role of personnel departments as they concentrate on short-term operational issues. As we saw in Chapter 4, the strategic capability of social services and local authorities is undeveloped and at a cost to care management and children's services. How such preferences for personnel management are expressed at local level will be shown to have an important effect on how residential care staff have been managed.

7.3   Managing staff and residential care in the case authorities

Our study has examined the responses of the 12 local authorities to the recommendations and practices outlined in Section 7.1. In addition, we have used the observations on the management of people in local government, and more widely, to inform the research. We have paid attention to the nature of the authorities as employers and the orientation of their personnel function. The concern is not simply with training but also staff flexibility since redeployment appears critical to achieving the realignment of needs and provision within SSDs. The result is that the actions of the case authorities are best understood under five main headings: their relation to national agreements; the implementation of Warner; the style of personnel management; the achievement of flexibility and redeployment; and the linking of training to needs analysis.

National agreements The dominant role of national level agreements (identified in Section 7.2) is amply confirmed by the experience of the 11 authorities. All have honoured the main conditions concerning pay levels, grading and service contained in the National Joint Council (the 'Green Book'). Even the larger metropolitan and shire authorities, where the implications and costs could be extensive, signed up to the agreements with minimal variation. Shire 2, for example, adopted the national pay award and the principle of 'benchmark grades'. The personnel manager accepted that:

> The national negotiators came up with the notion that residential social workers ... should be on a grade which recognises this notion of benchmark duties. And anybody who was working along these bench mark duties would be paid accordingly. So that dictated your benchmark grade.

Metro 2 showed only minimal variations from the agreements. The differences, however, exist mainly where the agreement's general framework make space for local negotiation. As a result, Metro 2 has developed locally negotiated staff structures/establishment rates for its children's homes. It has also used the framework to raise pay and conditions of work for residential staff. Metro 3 has gone furthest in interpreting parts of the national agreements in order to meet its own needs. The move to place heavy reliance on preventative, family-based work and reduce long-term residential provision meant that costs had to be adjusted. In the words of the personnel manager:

> We have moved away in some degree from the national scheme and recommended something that suited us and we could afford because basically, we were sticking with the residential recommendations that we couldn't afford any more.

The influence of Warner As we saw earlier in the chapter, the recommendations contained in the Warner report of 1992 on the management of staff in children's homes were the most far reaching of their kind. Early meetings during the study with UK experts in the field suggested that SSDs have complied with these recommendations in an incomplete way.

None of the local authorities in the study would claim to have introduced every element of Warner. It is very clear though, how the pattern of recommendations have come to dominate the thinking of their personnel managers. Most of the authorities have a firm grasp of the standards required for recruitment, selection and training. London 1 illustrates how the Warner framework may be used by managers to challenge the position of trade unions on points of negotiation. Metro 2 is representative of a wider view among the case authorities; they have treated the main conclusion seriously and it is the more technical aspects of personnel which they have yet to complete (such as psychometric testing). The social services director of Metro 2 makes a reasonable point when he comments:

> We've been fairly conscientious ... in following most of the recommendations of the Warner report. I say most of it because I readily admit in some of them we haven't done anything and we're not certain that we know how to do it, because nobody else does; I am thinking of personality testing in recruitment selection for example.

The same is true for Metro 3. All the authorities are concerned about attaining consistency of practice across their personnel and residential mangers in relation to Warner.

The personnel function The position of the personnel function in the case authorities is a more varied one. In Section 7.2 of the chapter, a distinction was made between two approaches to personnel management. One is the traditional orientation, founded on ensuring adherence to rules and procedures together with a reactive mentality. The other, more recent version, known as human resource management, emphasises a developmental orientation, the maximisation of individual and collective abilities and a concern for clients' problems within the organisation.

In general, the sample of authorities are some distance away from the model of HRM which is better known in some other sectors. No instances were observed of contracting out parts of the personnel function's tasks, for example. Metro 2 stands by itself as the one personnel department which concentrates on its professional responsibilities first. The client orientation of the HRM approach does not yet provide its raison d'être.

Conversely, Metro 1 and 3, Shires 2 and 3 and Unitaries 2 and 3 are all striving to make such a transition. All admit that their authorities have historically conformed to the role of guardian of policy and rules, outlined in Section 7.2. Each is attempting to devolve personnel issues to line and unit managers in residential care and adopt a more enabling position. Metro 3, for example, is now organised into three teams (each headed by a personnel officer with clerical support) within the SSD. As the personnel manager explains:

> Instead of providing a generic service to anybody who happened to want something, we have streamed into children['s], adults and learning disability. The idea is that you get specialism within the team, and they have more awareness of the needs of their 'client group' and, again, familiarity with the things that are going on in that area of the service.

The direction of development is broadly similar in Shire 3. According to the personnel manager in the SSD:

> Traditionally we have had a central personnel function ... and up to fairly recently, it has been very much about the centre. You know they pass out the policies and the judgements and the pieces of paper and they make demands on departments about statistics and other things that they need and there has been very little communication between the two ... We are actually entering a new era where the central personnel function is becoming far more of an enabling function.

The two London boroughs form a third group where devolution to line managers of personnel issues was weak and problems of control and centralisation dominated.

Flexibility   The profile which emerges from the case authorities largely conforms to the nature of personnel management in the public sector in the United Kingdom. In other words, the personnel specialists are constrained by national agreements and struggling to adopt more advanced techniques associated with HRM. Whilst they all have embraced the conclusions of Warner, what has been the impact of the personnel function on the major tasks of linking needs analysis with training, or, the problem of flexibility which redeployment raises as residential care is reorganised?

Flexibility has proved to be a serious problem for the local authorities studied. Half have been unable to renegotiate staff contracts to enable the appropriate movement of residential staff following the redesign of provision. In this group, Shire 3 has resorted to agency staff at a cost of £3.5 million, with an overspend in 1997 of £250,000. The more traditional personnel function had not helped to overcome the difficulties in creating more flexible working arrangements. London 2 had found flexibility difficult while introducing a major programme of centralisation.

Metro 2 has been particularly sensitive about staff movements between homes. Staff may be moved for short periods on a formal acting basis. Personnel managers were also concerned about the Warner recommendation of the importance of recruiting for a particular unit. The result has been a heavy reliance on overtime from staff employed on 39 hour contracts.

Those who have enjoyed more success include Metro 3, Shire 2 and Unitaries 1 and 3. In Metro 3, staff are employed on part-time contracts based on 15–20 hours per week. Additional work can be 'made up' through using the difference between 20 hours and the 37 hours full week. The system also makes it easier to cover for staff holidays and absence. Use is also made of a reserve pool. The personnel manager for social services explains:

> We should only have ratios which reflected the needs ... As opposed to staffing up to the maximum, staff up to the average, have this pool that you use on a temporary basis, so that you topped-up at peak times but you didn't staff up to that.

In a partly similar way, Shire 2 used a 'known casuals pool'. Both Metro 3 and Shire 2 do not use agency staff as a consequence.

The unitary authorities in the sample have taken the opportunities offered by local government reform to re-work employment agreements. Unitary 1 has moved all staff on to field social work grades and is breaking down the mentality where residential staff work in one home for large parts of their career. Unitary 3 has used a parallel approach of appointing staff to the resource group rather than individual units.

Needs and training Observation of all the case authorities and their SSDs reveals widespread training activity of all kinds. Where the cases differ is in their ability to link the needs of children and service provision with appropriate training. Training may enhance the skills and career of the trainee but there is no necessary reason why such training should positively affect the standard of residential care.

In common with many organisations in the private sector, the measurement of training effectiveness is only just starting. There is, however, a split between two types of authority in our findings. The first category is made up of those who addressed the issue but slightly, often hampered by major problems confronting the department. The upheavals following scandals and restructuring in London 2 and Shire 1 are cases in point. It is interesting that in London 1, the pressure for relating training to emerging care needs came from the training area in the following way:

> When the residential review was going on, what we did was make sure we were represented on the group there, so that training was thought about ... we actually got to hear about that work whereas before we wouldn't necessarily hear about it direct from anybody. (Training manager)

The second group is best described as aware of the problem of combining needs and training but with varying results. The departments in question obviously have emphasised aspects of training which are relevant to their circumstances. Unitary 2 has benefitted from a Welsh Office initiative on training which is reflected in the way the department's new emergency home opened in 1997 with all staff given specialist training. The same department has also appointed an officer to support all residential staff through their NVQ work.

The mixed picture of achievement is well illustrated in the shire and metropolitan authorities. Metro 2 has a strong commitment to bringing training and residential plans together at departmental level but has not yet translated the intention down to individual staff. Their management programme which incorporates all unit managers is impressive. Shire 2 has a large training operation, including its own training centre for residential care. The irony is that local residential care courses tailored to the pattern of needs in the county's zones have, as a result, proved more difficult to set-up. In Shire 3, the major restructuring of residential care clearly drove an associated programme of retraining and redeployment. All unit managers are qualified, as are most assistant managers. The belief in therapeutic skills at senior level has ensured a complete implementation of unit-based training led by outside experts. Metro 3 meanwhile concentrated first on its reorganisation around family-based care and has (since 1997) created a training plan which reflects the new structure.

Conclusion

This chapter has tried to take a constructive view of the way SSDs manage their staff in relation to residential care. Examining the way such departments manage people does not only reveal a core element of their model of management and its context (aim 1 of the project), it also highlights how appropriate, or otherwise, such models are in supporting the external management of children's homes (aim 2). In order to present an accurate picture this requires building an account through a number of steps.

First, at the sector level, public services are heavily influenced by the weight of traditional institutions, built up over a century. These include, highly regulated employment practices, an administrative personnel style and the expectations attached to the state as a model employer. Human resource management approaches have appeared in a fragmented way, associated partly with new attempts at cost control and the increase of private provision.

Second, those in the residential care field have been subject to a wealth of advice and imperatives concerning the management of staff. Reports from Wagner (1988) through DH (1992) to the Support Force (1995c) produced both general and specific recommendations. The details of recruitment, selection and staff development were well covered. The general injunction to develop a more managerially led staffing approach was seen as a means of integrating residential care within social services. Similar emphases are apparent in the emerging framework that seeks to join delivering services, social work training and workforce planning with the establishment of a Social Care Institute for Excellence and a General Social Care Council in England. Different arrangements are being developed in each county in the United Kingdom, reflecting contrasting patterns of social care (Orme 2001: 615–16).

In this context, it is possible to understand the main features of the management of residential staff in the case authorities. It is entirely consistent with practice in the public services that all the cases honour national employment agreements. Local negotiation over certain elements is increasing. In a broadly comparable way, the response to Warner and others seems to share the same mentality. The recommendations have been accepted and they influence practice. This finding would appear to run contrary to the expectations of some involved in the Support Force and subsequent initiatives. SSDs are open that they have been less able to meet details of Warner where it exceeds their expertise (e.g., psychometric testing).

In terms of the project's aim to suggest forms of management which help to solve problems in the external management relationship (aim 2), one main finding stands out. Overall, there is a genuine movement towards the use of more advanced approaches to personnel management. This includes the reorienting of personnel departments from a central guardian role to that of an enabler to client groups in the organisation. Those who have consciously thought through this change have also been the most able to deliver the conditions required for new children's services provision. Even though most SSDs are at an early stage, it is clear from the evidence that the adoption of HRM planning linked to needs and care reviews, for example, has been of *mutual* benefit. Greater flexibility in employment terms has resulted and redeployment has made possible the redesign of residential and children's care, problems that have dominated the case authorities.

There are a number of recommendations that follow on from these findings. The adoption of useful elements of the HRM orientation to the management of people in SSDs should be extended and the results shared more widely across the sector. The practical benefits could be extensive. Personnel issues would become an integral part of planning processes rather than employment practices having to 'catch-up' with wider policy initiatives. Recruitment, qualifications and training should be considered at the same time as the results of needs analyses and care reviews are discussed by planning groups. Major decisions about residential care practices would be more robust at the outset as a result.

The use of a more integrated conception of residential care and personnel issues from the start of planning exercises would also lead to better prospects for dealing with some of the most widespread problems in the sector. It would appear that the high cost of employing agency staff in order to ensure adequate cover, could be avoided by creating 'established hours' schemes. The cost of overtime is far less damaging to SSD budgets than the bill for hiring at agency rates. The creation of pools of approved temporary staff, run from the centre, is a necessary requirement. In a similar way, senior management must create the conditions for meaningful appraisal schemes to operate. The need is all the more urgent given the limitations of the monitoring and control devices which will be shown in Chapter 8. In the same spirit as our earlier remarks concerning strategic thinking in SSDs, a more reflective approach to training and development of staff is imperative. As needs analysis and care plans become more precisely targetted, so the links (or otherwise) between training and the standard of care should be more exactly demonstrated.

8
Monitoring and Control

Introduction

The concept of 'corporate parenting' requires that a Social Services Department (SSD) establishes an effective management information system (MIS) which allows managers to monitor the safety of children placed in local authority homes (DH 1991a, 1997). In the past, managers in SSDs have tended to rely on data sources such as supervision sessions, visits by field social workers and by members. However, in the wake of the well-publicised scandals in homes a succession of reports have questioned the effectiveness of these procedures and the extent to which they guarantee the well-being of children looked after (Berridge and Brodie 1996). As one Social Services Inspectorate (SSI) report concluded, there exist 'considerable weaknesses in the external management and monitoring of residential care services' (SSI 1993).

In line with broader trends across the UK public sector (Power 1997; Sanderson 2001), policy-makers sought to address these deficiencies by implementing a regime of audit and inspection in local authority children's services during the 1990s. This meant greater involvement of external agencies such as the SSI and, to a lesser extent, the Audit Commission. It has also led to the development of *internal* mechanisms of inspection of children's residential care, for example, with the requirement for routine management visits to homes (regulation 22) and the use of 'arm's length' inspections carried out by Registration and Inspection (R&I) Units. A key aim of these practices was to provide senior managers, local politicians and the public at large with the information required to protect the safety of children looked after.

The purpose of this chapter is to address the third main research aim of the study, 'to discover how far techniques of monitoring performance and of remedial intervention have been developed'. To complete this task, attention in this chapter is devoted to the internal mechanisms of inspection: Regulation 22 (reg. 22) visits and arm's length inspections. A key question is how far these practices enhanced MIS within SSDs? We also explore the way in which the information collected has been used in a broader sense, whether it has led to changes in the quality and standard of services.

To address these issues the chapter contains four main sections. The first discusses the development of new audit and inspection regimes across UK public services during the 1990s. Section 8.2 turns to the specific policy and guidance relating to the inspection of local authority run children's homes. Section 8.3 contains the experience of the 12 case study SSDs and the practice of reg. 22 inspections. In Section 8.4 we examine how arm's length inspections were conducted and to what effect. The conclusion summarises this experience, as well as linking its implications to the recently announced plans for social care regulation and inspection.

8.1   Inspection in public services

As noted in Chapter 2 a key characteristic of professional bureaucracy is the tendency of front-line practitioners to demand autonomy, not only over the means of service delivery, but also to determine methods of evaluation and assessment (Ackroyd *et al.* 1989). As Pollitt (1990: 435) suggests, 'the control of quality lies at the heart of the notion of professionalism'. In the United Kingdom this assumption was central to the 'organisational settlement' of the 1960s and '70s whereby qualified professionals were trusted to manage services in the public interest (Clarke and Newman 1997). In health, education as well as social care, professional peer review and self-regulation served as the primary mechanisms for the control and evaluation of public services (Hallett 1982).

In the United Kingdom these arrangements were largely reinforced by the practices of government evaluative agencies, such as the Social Work Advisory Service and the Health Advisory Service. According to Harris (1998: 845) the work of these agencies was characterised by 'a lightness of touch' (Harris 1998: 845) and shaped by notions of 'professionally led, liberal and interactive evaluation' (Henkel 1991: 121). This meant a regime in which the autonomy of professional groups to regulate themselves was largely preserved and where the role of external agencies was essentially 'advisory'. While central government did try to influence practice the emphasis was on achieving change by relying on persuasion and 'rigorous argument rather than conclusive judgement' (Henkel 1991: 122).

By the early 1980s this mode of evaluation in UK public services was increasingly questioned by politicians, policy-makers and consumer groups. For central government a key difficulty was the emphasis on 'resource needs, inputs and on processes' (Henkel 1991: 122). This meant that less attention was given to the question of measuring performance in terms of outputs or the cost effectiveness of services. Concerns were also growing about 'provider paternalism' (Day and Klein 1990) and doubts as to whether professional groups could or should be trusted to regulate their own practice. As Foster and Wilding (2000: 145) put it: 'accountability to themselves, to a professional ethic or to their professional peers was criticised as little more than a fig leaf on a naked unaccountable, unmanaged, unresponsive independence'.

From the mid-1980s these criticisms led to policies aimed at developing a new regime of audit and inspection in UK public services (Day and Klein 1990). A central feature was the change in the role of agencies involved in evaluation, notably the SSI (previously SWAS until 1985) and the Audit Commission (formed in 1983). Increasingly these agencies rejected the model of peer review and 'professional consultancy' that had been dominant in the 1970s. Instead it was

> Assumed that complexities of provision could be broken down and objectively assessed on measurable indicators of performance according to nationally established standards. Resource constraint and control were taken as incontestable priorities. (Henkel 1991: 122)

Gradually, the role of evaluative agencies shifted from offering advice and support to public organisations, to one of helping 'to implement national policies or hold the inspected to account for what they had done, and how'. (Day and Klein 1990: 4).

In addition to this growing emphasis on external inspection, public organisations also faced pressures to develop their own internal management control systems. As Power (1997: 92) suggests, the aim of government was to achieve a 'steady transformation of internal control cultures (that were *ad hoc*, process driven) into externally auditable objects'. To comply with this, local managers were required to find ways in which to quantify and simplify even the most 'complex' and 'internally controversial' (ibid.: 114) professional operations.

There remains some disagreement over the impact and consequences of these policies. For many, the introduction of these regimes of audit and inspection represents a radical change in public services.

Hoggett (1996: 29), for example, suggests that 'the diffusion of performance management systems has clearly had the effect of reducing professional autonomy across a wide number of different sectors'. The argument put forward by such scholars is that new inspection regimes have been largely effective in reconstructing professional work, making it more transparent and accountable. Ultimately, new forms of inspection and audit might 'colonise' professional work, leading to 'the creation over time of new mentalities, new incentives and perceptions of significance' (Power 1997: 97).

Others contend that processes of audit and inspection have had less dramatic consequences. New inspection regimes are difficult to implement in professional bureaucracies. As we saw in Chapter 2 there exist powerful sources of inertia and resistance to change in these contexts. According to Ackroyd *et al.* (1989: 611) 'attempts by management to apply standardised performance measures' are likely to be 'fraught with difficulties and give rise to effective resistance by practitioners'. There is also the possibility that systems of inspection, even when they are established, may not have their intended effects. Power (1997: 95), for example, notes the possibility that an inspection regime could be 'decoupled or compartmentalised in such a way that it is remote from the very organisational processes which give it its point'. This implies that organisations may engage only in surface compliance with external demands for inspection. While systems may be established they could take on a ceremonial character, remaining loosely-coupled or buffered from core professional operations (Meyer and Rowen 1991).

8.2 Inspection and local authority children's residential care

In the context of children's residential care, the development of new regimes of inspection became a priority during the 1990s. A succession of reports into abuse scandals pointed to the inadequacies of line management control and a failure to detect malpractice in homes (Shaw 1995; Berridge and Brodie 1997). To counter this problem, central government produced extensive policies and guidance detailing the need for new mechanisms of inspection. A key change was the enlarged role played by the SSI as the main external body involved in the monitoring of residential care. In addition, local authorities were required to develop their own *internal* arrangements for the inspection of children's homes. Two main systems were prescribed: arm's length inspections and reg. 22 visits.

The first of these internal systems – arm's length inspection – became the responsibility of local authority R&I (Registration and Inspection) units. These units were set up following the *NHS and Community Care Act 1990*, primarily to regulate the growing private sector market for adult residential and domicilary care (Challis 1990; DH 1997: 176). With regard to children's homes, policy stated that all establishments should be audited twice a year, with one visit being planned in advance and the other unannounced. Both staff and children had to confirm that the inspections have occurred and that they were conducted in a manner that respected them. An annual report of the inspection had to be prepared both for members of the authority and the SSI (LAC 1994b: 16).

The second mechanism for internal inspection is what came to be known as the 'regulation 22' visit. This related to Regulation 22 of the *Children's Homes Regulations 1991* stating that 'the local authority who maintains a community home shall cause the home to be visited once a month'. The *Children Act 1989* (Volume 4) also prescribed that 'an important part of these visits is to ensure that the day-to-day conduct of the home is seen by someone not involved in its operation and who can provide an independent report to the responsible authority'. It was also mandatory that the responsible authority receive each month, directly from the appointed visitor, a written report on the conduct of the home (CH reg. 22, Vol. 4, 1. 170).

The assumption was that these new systems of internal inspection would help to advance two main goals. The first, and perhaps most important, was to enhance management control over the service, providing reassurances that young people looked after are safe. According to Utting (1997: 176) inspection can offer management 'an expert appraisal of services from a viewpoint independent of the vested interests involved in supplying them'. It is therefore 'serving the public interest by providing an additional safeguard for vulnerable people' (ibid.). A key aim of inspection was therefore to feed into a wider management information system 'designed to recognise differences between current and desired levels of performance and to trigger adjustments when discrepancies are noticed' (Hatch 1997: 330). Alongside other sources of information, inspection reports should greatly enhance this MIS.

The second goal of such inspection in children's residential care was to act as a mechanism for quality assurance and the gradual improvement of services. In the wider literature it is acknowledged that evaluation systems have a 'dual rationale' (Sanderson 2001: 301). As such, the emphasis is not simply on '"top-down" systems oriented primarily to accountability and control', but also on '"bottom up" systems with a greater concern for promoting improvements in performance' (ibid.: 302). In the context of SSDs, this latter role was regarded as being extremely important. R&I units were required to produce annual reports detailing the condition of children's homes and including formal requirements on how local authorities should improve standards [WOC/LAC]. It was also assumed that R&I units might take on a developmental role, offering expert advice and making recommendations to managers on how they could improve the quality of residential services (DH 1991a). As Challis (1990: 130) suggests, in addition to their policing role, it was envisaged that R&I will 'become the arbiters of practice, the exponents of the moral and professional arguments against poor performers, and the confidants of the director and possibly of members'.

Policy and guidance therefore placed considerable emphasis on the role played by inspection in children's residential care. However, questions remain over how far new structures and practices have been fully implemented in SSDs. For example, an SSI study (1998: 1) of 17 authorities reported that:

> Although all SSDs had developed a range of planning, policy and procedural documents, these were not always followed by staff. Managers did not have systems to check that workers complied with procedures and guidance.

These (and other) studies raise questions about how far new inspection regimes have been fully implemented in children's residential care. They also imply that new systems may not have achieved their desired goals and that, possibly, have become 'decoupled' from core professional decision making (Power 1997). To address this issue, in Section 8.3 we examine the experience of the 12 case study SSDs, dealing first with the practice of reg. 22 inspections and second the arm's length inspections conducted by R&I units.

8.3   The practice of reg. 22 visits

With regard to reg. 22 inspections, a wide variation in policies and practices was noted between the local authorities in our study. To understand this complexity it is useful to compare management arrangements along four main dimensions (see Table 8.1 for a summary): the general procedures for conducting reg. 22 visits, the variations in the format or content of such inspections, the differences in the frequency with which

Table 8.1 The conduct of regulation 22 visits

Local authority	Procedure for reg. 22 visits	The format/content of reg. 22 inspections	Evidence to suggest that reg. 22 visits are conducted 100% (Y/N?)	Integration of reg. 22 reports in wider MIS
Metro 1	Rota of line managers	Tick box	No	Low
Metro 2	Single responsible officer	Tick box and more general observations relating to practice	Yes	High
Metro 3	Line manager and rota of unit managers	Tick box	Yes	Low
Shire 1	Rota of line managers	Tick box	Yes	High
Shire 2	Line managers (own homes)	Tick box ('doing the books')	No	Low
Shire 3	Rota of middle managers	Tick box and more general observations relating to practice	Yes	Low
London 1	Line managers (own homes)	Tick box	No	Low
London 2	Rota of line managers (including FSW managers)	Tick box	No	Low
London 3	No. in house provision	NA	NA	NA
Unitary 1	Line managers (own homes)	Tick box	Yes	High
Unitary 2	Line managers (own homes)	Tick box	No	Low
Unitary 3	Rota of middle managers	Tick box	Yes	Low

they were conducted, and the questions relating to how far information produced from these inspections was used as part of a wider MIS.

Procedures for conducting reg. 22 visits

Given the vagueness in the guidance relating to reg. 22 inspections (see earlier) it is perhaps not surprising to discover a wide variation in the procedures used by the case SSDs. While some adopted a systematic approach, in others the practice was less well organised. In general, three main approaches could be identified.

The first is the practice adopted in six of the case SSDs of establishing a rota of managers to conduct reg. 22 visits on establishments for which they were not directly responsible. In one case, Metro 1 this was achieved by relying exclusively on residential care line managers who would conduct visits on each other's homes. However, in those SSDs where fewer line managers were employed (see Table 6.1) the rota also included middle managers, field social work managers and (in Shire 1) Assistant Directors. Typical of these arrangements was the system adopted at Shire 3:

> All our middle managers across the department, of which we have a huge number [36], are rota'd to do a regulation 22 visit to all our children's homes. (Assistant Director, Children)

The only exception to this rule of using higher level managers in the rota was Metro 3 where, due to its small size, unit managers of homes in the rota had been included making them responsible for visiting and 'inspecting' homes run by their colleagues.

The second approach, adopted in four case SSDs was for line managers to conduct reg. 22 visits on the homes for which they were directly responsible. In these authorities the expectation was that reg. 22 visits would be unannounced and conducted separately from supervisory sessions. However, in the majority it appeared that reg. 22s were being conducted at the same time as the scheduled supervisory session. For example, in London 1 a unit manager explained that: 'she [the line manager] comes in for supervision and then, at the end of the supervision, she checks things that were meant to be part of her unannounced [reg. 22] visits'.

This practice of linking supervision and reg. 22s was, of course, contrary to the regulations and, in some SSDs, had been strongly criticised. In Unitary 2, for example, an SSI report concluded that 'line managers were organisationally too close to the operation of homes to satisfy the requirement that visits be undertaken by someone independent of operations' (SSIW: 1997: 45–6). Generally it was admitted that the practice of relying on line managers was a largely pragmatic response to guidance driven mainly by the lack of time and resources to set up more elaborate systems. The only exception to this was in Shire 2 where managers defended the practice on the grounds that it contributed to the maintenance of good relationships between the centre and front-line staffs. It was assumed that 'If a manager from outside that relationship was to get regular access into the home it might unsettle the relationship which can get rocky at times anyway'.

The third approach towards conducting reg. 22 visits was apparent only in Metro 2. Here the decision had been taken to appoint a single officer (an ex-unit manager of a children's home) whose entire responsibility would be to conduct reg. 22 visits on all children's homes. It was acknowledged that the reg. 22 manager was not fully 'independent' (given his background in residential care), it was felt that the system was superior to past practice in the terms of the information produced and also in terms of meeting the formal requirements of the Children Act 1989.

Format and content of reg. 22 inspections

All 12 SSDs had produced a standard *pro forma* of some kind for the conduct of reg. 22 visits. However, there was some variation in the type of information these *pro forma* were designed to collect. In general, two broad approaches were evident.

The first practice, adopted in the vast majority of SSDs, relied on a tick-box questionnaire composed of easily quantifiable issues such as record keeping and the condition of the premises. According to a unit manager at Metro 1, the emphasis was mainly on 'trivial' issues such as 'the temperature of fridges and bath water'. In a similar fashion, a line manager at Shire 2 described it as 'doing the books'.

This tick-box approach towards conducting reg. 22s reflected a widespread view amongst managers and staff, in this and other authorities, that the process was primarily about minimal compliance with external demands for audit and record keeping. It also reflected a more general confusion over the nature and purpose of the reg. 22 inspections. According to a line manager at London 1, 'I think regulation 22 is extremely unclear. It seems to apply much more to the private and voluntary sector and the language doesn't seem to fit with ... ourselves.'

By contrast, in two SSDs – Metro 2 and Shire 3 – attempts were made to go beyond straight compliance and broaden the scope of reg. 22 to incorporate more general observations about the nature of professional practice and the standards of care received by young people. In Shire 3, for example, the line manager explained:

> We have a standard schedule, although we are about to change it because we think it's a bit too inspectoral. We want it to be more about ethics and culture and ethos within the children's home. You know, 'do the kids like the food?', 'do they have access to a homework room?'

Frequency of visits

Given the nature of our data it was not always possible to confirm exactly how far the 12 SSDs were in full compliance with the formal requirement that reg. 22 visits be conducted monthly. In six cases senior managers asserted that all visits were routinely conducted, a claim that was not disputed by unit managers and other staffs. However, it was evident that in some of these authorities, new procedures for checking up on the conduct of reg. 22s were a fairly recent development. For example, Shire 3 had only just implemented a new policy designed to 'close loops' in the MIS. This followed an SSI report, published in 1997, that was critical of the fact that only 60 per cent of reg. 22 visits were being conducted.

In the remaining five SSDs it was apparent that not all reg. 22 visits were being conducted. A number of reasons were given for this, by far the most common of which were constraints of time and resources (see also Chapter 6). A resource manager at Shire 2 noted that:

> If you have line managers who manage an average of six units plus a number of teams, things stack up. So I can easily see how we can get into a mindset of, you know, 'it's a bit like the MOT on a car, really, it can wait'.

Although limited resources were clearly an important factor in preventing the full completion of reg. 22 visits, the point should not be exaggerated. The failure to conduct visits in these cases also had much to do with a prevailing culture in these SSDs that tended to view the reg. 22 process as merely an outward compliance exercise and therefore less of a priority than other tasks requiring management time and attention.

Integration of information into MIS

The final issue to consider is how far the information collected from reg. 22 visits was relayed to senior professionals and members and then acted upon. As Table 8.1 shows, evidence could be found in only three SSDs – Metro 2, Shire 1 and Unitary 1 – which suggested reg. 22 reports were systematically used in this way.

At Metro 2, all reg. 22 reports were read and 'signed off' by the reg. 22 manager, the line manager of the home (who adds his/her comments) and senior managers. There is also some evidence to suggest that these reports are used consciously both by senior staff and by members. As the Director explained:

> Members pick up things like, 'hang about, you said that you were going to repair the washing machine, it's been broken for six weeks, when are you going to do it', or 'we notice from the last report that this kid was missing, they've come back and gone again, what's the problem, why are they running away, where are they going?'

At Unitary 1 and Shire 1 we also found evidence that reg. 22 reports were well-read amongst senior managers and members and that they did inform management practice. The line manager at Unitary 1 explained this process and why it had developed:

> The one thing that all the scandals have told us is that you can't assume that nothing is happening, you must find out what is going on. ... On a monthly basis, the Reg. 22 reports are sent through to members of the social services committee, the AD, the director and the unit managers. I'll give you an example of what comes out. I was involved in one home when we identified that the information stored on kids was grossly short and there were concerns about staff supervision. It was only the Reg. 22 visits that I do that could really pull those issues out. So, we spent 4 weeks putting them right so that the next visit, 4 weeks later, they had to be in place, or there was going to be trouble.

By contrast, in the remaining SSDs there was far less evidence to suggest that reg. 22s formed part of a systematic MIS. In some cases, while reports were passed up to committee and senior management levels, little energy was devoted either to reading or acting upon them. For example, at Metro 3;

> We report them to committee. They're not interested [the members]. They don't read any committee reports. They just read the front page with the recommendations. (Assistant Director)

In other cases it was clear that reports were not even being passed to higher levels. For instance, in Unitary 3 a committee member admitted: 'I have heard of the reg. 22 reports, but I can't remember what it is ... We don't get specific reports back to committee on that.'

In these SSDs the failure of managers to read reports and act upon them may have exaggerated the cynicism amongst many lower level staff regarding the purpose and usefulness of reg. 22 visits. A typical comment came from a unit manager at Metro 3.

> The senior managers can't possibly say that the monthly visits are here to help us. Its all right people coming in with pens and a bit of paper and saying 'have you done that?'. Most of the time we just have to say 'no, because we told you last week that we needed more staff'. I don't see the point.

Partly in recognition of this problem (and in response to external demands, such as the SSI) some SSDs had begun to develop more systematic procedures for using reg. 22 information, including the intro-duction of a rota system and a series of checks to ensure reports were conducted and passed back up the hierarchy in Shire 3.

8.4   The practice of arm's length inspection visits

In this section we now turn to the practice and outcomes of arm's length inspections on children's homes that were conducted by local authority R&I units. The main issues concern the organisational characteristics of R&I units and the general practice of arm's length inspections, the extent to which information produced from inspection had contributed to greater management control and surveillance, and the issue of how far SSD managers implemented the recommendations from inspection reports and how far this led to improvements in the standard of services.

Approaches towards the conduct of arm's length inspection

The organisation and staffing of R&I units

The first point to make with regard to the R&I units is their location in the wider organisational structures of the 12 SSDs. Following the national trend (Challis 1990: 131) the majority had established these units as free standing operations, accountable either to the Director of Social Services or (in London 3) to more junior managers (such as assistant directors). The only exception to this in the sample was London 2, where the R&I unit was not formally attached to the SSD, but reported directly to the chief executive's department. In two cases (Shires 2 and 3) procedures had been introduced to preserve the independence of the R&I unit, allowing the chief inspector to submit reports directly to the social services committee, thus by-passing the management hierarchy.

Turning to the internal organisation of R&I units, as one would expect there were wide variations in size. This reflected not only differences in the amount of local authority residential care but, more importantly, in the size of the private sector in each local area. Also notable were different internal structures of the R&I units. In many cases, separate teams had been established in which inspectors specialised according to client or function (including children's homes). In other cases, however, these divisions were less explicit, with specialisation in children's residential care being largely 'informal' (Metro 2).

With regard to staff skills and training it is perhaps not surprising that the vast majority of staff involved in the inspection of children's homes were social work qualified. It was also notable how a large number of these staff had previous residential care experience. In many instances this had resulted from a deliberate policy of targeting these staff in recruitment and selection. For example, the chief inspector at Shire 2 explained that:

> Our general approach ... is that we want our inspectors to have walked the job before we appoint them. To walk the job, to have actually worked in the area that they are inspecting.

For many informants across the sample, previous experience in working in residential care was seen as an essential prerequisite for the conduct of effective inspections. One reason for this was that such staffs were thought to be more likely to appear credible in the eyes of staff groups and managers when passing judgement on the standard and quality of services. Past experience in residential care was also thought to produce a deeper understanding of care practice in homes and make it more likely that staff would identify examples of malpractice. According to a unit manager at Unitary 1, for example, with the less experienced inspectors:

> if you want to con them, you con them. Its reality. If you have got plenty of books and the place looks nice you will get away with murder in my opinion. You could get away with it because there is so

much of an emphasis on things like the temperature of the bath water. They are happy with testing that sort of thing because they can understand that. They just don't get what it's like to look after some of the disturbed kids we have to look after.

Similar conclusions were reached by the chief inspector at London 3.

The experience of inspectors was therefore regarded as an important issue both by R&I managers and by residential managers and staff themselves. Crucially, experience seemed to impact on the extent to which inspectors where 'informationally dependent' (Power 1997: 132) on staff and therefore on how far it was possible to make effective judgements about standards. While a number of informants also emphasised the growing importance of generic 'inspectoral skills' (Shire 3), these were seen more as complementing experience rather than offering an alternative to it.

Approaches to inspection

Prior to looking at the practice of arm's length inspections it is important to note some emerging differences between R&I units in terms of broad philosophy. The dominant view was that inspection should follow what others (DH 1990, 1991a) have described as an 'inspectoral' or 'regulatory' model. According to Utting (DH 1991a: 48), this denotes 'the type of scrutiny which checks adherence to statute, regulations and guidance' and 'is most effective in scrutinising processes which are readily observable and measurable'. The emphasis is on having a standardised *pro forma* or check lists for inspection, with essentially the same issues and subjects being covered on each visit. As the chief inspector at Shire 3 explained:

> What we do is external quality control … What quality control does is just to basically describe and to identify those areas that need to be addressed and it is the management responsibility to address them … we aren't actively responsible for the change, we are responsible for ensuring the managers bring about change.

While inspectors can make recommendations for how to change and offer advice, the 'regulatory' model assumes that inspection is primarily about monitoring current practice and identifying deviations from the rules.

By contrast to this, were moves in a small number of SSDs to supplement regulatory inspections with a 'developmental' approach (DH 1991a). Here, the emphasis is not simply on measuring standards according to fixed, predetermined categories, but also focussing on the 'assessment of outcome, quality and standards' (DH 1991a: 48). One example of this was Shire 1 where, according to the chief inspector

> Our approach is very much one of ensuring that requirements are met and, other than that, discussion and negotiation and talk about good practice and making recommendations about good practice. Its a very much negotiative, developmental type relationship ... rather than going in and inspecting in a very mechanical way and ticking boxes.

In Metro 1, inspectors had also been encouraged to follow a departmental *Aide-Memoire for the Inspection of Quality of Care and Quality of Life*. This emphasised the need to collect qualitative outcome data on issues such as the education of children in the homes. Finally in Shire 2 it had been decided (in 1997) to introduce a third annual inspection aimed exclusively at care practice issues. Following a model originally proposed in an ADSS (1993) publication *Homes are for Living in* nine themes were identified, each of which would form the basis of a separate inspection: planning, relationships, development, fulfillment, rights, choice, independence, respect and privacy. According to the chief inspector, the aim was to: 'move from the age old criticism of inspectors that we get around the counting books and measuring things, and don't look at quality issues. It's a means of moving into child care, an approach that's based on quality rather than measuring'.

Staff in R&I units disagreed over the costs and benefits of this 'developmental' model. On the positive side it was argued that it could produce richer, more 'qualitative' information about local practice and therefore also serve as a method of improving the quality of services. In addition, it was believed that developmental inspections were preferred by residential staff groups and that this, in turn, would help to raise the credibility of R&I units. According to the chief inspector at Shire 1: 'common sense tells you that we are in the business of not just enforcing things. We are in the business of influencing change'. However, not all agreed that the drift away from a standardised regulatory model was sensible or desirable. At Shire 3, for example:

> My personal view is that they are in danger of getting into all sorts of areas that that they ought not to be getting involved in ... which is going to complicate the legal process more than I would like. (Junior Inspector)

In addition to this it was felt that the developmental approach might lead to confusion over the proper role of the R&I unit and work against the formal requirement to 'preserve the responsibilities of management' (DH 1990).

The general practice of arm's length inspections

A number of points can be made about the general practice of inspection in the 12 SSDs. First, with regard to frequency, in the majority two annual visits to homes were conducted in accordance with regulations: one announced and one unannounced. The only exception to this was in London 3 where the chief inspector admitted that due to resource constraints 'we try and do them all, if we can'. In some instances, for example, London 2 and Shire 2, management had set itself the objective of conducting a third annual visit to check up on new unit managers or as a method of responding to complaints or concerns.

Turning to the process of the arm's length inspection itself, there were few notable differences between the SSDs. In most cases the announced visit lasted two or three days depending on the size of the residential establishment and normally involved two or more inspectors (and, occasionally, lay assessors). As noted earlier, most inspections followed the 'regulatory model', using a standardised proforma (sometimes proceeded by a questionnaire) focussing on the condition of the premises and on record keeping. In addition to this, most inspections included what one informant at Shire 3 described as 'informal time ... with the young people in the home, staff ... and any visitors who come to the home'. By contrast to this, unannounced visits were generally of a shorter duration and far less detailed.

In the wider literature it is often been noted how processes of inspection and audit involve considerable negotiation and compromise between regulatory bodies and local managers and professionals (Power 1997). Day and Klein (1990: 5) for example, suggest that 'the pure or ideal model Inspectorate which automatically enforces a set of norms or benchmarks, exists only in the text books'. Moreover, in practice 'reports are frequently the result of compromises and bargains between inspectors and inspected' (ibid.: 59).

In the case of the 12 SSDs we found numerous examples of such compromise and negotiation. This was most evident at the stage when reports were being written up. Usually this allowed for a practice in which managers at different levels were invited to comment and revise conclusions, both formally and informally. As the chief inspector at Metro 2 explained:

> Generally after each section has been gone through in the reports, there is feedback. There is continuing dialogue throughout. Generally

there is a verbal feedback after inspection on what we're going to say in the report in terms of requirements and in terms of advice, so that when they get the report there are no surprises. If you like, it's an agreed report, both in terms of requirements and advice.

An obvious question raised by these observations is how far the negotiated character of inspections compromised the ability of R&I units to criticise management practice? From the data available it is hard to draw firm conclusions. In some SSDs concern was expressed about management interference, or what the Chief inspector at London 1 described as 'maddening after changes' to reports. However, in the majority, we found little evidence to suggest that this process of negotiation prevented R&I units from criticising management practice. Generally the study confirms the observations made by Utting (DH 1997: 177) regarding the 'robust tone' of inspection reports and their willingness to be critical of 'poor policies, management and practice in their own authority'.

Arm's length inspection reports and MIS

A major issue was how far information produced by arm's length inspection reports was relayed to senior levels in the SSDs. As with the regulation 22 reports, discussed earlier, our concern is with the extent to which each organisation had developed an effective MIS that would ensure greater control and accountability.

In general the research revealed that in the majority of SSDs arm's length inspection reports were being passed up to senior management levels and also read by members of the social services committee. In Shire 1, it was also claimed that, in recent years, systems for relaying information to senior levels and for scrutinising front-line practice had been greatly improved:

I think in the past what has happened is selected bits of inspection reports, usually the positive ones, have gone to committee. Obviously somebody got wise to this and now they look at all the reports. So therefore the involvement of committees in terms of the external management via the inspection is far greater. I think that inspection is destined now to have a greater influence on what goes on. (Unit Manager)

In this case and more generally formal procedures had been agreed in which managers at different levels were required to address problems and issues raised by inspection reports.

The only significant exception to this general pattern was Shire 2. In this case, the size of the residential provision meant that it had become impractical for all reports to be scrutinised by senior managers or members. As the Director explained:

> It's impossible with the size of the organisation and the diversity of my responsibilities, it just doesn't allow for that.

To compensate for this, all reports were read by the Assistant Director for Children services who then passed on summary reports both to the Director and to Members.

Taken together, these observations suggest that arm's length inspection reports were being used as part of a management information system. One might conclude that the risks of malpractice in homes remaining undetected were lower as a consequence of these internal mechanisms for inspection. However, when drawing this conclusion it is vital to recognise that the system was by no means perfect or that it ensured full transparency. The question of how this information was used must be considered.

The use of arm's length inspection reports to improve services

Earlier we noted that a key function of arm's length inspections was to contribute to ongoing improvements in the standard of services. For this reason inspection reports set out formal requirements stating how services and facilities needed to be changed. However, while central guidance insisted that local authorities work towards the implementation of these requirements (WOC 68/94), in practice there was no guarantee that change would occur. A key reason was that R&I units had no legal powers (comparable to the regulation 20 notice used against private sector providers) to enforce their requirements with regard to local authority-run services. As such, the power of R&I units in this context was chiefly hortatory, linked to their ability to cajole and persuade managers to change.

Given this picture, one would expect that wide variations existed in the level of compliance to inspection reports. At one extreme were those SSDs where R&I units found it very difficult to persuade managers to accept or implement changes. In Shire 2 and elsewhere there was a tendency to resist change on the grounds that inspection reports made, what many believed to be, naïve and unrealistic requirements. For example, at London 1:

> The inspectors say that the fabric of the building needed thousands of pounds worth of work, that causes problems because neither the Inspectorate, nor the child care sub committee, are the ones that have the power to give that money.

These attitudes did not mean that inspection reports were completely ignored by managers and local politicians. Rather the pattern was one in which changes were implemented in a piecemeal and 'select fashion' (Day and Klein 1990: 57).

In stark contrast were the SSDs where the requirements of inspection reports were generally implemented in a more planned and systematic way. This was most notable at Shire 3 and Metro 2. In the latter, there had been 'an enormous increase in expenditure on the children's side' with managers accepting the need to raise standards in children's residential care (chief inspector). According to the Assistant Director Resources:

> We act on all those [arm's length inspection] reports. If there's something there we need to act on that's been picked up by those people we act on it instantly. We don't wait, we get on with it. The yearly major inspection we have to respond to formally in writing, to show what we are doing to the recommendations that the inspectors have made.

At Shire 3 we also found evidence to suggest that many of the recommendations made in inspection reports were being routinely implemented. In this case local politicians and managers had formally agreed to 'accept the same regime as the private sector'. To achieve this a quasi legal procedure had been agreed in which managers and local politicians were issued with a 'notice of concern' when homes failed to meet the required standards.

There were also variations in how SSD managers responded to and implemented changes required in inspection reports. Partly this can be explained by differential access to resources to invest in residential care. Also important is the extent to which each SSD had developed a strategic plan for children's residential care and had made commitments to improve the service (see Chapter 4). Beyond this, however, it seems that relationships between R&I units, managers and members were a key factor determining levels of compliance.

Positive, or 'co-operative' relationships had been established in some instances (most notably at Metro 2 and Shire 3). In seeking to understand why this had occurred two main factors stand out.

First, and perhaps most importantly, was a strong commitment on the part of senior managers and politicians to the whole process of inspection and the goal of improving services. According to the chief inspector at London 2:

> If what you have is a director who generally wants to improve services and wants to work closely with organisations who are going to do that, then that's fine. There's going to be discrepancies and there's going to be differences, but by and large the person entrusted to go and inspect and report back should be free from any pressures to accommodate.

What these accounts suggest is that co-operative relationships that promote greater compliance are most likely to emerge when senior managers and politicians are committed to the process of inspection and value the information that is produced.

By contrast, change is less likely when there exists what Day and Klein (1990: 39) refer to as a 'collision model', where managers and politicians view the R&I as an 'unwelcome intruder offering unwanted advice'.

The second factor that seemed to contribute towards more co-operative relationships were the strategies of the R&I units themselves. For many informants in R&I units the key to developing this kind of 'partnership' was a willingness to understand and work within the constraints faced by local authority managers. The chief inspector at Shire 3, for example, explained how it was necessary to 'recognise local authorities' limitations' and be prepared to negotiate change:

> If you blindly insist on something and make as big a deal about a small issue as you do about a big one, you won't deserve those people's respect. If you are prepared to say to people 'OK, its a relatively minor issue, I understand the position you are in, we will let that one go – at least for the time being. But this one is important, and I can demonstrate to you why.' I think you command respect. But its something you have to earn and people need to believe that you do actually have an understanding of what is going on.

The implication is that co-operative relationships leading to improvements in services will only emerge if R&I units are prepared to act pragmatically. As such, inspectors should be prepared to negotiate over recommendations made in reports (DH 1997: 177) and also devote time to the essentially political task of building relationships. In short, compliance depends as much on 'the credence that inspection has generally ...' (Chief Inspector: London 2) as it does on having legal powers to enforce change.

Conclusion

This chapter has sought to address the third key aim of the study – 'to discover how far techniques of monitoring performance and of remedial intervention have been developed'. To accomplish this we reviewed evidence from the 12 case study SSDs relating to how far new modes of inspection had been implemented and their operation. There is an opportunity to turn now to a more general review and discussion of these findings. The three main issues which require attention include: the extent to which SSDs have been in compliance with policy in developing internal inspections regimes, the effectiveness of these systems, and the more general implications of the findings for policy-makers.

In the early sections of this chapter it was noted how, from the early 1990s, local managers and politicians faced growing pressure to implement mechanisms for the internal inspection and audit. In part this change was driven by a 'decline in trust in professionals as the basis for ensuring value for money in public services ...' (Sanderson 2001: 300). However, consistent with the findings of other studies (SSI 1998, 1994a), our evidence suggests a mixed and uneven picture of change. In many respects SSDs conformed to the expectations of policy and guidance, most notably in terms of establishing R&I units and new systems governing the conduct of arm's length inspections. By contrast, in other areas, change has been far less pronounced. This was especially the case with reg. 22 visits. While all SSDs in our sample had established 'systems' for the practice of these inspections, there were marked differences in how far these were operational and in the extent to which they conformed with policy and guidance.

Given these observations, our overall conclusion is that across the 12 SSDs the new inspection initiatives were not adopted either universally or in full compliance with policy expectations. However, at the same time, one should not underestimate the significance of the change that took place. In a majority of SSDs new systems were established. As a consequence, inspection became more ubiquitous in SSDs and a core part of the work experience of front line professionals (also see Whittaker *et al.* 1996). While it seems unlikely that inspection has 'colonised' professional decision making in this area (Power 1997), there has nevertheless been a significant movement away from older practices of self-regulation and operational autonomy.

In order to comment on the effectiveness of internal inspection regimes in the case study SSDs, it is necessary to recall the dual purpose of inspection, described in Section 8.2. As noted, the intention is for inspection regimes to serve both as mechanisms for control and accountability and also as a means of improving services.

With regard to the first goal, a key indicator of success is the extent to which information contained in reports is relayed to higher levels and fed into a wider MIS. Once again, however, our findings reveal a very uneven picture of change. With regard to reg. 22 inspections, for example, in more than half the SSDs, information was not being passed to higher levels. By contrast, there was more evidence to suggest that information collected through arm's length inspections had been reported to senior managers and committee members.

Our overall conclusion, therefore, is that the new inspection regimes in SSDs led to an increase in the amount of information available to senior managers. This, in turn, made local practices in children's homes more transparent and reduced the risk that poor performance would go undetected. However, at the same time it is important to keep these changes in perspective. Questions remain about the *quality* of the information that was produced from inspections. While R&I teams were often critical of practice, we also noted a tendency for many inspectors to concentrate only on the more quantifiable or measurable aspects of professional work. In addition, there are questions about how information, once received, is *used* by senior managers in SSDs. There was some evidence, for example, that inspections (especially the reg. 22s) were being conducted in a ritualistic fashion, with information being 'kept on file' simply in order to satisfy external stakeholders (Meyer and Rowen 1991). Even in those cases where committee members did receive reports it was far from clear how far these were being used to monitor practice in a systematic way.

The second goal of inspection in this context was to serve as mechanisms for quality assurance and service improvement. One way in which this occurred was through the process of inspection itself. This was especially so when R&I units adopted a more 'developmental' approach, seeking to offer local managers' advice and assistance. More concrete changes, however, are only likely to follow when SSD managers implement the recommendations made in inspection reports. In the case SSDs, we saw how a key obstacle to such compliance were the growing resource constraints. Of equal, if not more importance in determining compliance were the relationships formed between R&I units, local managers and committee members (Day and Klein 1990). In some cases these relationships had become antagonistic and instrumental, while in others, more co-operative patterns had emerged. Generally it was in the latter that most progress had been made towards implementing the requirements of R&I reports and the development of services.

There are also the wider implications of these findings for policy makers and practitioners. The first concerns the balance of responsibilities between inspectors and line management in children's residential care. According to Utting (DH 1997: 176), the aim of inspection is to support management. As such inspection should not become a 'substitute ... for the routine monitoring which is a fundamental responsibility of management' (ibid.). A key question, however, is just how much 'support' do management need in this basic task of monitoring and control? Policy and guidance assumed that the need was high, especially given the widespread view (partly confirmed by Chapter 6) that line management supervision in SSDs was largely ineffective as a top-down control system. At the same time, it is also recognised that attempts to compensate for the inadequacies of line management are not problem-free. The risk of 'inspection overload' (Day and Klein 1990) was real, accompanied by a growing cynicism amongst staff groups regarding the value of regular visits aimed at monitoring practice. This, in turn, could exaggerate the tendency for inspection regimes to become 'decoupled' from core practice (Power 1997).

Given these problems it might be argued that, while some inspection (especially the arm's length variant) will always be necessary, serious thought should be given to how far existing levels of inspection are helpful. This raises the wider question of whether the resources devoted to inspection might be diverted and used more effectively elsewhere? One possibility is that the resources used in this area might be better used to train line managers, develop systems of performance appraisal and to create slack for more effective supervision (see Chapter 6).

The final issue raised by our investigation concerns the future balance between regulatory inspection, concerned primarily with 'policing', and developmental inspection. As we saw, a minority of SSDs had started to experiment with the second. A key aspect of this approach is the way inspections emphasise care practice and become more concerned with the ongoing improvement of services by offering advice and assistance to unit managers. A developmental approach may also be useful in terms of offering extra support for unit managers and staff groups, beyond what is received from their immediate line managers (see Chapter 6). These advantages raise questions about how far inspectors should invest more time and effort in this kind of activity or concentrate on a more detached model of 'regulatory' inspection.

Of course the future role of inspection in children's residential care will depend on wider policy developments beyond the control of individual SSDs. These include the changes set in motion by the White Papers on *Social Services: Achievement and Challenge* (Burgner Report) (1996) and *Modernising Social Services* (DH 1998b). A National Care Standards Commission (NCSC) became operational in April 2002, replacing the existing 150 local authority inspection units and with the remit of regulating services across all social care areas. The transition did not go well (Williams 2001). Inspections have been criticised for being overly bureaucratic and of variable quality. The government intends that in 2004, the NCSC will merge with the SSI to create a new Commission for Social Care Inspection and with responsibility for children's services moving from the Department of Health to the Department for Education and Skills.

A key element is that R&I units are formally separated from the control of local authorities. Such change has major implications for the inspection of children's residential care. There is a risk, for example, that in larger (regional) organisations, the specific needs of inspection in this area will not be met. As Utting (DH 1997: 178) suggests 'inspecting services for children is likely as a result of the proposed change to engage an even smaller proportion of unit resources and attention'. This could mean less specialisation within R&I units and also less emphasis on the employment of staff with specific residential care backgrounds. A further implication of the move is that it may be harder to pursue the kind of developmental inspection described in this chapter.

9
The Management of External Residential Placements

Introduction

In this final chapter reporting the findings of our study we turn to the question of how SSDs manage relationships with external providers of children's residential care. Over the past decade the role of the independent sector in this area care has increased dramatically. This change is demonstrated most clearly in statistics revealing a sharp decline in the share of local authority run provision in England. Between 1993/94 and 1996/97, the proportion of 'own provision' fell from 63 per cent to only 53 per cent (CIPFA 1997). Many authorities, even those with large in-house resources, now rely heavily on independent sector provision. The trend has been especially marked in the new unitary authorities, many of which are now too small to provide for all their residential care needs locally (SFCRC 1996: 28).

These changes have placed new demands on the management of local authority children's services. There is an overwhelming need for effective control, both to ensure value for money and to guarantee the safety of young people placed in non-local authority provision. Such control requires the development of effective management systems for collating information and the negotiation, specification and monitoring of contracts. Evidence suggests, however, that by comparison to adult services (Lewis and Glennerster 1996), these systems remain underdeveloped in local authority children's services (SFCRC 1996; SSI 1995b). The implication is that reliance on external markets for residential care has been costly both in terms of resources and poor outcomes for young people.

In this chapter the goal is to assess how the 12 case authorities have dealt with these issues. In particular, how far have new systems for contract management been established and with what outcomes? To achieve this, the chapter is divided into four parts. First we look at general trends in the market for children's residential care and review arguments for and against further change. In Section 9.2 the attention shifts to the management literature and guidance relating to contract management. Finally, in the main section of the chapter, the management practices of the 12 case SSDs are compared along four main dimensions: general decision making, management information systems, approaches towards contracting, and monitoring arrangements. In so doing, the chapter will be responding to the first two major aims of the study by exploring and evaluating one of the more recent yet central elements of the model of management which informs the external management of children's homes.

9.1   The expanding role of markets for children's residential care

A combination of factors helps to explain the increasingly important role of markets for children's residential care. First, it has been suggested that 'over-optimistic closure plans' for in-house resources left many authorities unable to meet need (Simm 1995: 17). In this situation most have had little choice but to rely on some external provision. Second, there has been a demand for specialist services for more varied and complex needs of children and young people which most SSDs, with limited resources, have so far been unwilling or unable to develop (Sinclair and Gibbs 1996; also see above Chapters 4 and 5).

Not only has the market for residential care expanded, but important shifts in its composition have also occurred. Most notably there has been a decline in the voluntary sector's share and a 'dramatic increase' in the role of the private sector (Warner 1997: 25). Statistics relating to the sector reveal a steady rise in both the number of establishments and in the number of placements made by local authorities. In the early 1980s, for example, the private sector accounted for only a small proportion of the total number of children's homes in England and Wales: 71 compared to 1634 local authority run and 288 voluntary (Berridge 1985: 4). By the early 1990s, this picture had changed markedly. In 1991 Warner (DH 1992) surveyed 180 private homes in England, a figure which had increased to 202 private registered homes (with 1500 places) by 1996 (DH 1997: 210). There was a consequent increase in the number of placements made by local authorities, from 440 in 1992 to 830 in 1996 (DH 1993–96). The growing importance of the unregistered children's homes sector is also apparent. Although hard to assess, one national survey (SSI 1995b) found over 120 establishments providing approximately 250 child places in England and Wales.

There are signs that the market for residential care has developed unevenly across different parts of the country. In particular, there has been a concentration in London, the South East and Wales. In 1996, the 15 authorities purchasing over 80 per cent of children's residential care externally were almost entirely located in those regions (CIPFA 1997). In many cases, this unevenness of the market has made it difficult to plan and commission supply to meet local needs (Simm 1995). Problems of market structure have also led to the development of a sellers' market in which the demand for certain kinds of residential provision is now out-stripping supply. In London, for example, this sellers' market was demonstrated by a 16 per cent rise in prices for all residential provision in the 1996/97 financial year (Carebase Annual Report 1997). While figures are not available for other regions, anecdotal evidence suggests a similar picture.

The growing role of the mixed economy for children's residential care occurred largely in the absence of a clear policy framework or guidance from the Department of Health (Platt 1994; Kirkpatrick *et al.* 1999). This is in stark contrast to the picture in adult services where, following the *NHS and Community Care Act 1990*, local authorities were required to contract-out a significant proportion of residential and domiciliary provision (Lewis and Glennerster 1996). In children's services the role of markets is far less obvious. At one level, the legislation seems to imply that local authorities should not engage in a wholesale externalisation policy (Hallert 1991: 287). For some a 'divergent model' of professional organisation is required (Clarke 1995), where local authorities continue to be large providers of services (Challis 1990; Jones and Bilton 1994).

Serious concerns have also been expressed about the likely effectiveness of market mechanisms in children's services. One issue is how local authorities can ensure that adequate safeguards exist and that they will be able to fulfil their 'parental responsibility' for children who are placed outside the local area. Berridge and Brodie (1997: 42) note problems of drift in care planning in some private establishments where 'distance and dispersion might make it difficult for planning to be sufficiently proactive'. There are also concerns about the variable quality of some parts of the private sector, in particular in small, unregistered children's homes (Downey 1995; SSI 1995b; Burgner 1996; DH 1997). These concerns and others have led many to argue that local authorities should retain their own provision and avoid 'an unplanned incremental approach to a full blown market economy' without 'a great deal more analysis, option appraisal, and greater clarity about objectives' (Walby 1993: 355–6).

A contrary view centres on arguments in favour of expanding the role of the independent sector. The *Children Act 1989* (17 (5) [A]), for example, proposes that SSDs should 'facilitate the provision by others (including, in particular, voluntary organisations) of services which the authority have power to provide'. Beyond this, at least three reasons are given for why *some* externalisation is desirable. First, although comparisons of the service quality of independent and local authority providers are hard to make (Sinclair and Gibbs 1996), it is generally agreed that the former can offer highly innovative and flexible services (Burton 1993). Second, there is a possibility that the cost of some private and voluntary services might be lower than local authority provision (Knapp and Lowin 1997: 5.4). Finally, some argue that the process of contracting itself is a useful management discipline. Warner (DH 1992: 6.56), for instance, states that '… A clear contract is at the heart of good social work practice for developing secure futures for children.' The use of contracts, he believes, can help SSDs to achieve greater accountability, cost effectiveness and clarity about assessed needs, care plans and outcomes.

From this discussion it is clear that the role of the mixed economy in children's residential care (in particular of the private sector) has increased in recent years. However, it has done so in an unplanned way, leading to the development of a market with structural problems. Change has also taken place in the absence of a clear national policy framework.

9.2   Key issues in the management of external placements

A specific concern of this chapter is how the externalisation of children's residential care has created a range of new demands and challenges for the management of children's services. As noted above, the key issue relates to control. Above all, this is necessary to ensure that adequate safeguards exist when children are placed externally and that drift in care plans is avoided. Effective control is also necessary to prevent the costs of external provision from rising to levels above what most local authorities can reasonably afford. In this section the question of how such control is established is addressed. In order to do so attention is given to both the management literature and recent guidance.

Observations from management authors

A premise that informs much of the management literature on markets is that there is always a potential for economic loss when principals (purchasers) contract-out services to agents (providers). The main reason for this is that agents are assumed to act opportunistically and to be looking for ways of shirking contractual agreements. This opportunistic behaviour manifests itself in a number of ways. One possibility is what Wistow *et al.* (1996) refer to as 'informational losses'. These are incurred 'when relevant information is incomplete or distributed asymmetrically between parties' and when 'the party with the better information' tries to 'mislead the other party and benefit accordingly' (Wistow *et al.* 1996: 141). A further source of opportunistic behaviour occurs with moral hazard. This is when 'providers put in fewer resources into the provision of the service than is consistent with the terms of their contract' (Bartlet and LeGrand 1993: 25).

The chief way in which purchasers can minimise these potential losses from opportunism is by investing in mechanisms for specifying and monitoring contracts. Two general types of contract are possible: spot or block. The former links payment directly to clients while they are using the service, with a high level of specification of services agreed in advance. This has the advantage of allowing the purchaser some flexibility to disinvest in the relationship if standards are unsatisfactory (especially where there is a competitive market and wide choice). Spot contracts may, however, be costly when services are complex and hard to specify in advance. Block contracts, by contrast, buy units of particular types of service at the agreed price regardless of whether the services are used. The price determined for block contracts is, therefore, not contingent on client characteristics because payment is not for services, but facilities. These contracts have the advantage of economies of scale in terms of drafting and negotiation. They also offer the possibility of developing effective long-term relationships based on greater trust. The disadvantage is that block contracts can involve payment for services that are not fully used by the purchaser.

Whatever choice is made by purchasers in terms of contracts and monitoring arrangements, the fact is that some kind of system of management is required in order to reduce (if not eliminate) costs incurred through opportunism. The problem is, however, that these systems also represent, in themselves, an important *transaction cost* for the purchaser. According to Ouchi (1980: 130) 'A transaction cost is any activity which is engaged in to satisfy each party to an exchange that the value given and received is in accord with his or her expectations.' Such costs are incurred both before a contract is agreed (the process of collating information, drafting and negotiation) and after (the expense of monitoring for compliance).

The literature suggests that some types of service will involve higher transaction costs than others. A key variable is the level of uncertainty and complexity in services and the extent to which it is possible 'to specify all future contingencies, and all possible adaptations to unforeseen circumstances which may at some point be required, in a written contract ...' (Bartlett and LeGrand 1993: 29). Put simply, the harder it is for a particular service to be specified in advance, the higher the costs associated with contracting are likely to be.

These facts clearly add to the difficulties faced by staff responsible for managing contracts. The implication is that a balance needs to be struck between two competing requirements. First is the demand for control to minimise the consequences of provider opportunism. Against this is the equally pressing need to ensure that these systems of control do not, themselves, become over-elaborate and a drain on departmental resources. The latter problem may be exaggerated by the complexity of children's residential care services (see Chapter 5) and the potentially high transaction costs associated with specifying and monitoring contracts in this area.

Management developments in children's residential care

The available evidence suggests that most SSDs in England and Wales have been slow to develop the contract management systems described in the previous section. The Support Force (SFCRC 1996: 38), for example, noted 'wide variations' in approach and suggested that: 'In the poorest of practice, what emerges is less a negotiated contract culture with a relatively stable number of partner providers but rather a series of one-off spot purchase placements usually driven by a crisis response.' An SSI report (1995b: 13) also found that many authorities had not developed clear management systems and were often relying on untrained, 'junior management staff' to make key decisions. Finally, Utting (DH 1997: 25) noted how many children in out-of-area placements had 'lapsed into a limbo out of sight, out of mind' due to incomplete controls.

These findings are surprising given that, in recent years, there has been no shortage of guidance from the Department of Health and other sources about how to improve management. Warner (DH 1992), for example, made a number of recommendations, stressing in particular, the need for 'a clear, written agreement (contract) with the home on the nature, duration, cost and anticipated outcomes of the care to be provided'. In a similar vein, the Support Force (SFCRC 1995a) recommended the development of a tighter framework for specifying and monitoring contracts in line with the statutory regulations of the *Children Act 1989*. The main thrust of these proposals was to abandon open-ended spot contracts in favour of pre-placement or call-off contracts, negotiated in advance with approved providers. This approach involves a general agreement over basic fee levels and service specifications within which more specific individual service, or 'spot' contracts are drawn up for each child. According to the Support Force (SFCRC 1996: 39) these arrangements 'should go a long way towards minimising the poor outcomes that can follow from a spot purchase contract in response to an emergency placement'.

Much of this guidance also makes various recommendations about the management of information databases. It has been noted that, within SSDs, there is often a 'lack of consistency and duplication of data sources' held by different groups – social workers, contract managers and Registration and Inspection units – and a failure to communicate information laterally (SFCRC 1995b: 13). Because of this it is suggested that, 'there are advantages in integrating databases into other parts of the department's operation which could use the same information about providers' (SFCRC 1996: 36). SSDs are encouraged to develop ways of collating and updating information held on independent sector providers, for example, by using checklists for pre-visits or monitoring systems (SFCRC 1994: 3).

It is clear that, in order to ensure both the quality and value for money of external provision, SSDs need to invest in contract management systems. This may be an especially important fact in children's services given high levels of uncertainty and risk. However, while there is a considerable amount of guidance on how such systems might be developed, the available evidence indicates that most SSDs have made little progress.

9.3 Purchasing practices: the 12 case SSDs compared

Prior to looking at the management practices of the 12 case SSDs, it is helpful to provide a brief overview of how they used external markets and to describe their purchasing practices and externalisation strategies.

The first point to make is that there were marked contrasts in the extent to which children's residential provision was externalised. This is

Table 9.1   Case authorities' residential care – own and other provision 1996/97

Authority	Own provision	Other provision	Own provision %	Other provision %
Metro 1	286	76	79.0	21.0
Metro 2	169	186	47.6	52.4
Metro 3	Not available	Not available	Not available	Not available
Shire 1	131	58	69.3	30.7
Shire 2	420	187	69.2	30.8
Shire 3	116	109	51.6	48.4
London 1	40	29	58.0	42.0
London 2	45	85	34.6	65.4
London 3	11	56	16.4	83.6
Unitary 1	17	4	81	19
Unitary 2	49	13	79.0	21.0
Unitary 3	22	6	78.6	21.4
Totals	**5,946**	**5,177**	53.0	47.0

Source: Personal Social Services Statistics (CIPFA 1994, 1997).

reflected in statistics showing the proportions of own and other provision for 1996/97 (see Table 9.1). While some authorities were large users of independent sector provision (e.g. London 3 with approximately 84 per cent of services externalised), others continued to rely on in-house resources. Table 9.1 also indicates differences in the average number of placements which were contracted out. This shows a contrast between the large authorities, such as Shire 2, averaging 187 placements, and much smaller users (e.g. Unitary 3 with only six).

There were few notable points of contrast between the 12 case SSDs in terms of the range and type of residential provision being purchased. In the majority, external placements were reserved for users with specialist needs. This was most commonly in areas such as therapeutic care, educational needs, secure accommodation and disabilities.

Despite this focus on specialist resources, informants in all 12 SSDs admitted that a large proportion of external placements (in some cases, the majority) were made in non-specialised, multipurpose establishments. Quite often, such placements were classified as emergency or unplanned. As one placement officer noted, 'we don't make as many planned placements as we make rushed placements' (London 2). This seemed to be a particular problem in the London area. In 1994, for example, statistics of Carebase referrals show that the number of same day 'emergency' referrals was roughly equal, at around 200, to the number of planned referrals (Annual Report 1997).

In total, four SSDs admitted that despite internal protocols and guidelines, placements were made in small unregistered children's homes. In some instances, this was without the knowledge of the placing authority, as young people were moved from registered homes into unregistered satellites (see also Berridge and Brodie 1997). In other cases, such placements were made because of the lack of alternative providers in the market able to cater for highly specialist needs.

In line with national trends, a large proportion of placements were made out-of-area, often considerable distances away from the home authority. In some cases, this was unavoidable given the lack of local children's residential provision of suitable quality. Of the 12 case authorities, three had no independent provision in their area, while three others (including Metro 1, with 76 external placements) had only one local provider. Not only were children often geographically dispersed, but some SSDs were also trading with a surprisingly large number of different organisations. This was particularly the case in the large Shires (2 and 3) where, as one fieldwork manager admitted, children were being placed 'all over the universe' (Shire 3).

With the exception of London 3, the decision to purchase externally was informed chiefly by pragmatic considerations. One reason given for contracting out was that this was necessary to make up for the perceived deficiencies of own resources, both in terms of quantity and levels of specialisation. This either meant purchasing specialist resources that could never be realistically provided in-house or, as was often the case, purchasing mainstream residential care when in-house resources were over-loaded. As the AD children and families of Shire 3 explained:

> One of the things that happens is that the children get bounced into external provision because ... we don't necessarily have the opportunity to assess the right placement for them.

The perceived or real failures of in-house provision was also given as a reason for externalisation. Finally, in three cases, organisational structures were cited as a factor leading to unnecessary external placements. One of the most striking examples of this was Shire 2, an authority with considerable own provision (39 children's homes). In this case, internal communication problems and rivalries between different regions meant that young people were referred out-of-area rather than into homes with vacancies in other regions.

There was considerable evidence in all the case SSDs of a growing reluctance of politicians and senior managers to use external provision. This seemed to be informed by a number of factors. One was related to the perception of increased costs of these placements and questions about their value for money compared to in-house provision. Rising costs are suggested by the fact that 7 out of 11 case authorities which had allocated an external placements budget were over-spent in the 1996/97 financial year (see below Table 9.2). In two SSDs (Shires 2 and 3) this overspend was by a significant margin, for example, by £2.5 million on a £7 million annual budget in Shire 2.

A further reason why many SSDs were increasingly cautious about extending the role of the independent sector was their interpretation of the *Children Act 1989*. Many remarked on the contradiction between placing in out-of-area establishments and the requirement of the Act to look after children close to their own communities. This informed a belief in many cases that external placements, while necessary in extreme cases, should increasingly be used only as a last resort. As a co-ordinator for NWASSA also explained, 'the reality is that most local authorities don't want to place outside their own resources ... in the main, the authorities are working to stop it'.

These concerns about the costs, quality of the independent sector and the lack of local provision led to a variety of initiatives. In most SSDs active gate-keeping of expenditure had been introduced. This occurred alongside attempts to (a) manage contracts more effectively through participation in regional consortia (see below), and/or (b) reconfigure or develop in-house resources to reduce the need for external placements. The second covered a range of initiatives. Six SSDs, for example, claimed that they were planning to substitute some external provision with in-house, localised alternatives. In two instances this was expressed only as a general aim of 'bringing the children back in borough as soon as is practicable' (AD children and families, Unitary 3). In the remaining 4 cases, however, more concrete policies had already been set in motion to reduce the reliance on external placements.

9.4   Management practices in the 12 SSDs

This section concentrates on describing the range of management practices in the 12 case SSDs. Four main issues are considered: decision-making structures and procedures; information systems; contractual arrangements and monitoring systems.

Table 9.2 External placements – decision-making arrangements

	Decision-making responsibility for approving expenditure	Main responsibility for co-ordinating external placements	Level of inter-agency collaboration over external placement funding	Involvement of 'contracts' staff	Status of external placement budget 1996/97
Metro 1	External placements panel (Inter-agency)	Placements team	High	Children's contract unit established early 1998	Overspend
Metro 2	External placements panel (Inter-agency) + Member's sub-committee	Operational managers (FSW and resources)	High	None	Overspend
Metro 3	FSW Managers with approval from AD Children and Families	Operational managers (FSW)	Medium	Central contracts unit involved from November 1997	Overspend
Shire 1	External placements panel (Inter-agency)	Operational managers (FSW)	High	Input from central Commissioning team	Underspend
Shire 2	External placements panel	Operational managers (FSW and resources)	Medium	None	Overspend
Shire 3	External placements panel (also in-house)	Operational managers (FSW) and placements Officer	Low	Contracts officer reports to Placements officer	Overspend
London 1	FSW Managers	Operational managers (FSW) and planning and Review manager	Medium	None	Overspend
London 2	Placements officer and AD Children and Families	Operational managers (FSW) and placements Officer	Medium	None	Overspend
London 3	External placements panel	Operational managers (FSW) and contracts unit	Medium	Contracts unit for children's services	N/A
Unitary 1	Resource Manager	Operational managers (FSW and resources)	Medium	None	Overspend
Unitary 2	External placements panel (Inter-agency)	Operational managers (FSW)	Medium	None	Within budget
Unitary 3	External placements panel (Inter-agency)	Operational managers (FSW)	Medium	None	Within budget

Decision-making structures and procedures

It is helpful to consider the decision-making arrangements along two dimensions. First, is the extent to which the power and authority to make decisions had been centralised in each case. Second, is the question of how far decision making is now supported by specialist staff with some training and expertise in the management of external placements.

Centralisation

A key finding of one SSI survey of contract management practice (SSI 1995b) was that external placement decision making was often delegated to the most junior and inexperienced staff. Encouragingly, in our study this practice was evident in only three case SSDs (see Table 9.1). Over the past five years the remaining nine authorities had introduced far greater central control and direction over external placement decision making.

The chief way in which this centralisation had been achieved in eight cases was through the establishment of gate-keeping panels. In six SSDs, these panels were established to deal primarily with external placements. In one authority (Metro 2) a members' sub-committee was also set up to approve expenditure. Importantly, in five SSDs, gate-keeping panels were inter-agency in membership, sharing costs with health and education. Increasingly this meant that no external placements would be agreed without joint funding.

The function of these panels was both to achieve more effective care planning for individual cases (see Chapter 5) and to establish central control over budgets. In most cases, field social workers were expected to approach panels only when all possible in-house alternatives to an external placement had been considered. For example, in Metro 1:

> If the social worker goes to panel, then they have to convince the rest of them that they've done their work ... They need to convince the panel that all the resources that are available within Metro 1 have been tried or experienced as being inappropriate for the young person to be placed there. (Placements officer)

There can be little doubt that the aim of the panels was to place a greater number of barriers in the path of fieldworkers seeking external placements. Whilst it is possibly too early to generalise, it did appear that these panels had succeeded in altering the perception of many social workers that external placements were an 'easy option'. This may be true even if panels had not yet managed to reduce levels of expenditure (see Table 9.1).

Support and co-ordination in external placement decision making

Five of the case SSDs had established a particular role or post with responsibility for co-ordinating or supporting external placement decision making. Three types of role were observed. First, were those SSDs (Metro 1, Shire 3 and London 2) where placements officers, primarily responsible for managing in-house placements, took on additional responsibilities for the support of field social work staff. In Shire 3, for example, the placements officer, appointed in early 1997, had been 'doing a lot of work on getting things up-to-date and sorting out proper contracts and contracting arrangements and so on ...' (disability manager). The second approach, found only in London 1, was for planning and review staffs to become involved in supporting and over-seeing certain aspects of management. Finally, one SSD (London 3) had established a contracts unit with three staff to manage external placements within children's services. Set up in 1993, this unit was responsible for maintaining a database (see later), negotiating contracts and also assisting field social workers in the process of monitoring external placements.

Whilst only five SSDs had established any kind of support post for external placement decisions, seven cases were beginning to draw on the expertise of contracts officers. These staff were either seconded from adult services or permanently based in children's services (London 3). In most instances, contracts officers were involved in the early negotiations with providers and in developing service specifications. Generally, this increased input from contracts staff represents an important management change in children's services. According to a co-ordinator for the West Midlands child care consortium, a large number of SSDs were now developing a contract function in children's services such that, 'field social workers' latitude for deciding and monitoring contracts is significantly being eroded'.

In some SSDs, the increased role of contract management staff was met with some initial opposition from field social workers. In London 3, for example, the contracts manager spoke of the initial hostility of many professional staff to her role:

> When I came in, I was NOT the flavour of the month, the feeling was very much around 'we could have had 2 social work posts, why do we want a contracts manager?'

In addition to this general dislike of the idea of contracting was also 'a total lack of ownership of the contracts and it seemed to be very much that happened in the far distance' (contracts manager, London 3). Such barriers, in this case, took some time to break down. Initiatives pursued by the contract unit included organising a number of workshops for staff in area offices and deliberate attempts to moderate the language of contracting.

Information systems

As discussed in Section 9.2, access to good information on the range and quality of services offered by the independent sector is of crucial importance. However, as the Support Force (SFCRC 1996: 34) noted, 'many [SSDs] lack access to information about the residential care service available beyond their own provision'. In this section the question of how far the 12 case SSDs had set up effective information systems is addressed.

The first point to make is that all 12 cases were relying on a variety of information sources. Not surprisingly these included word of mouth, adverts in *Community Care* and shared experiences of providers. In addition to the above, seven SSDs were also making regular use of regional databases, especially: Carebase (covering London and the South East), the NWASSA Directory (based in the North West) and the West Midlands Directory (see Table 9.3). In general, however, there was a perception that reliable information was hard to come by and that, in practice, social workers were expected to become 'amateur detectives and sleuths' (Metro 2).

In eight SSDs, information collected from these diverse sources had, to a greater or lesser extent, been centralised into some kind of file or database. This was held either by placements and contracts officers or, by senior managers. In some cases, the 'database' amounted only to a 'library of brochures and things' (placements officer, Metro 1) or a 'pile of booklets' that 'people sometimes come up and just look through' (planning officer, London 1). Only in London 3 had anything approaching a fully comprehensive, routinely maintained database of independent sector providers been developed.

Where they existed, central information systems did lead to a more effective lateral sharing of information within the case SSDs. This, in turn, helped to minimise the problems of co-ordination, noted in previous studies (SSI 1995b; SFCRC 1996). The new gate-keeping panels also assisted in the process of disseminating information, allowing managers to compare notes on external providers. According to a placement officer in Metro 1, for instance:

> ... we keep a record basically of complaints around external placements and if, for example, we are notified that there has been a child protection investigation in an establishment ... we will notify all the social workers that that has happened.

Table 9.3 Information held on the independent sector market for children's residential care

Authority	Central information held on providers	Responsibility for collating information	Use of regional databases	'Black list' admitted
Metro 1	'Library' of brochures/ comments	Placements team	West Midlands database	Yes
Metro 2	None	N/A	No use	—
Metro 3	None	N/A	NWASSA	—
Shire 1	Basic file	AD children and families	West Midlands database	—
Shire 2	None	N/A	NWASSA	Yes
Shire 3	'Library' of brochures/ comments	Placements officer	No use	Yes
London 1	'Library' of brochures/ comments	Planning and review manager	Care Base	—
London 2	None	N/A	Care Base	—
London 3	Database routinely up dated	Contracts staff and visiting social workers	Care Base	Yes
Unitary 1	Basic file	Resource manager	No use	—
Unitary 2	None	N/A	No use	—
Unitary 3	None	N/A	No use	—

In four cases, managers also admitted that this pooling of information had led to the creation of an unofficial blacklist of providers who 'we won't use because we have had bad experiences or have heard things about them' (placements officer, Shire 3).

In all 12 cases, senior managers claimed that fieldworkers were expected to conduct pre-placement visits to independent sector providers. However, the extent to which this always occurred in practice was questionable. As one fieldwork manager admitted:

> If you're doing a planned placement I think a social worker will be quite picky and quite well able to get a sense of the home. If they've got a person sitting in reception who they have to place that evening, that goes out of the window. (London 3)

A further issue related to the quality of these pre-placement visits and checks. In Metro 1, for example, a placement officer suggested that despite considerable guidance offered to fieldworkers, their lack of experience in residential care might mean that key information was often not collected.

In many cases, concerns about the quality of information extended to questions about the usefulness of registration and inspection (R&I) reports. A key problem was the perceived variability of registration thresholds in different parts of the country. In one case, London 3, the lack of faith in registration standards was so serious that a decision had been taken not to place children in a local registered children's home.

Contracting arrangements

In this section we describe the different approaches towards contracting in the 12 case SSDs. Generally, four main kinds of contractual arrangement were observed (see Table 9.4).

The first, and by far the most common practice in all 12 cases was to use spot contracts with individual providers. At the time of the research, ten SSDs were still relying exclusively on this method. This included some of the largest purchasers of children's residential care in England (Shires 2 and 3 and Metro 1).

In a majority of cases, spot contracts were relatively open-ended and limited in terms of specifying outcomes and costs. Many informants spoke of their lack of control over quality or guarantees that the cost of placements would not accelerate. As a development manager in Metro 3 explained:

> It has been an afterthought, 'God, what the hell are we going to do with this child? We have got nowhere for him to go in borough, they will take him on thank God. What are the fees? £1000 or £1200 a week. Thank you very much.' There has been no strategy there. We really haven't talked to these providers and said, 'This is what we need' ... It's just been 'go out there and see what is out there' and been totally non-tactical.

In Metro 1, the assistant director, planning, also suggested that 'we pay £400 a week or something to the organisation but we don't know what we're getting for our money ... we don't have a contracting framework that makes us feel like we're in control of the costs, or the standards'.

A second approach to contracting was the development of pre-placement agreements with approved lists of providers. This is similar

Table 9.4 Contract arrangements with independent sector providers

	Spot contracts	Block contracts	Approved lists/ pre-placement agreements	Participating in consortia	Management contracts
Metro 1	All	None	Under development	West Midlands	None
Metro 2	Some	With 3 voluntary sector providers	None	No	Idea floated, but lack of interest from voluntary sector
Metro 3	All	None	Under-development	ADSS/ NWASSA	None
Shire 1	All	None	None	West Midlands	None
Shire 2	All	None	Under consideration	ADSS/ NWASSA	None
Shire 3	All (pre-March 1998) Some/post	None	Under-development	Thames/ Anglia	None
London 1	All	None	None	London	None
London 2	All	None	Informal system based on contacts of placement officer	London	None
London 3	Some	With one voluntary provider	3 providers on approved list	London	With one private organisation
Unitary 1	All (pre-March 1998) Some/post	None	None	Thames/ Anglia	None
Unitary 2	All	None	None	No	None
Unitary 3	All	None	None	No	None
London X	Some	None	None	London	With one voluntary organisation – 4 children's homes

to the model proposed by Support Force (SFCRC 1995a) and others. By contrast to the spot contracts described above, these pre-placement agreements involved far more systematic attempts to agree to standards of care and to specify in advance the terms and conditions. Within our sample, one SSD (London 3) had pursued this model unilaterally, while three others (Shire 3 and Metros 1 and 3) were in the process of implementing change. In London 3, two private sector organisations had been signed-up to a pre-placement agreement that guaranteed the Authority a 5 per cent reduction in fees for every child placed.

Closely related to this approach was the development of pre-placement agreements between providers and SSDs co-operating through regional consortia. During the study, the activities of four such consortia led by regional Association of Directors of Social Services (ADSS) representatives were noted. These included London, the North West, the West Midlands and Thames Anglia. In total, nine of the case SSDs were actively participating in these negotiations.

The common thrust of these consortia was to develop standard pre-placement contracts with registered providers in order to ensure base-line guarantees about fee levels and general quality standards. According to a representative of the ADSS/NWASSA group:

> Part of the reasons to come together is that we are each trying to tackle it ourselves and what I have been saying is 'we cannot'. I certainly, as an authority here, cannot tackle it on my own. I cannot challenge providers. But collectively we can.

The four consortia were at different stages of development and only in Thames Anglia had the standard contract been agreed by the selected providers. In the remaining three cases, the time-consuming process of negotiation and accreditation of providers was still ongoing with full implementation of the standard contract planned for mid-1999 or later. With the exception of Thames Anglia, there were plans to link-up regional lists of approved providers to existing information databases. In the West Midlands, for example, the objective was for all providers 'hitting basic standards to be introduced on the inner shell of the data-base' accessed by seventeen local authorities (West Midlands representative).

A third approach towards contracting was that of long-term, block contracts with established voluntary organisations. This was observed in only two SSDs, London 3 and Metro 2. Contractual arrangements in these cases were of two kinds. First, were historical block agreements with providers which were largely informal and unspecified. According to a contracts officer in London 3, 'We made the decision ... that to try and formalise it in any way would rock the boat and it would detract, rather than add, from the service.' A second variant of block contracting was found only in Metro 2. In this case, a decision had been taken to engage in a block contract with two voluntary organisations (for approximately 15 beds) as a strategy of responding to the pressure of rising fees in the open market. According to the director, this strategy meant a trade-off between the risk of financial loss due to under-occupancy and the security of having guaranteed beds provided by a 'reputable provider'.

The fourth and final approach described here is 'management contracts'. These bear many similarities to block contracts, the main difference being that the local authority retains ownership of the premises. Only one SSD from the main study, London 3, had entered into such an arrangement. In this case, a management contract had been agreed with a private organisation to run a local, multipurpose unit, providing 4 beds. Whilst this arrangement was described as satisfactory, there had been difficulties. One problem arose when a previous provider had lowered the standard of service, a move that forced the SSD to re-tender the contract. Informants in London 3 also referred to high costs involved in monitoring the contract (see later) and losses incurred through under-occupancy.

Another example of a management contract, not part of the main study, was in London X. This authority had taken the radical step of entering into an agreement with a local voluntary organisation to manage five of the authority's children's homes. In this case, a key motive had been to combine the need for developing local services with a desire to commission them from the independent sector. The latter, it was assumed, was likely to offer more efficient, higher quality residential care than could be achieved in-house. The arrangement was also believed to have a number of additional benefits. One was the possibility that independent providers would invest their own resources to improve the service. Another was that management contracts allowed the SSD to purchase total care packages of multidisciplinary services from the same provider, including education support and psychiatric input.

A number of points can be made about the different contract arrangements described above. First, the predominance of spot contract arrangements suggests much continuity in management arrangements from that which was observed in previous studies (SFCRC 1996; SSI 1995b). However, our study also points to a number of important changes away from these management practices. This was most evident in the way many SSDs, either unilaterally or through consortia, were developing more rigorous pre-placement agreements and approved lists. These arrangements, although still in their early stages, may represent a tighter arrangement for contracting, one less likely to result in high losses.

A second issue raised by our findings is the limited use of longer-term block and management contracts. Despite their appeal, there seems to be important limits on the extent to which these can develop, notably the costs of underutilisation of beds, which most SSDs would be unable to sustain. Management contracts are also limited by the fact that most SSDs will only consider using voluntary providers which themselves may be reluctant to step into the breach (Thompson 1997: 22).

Arrangements for contract monitoring

Essential to the effectiveness of any system of contracting provision is the process of monitoring post placement. In children's services this monitoring should take on a dual role. Not only is it essential for ensuring that the care plans of individual children are implemented through statutory reviews, but it is also necessary for the control of the quality and value for money of external placements (SFCRC 1995a: 29). The aim of this section is to address how far effective contract monitoring arrangements were in place in the 12 case SSDs (see Table 9.5).

In a majority of cases monitoring arrangements were at best imperfect and at worst, 'haphazard' (resource manager, Unitary 1). In Shire 3, for example:

> In the past ... the amount of monitoring of that [external placements] has been fairly, well, *ad hoc* is probably the politest way of putting it ... I don't think we actually often have been very clear about what we want ... So how do you know that you are getting what you are paying for? (Disability manager)

Linked to this was evidence to suggest that many SSDs were losing money as some providers took advantage of the situation (Berridge and Brodie 1997: 43). In most cases, examples were given of providers shirking on contracts and not offering what had been agreed. In London 1, for instance

> A major problem was to do with a unit who promised the earth. When we made the initial placement and perhaps 3 months down the line or at the first review, we were finding that the unit hadn't delivered all the therapeutic treatment that they said and that, in fact, the child was being warehoused. (Planning officer)

Across the 12 cases there were also concerns that ineffective monitoring had meant that the care plans of children placed out of area were being effectively dictated by providers. According to a development manager

Table 9.5 Monitoring arrangements for external contracts

Authority	Support offered to FSWs	Financial control mechanisms	Additional mechanisms
Metro 1	General oversight and guidance by placements team	External placements time-limited and reviewed by panel	None
Metro 2	None	External placements time-limited and reviewed by panel	Quarterly reviews of providers on block contracts conducted by resource managers
Metro 3	None	Oversight by AD children and families	None
Shire 1	None	External placements time-limited and reviewed by panel	None
Shire 2	None	External placements time-limited and reviewed by panel	Occasional visits to providers by resource managers
Shire 3	Placements officer developing guidelines linked to new contract arrangments	External placements time-limited and reviewed by panel	Occasional visits to providers by placements officer
London 1	None	Scrutiny by planning and review manager. Placements review group established 1997	None
London 2	General oversight and guidance by placements officer	Placements officer and AD children and families review all cases 3 – monthly	Occasional visits to providers by the placement officer

Table 9.5 Continued

Authority	Support offered to FSWs	Financial control mechanisms	Additional mechanisms
London 3	Checklists developed by contracts department – some visits conducted with contracts staff	External placements time-limited and reviewed by panel	– Quarterly monitoring of approved providers by contracts unit – Quarterly monitoring and 6-weekly reviews of management contract providers conducted by contracts unit
Unitary 1	None	In process of setting up a planning and review team to oversee external placements	None
Unitary 2	None	External placements reviewed by panel	Occasional visits to providers (out-of-area) by R&I unit
Unitary 3	None	Annual reviews of external placements by panel	Establishing a standards and development unit to conduct visits to all young people in external placements

at Metro 3

> Quite often the responsibilities for managing the careplan haven't been agreed. There is evidence that it's been the providers that have been dictating what the careplan should be for that particular child rather than the social workers dictating to them after some negotiation. So it's been provider-led.

These problems stemmed largely from the inadequacies of existing arrangement for monitoring. In most cases, the only method of control was statutory visits by field social workers to establishments. In all 12 SSDs it did seem that case reviews were being carried out most of the time, especially where gate-keeping panels and planning and review units had been established (see later). However, there was also evidence in most cases that pressures related to work loads and the long distance of some out-of-area placements meant that not all reviews were being conducted. As a fieldwork manager in Shire 3 explained, 'obviously if we have only got one or two children in residential units at some distance, the frequency of visiting and the amount of people going in and picking up any duff dealings is less than we would otherwise have at our own residential units'.

A further problem was that of reconciling the different roles of social workers with regard to monitoring. There were tensions between the social worker's role as the manager of each child's individual care plan (the primary responsibility) and his or her other (potential) role as contract manager, concerned with the value for money of the placement. As a development manager in Shire 2 remarked:

> We rely on the social worker when they go to the review but, again, I suppose they go to the review with a different intention really. And that is, 'is it working for the child?'. They are not looking at it beyond those sort of terms although I think, if there are obvious problems, they would report it, but I don't think staff go with a monitoring/quality assurance perspective.

In many cases, field social workers were reluctant to take on what many considered to be additional responsibilities for monitoring the cost effectiveness of external placements. In London 3, this meant that it was extremely difficult to acquire certain kinds of feedback information from social workers following reviews:

> I think when they [FSWs] visit young people they are very parochial and will focus on that young person. What is nice to get feedback on

is what the ambience of the unit was like, how the staff treated them, how the staff appeared to treat the young people. That's the sort of information that the social worker won't think to pass back ... . They would never think about it. (Contracts manager)

For some senior managers, this failure to adopt a greater monitoring role was seen as deeply rooted in a professional ideology and practice that is incompatible with the growing necessity to manage and control external placements. According to the AD children and families in Shire 3, for example, 'a fundamental change of philosophy' was required to move away from the traditional approach of 'place and hope' towards a 'focused intervention agency that is setting out to achieve something'.

The case SSDs had attempted to improve the effectiveness of monitoring by fieldworkers in two main ways. First, some had attempted to impose greater financial control and managerial oversight of the reviewing system using the gate-keeping panels that had been set up (see Table 9.1). In these cases (and London 2), a policy of three or six-monthly reviews of external placements by panels had been introduced with time-limited budgets. This had led to some improvements in the process of monitoring and, it seemed, had put a stop to some of the worst examples of drift that had existed previously.

The second way in which some SSDs had attempted to develop more effective monitoring was by offering field social workers additional support and guidance from placements officers and contracts staff. Often this involved general advice and the occasional visit conducted by resources staff. The most developed example was London 3 where the contracts staff had developed general guidelines and issued feedback pads to social workers to record general information about homes. Because of the wider problems discussed earlier, however, this system was not fully effective in terms of closing feedback loops. As the contract manager admitted, 'some social workers are excellent, some are appalling. They don't feed back as often as we would like'.

So far attention has been paid exclusively to monitoring conducted by fieldworkers. In some SSDs, however, resource managers, placements officers and contracts staff were also involved in the monitoring process. This was especially the case in those SSDs that had set up approved lists or entered into block or management contracts. In Metro 2, for example, quarterly reviews were made of local voluntary organisations by one of the line managers for in-house children's homes. In London 3, regular monitoring visits to both approved and management contract providers were also conducted by contracts staff. The latter, for instance, was reviewed quarterly and visited monthly. Generally, however, the involvement of contract staffs in visits to non-approved providers on spot contracts were less frequent, mainly due to limited resources.

Conclusion

In this chapter the aim has been to describe how far the case SSDs had established effective systems for the management of external placements. Now that our main findings have been presented it is possible to draw a number of conclusions that relate to the first two aims of the project: to not only explain the models of management which shape the external management of children's homes but to evaluate their appropriateness and suggest which forms may contribute to the solution of key problems. Three main issues stand out with regard to external placements: the range of management practices, the appropriateness of existing models of management, and any future changes which might be required.

First, it is helpful to comment on the range of management practices in the 12 case SSDs. Looking across the sample, what is striking are the similarities in approach towards managing external placements. A majority of cases continued to rely on spot contracts that were relatively under-specified. Most authorities relied heavily on overworked and poorly trained social workers both to negotiate and monitor contracts. The SSDs also seem to have responded to problems in similar ways. Most had sought to establish rigorous gate-keeping arrangements with (often inter-agency) panels, imposing tighter central control over external placement budgets. In addition, there was a trend in a majority of SSDs towards the development of pre-placement contracts as a mechanism for reducing problems.

In contrast to these similarities, the differences in management practice within our sample are far less pronounced. Possibly the most marked differences were between those SSDs (London 3 and Metro 2) which had sought longer-term block contractual arrangements or management contracts and the remainder which relied on spot contracts. London 3 was also an exception within the sample, having a range of contractual forms and, more importantly, having gone furthest in terms of developing a dedicated contract management function for children's services.

Interestingly, variables such as authority type and size were of little importance in explaining differences in management practice. Large authorities such as Shire 3 and Metro 1 tended to be just as poorly managed as were their smaller neighbours. The only factor that may explain some variation in practice was the geographical location of the SSDs. It was clear, for example, that those SSDs located in a region with an effective database of independent sector providers – London, the North West and the West Midlands – were slightly better informed about the range and quality of external provision. Regional location will also be important in terms of the development of future contractual arrangements. Those authorities that are part of a major consortia involved in developing pre-placement agreements and approved lists could be at a distinct advantage in this respect.

A second set of issues relates to the appropriateness of management practices. As was discussed earlier, the literature offers some guidance on what 'appropriate' or 'effective' management looks like in this context. To reiterate, such a system would need to ensure effective control having adequate information about the market, clear contractual specifications and some method of monitoring compliance. In the context of children's services, control is not only financial, but also necessary to ensure that safeguards are in place to protect children and to progress their care plans.

What is evident from our study is that existing management systems only partly met these criteria of effectiveness. In some respects, little had changed from what was reported in earlier investigations (SFCRC 1996; SSI 1995b). In particular, there were few signs of developed contract management structures for children's services (with the exception of London 3) and a continued reliance on social workers to monitor compliance. These arrangements are clearly inappropriate. Although hard to quantify, the findings did suggest a link between underdeveloped management and negative outcomes such as spiralling costs and drift in care plans.

Despite these difficulties there was also evidence to show that a majority of SSDs were seeking to introduce change. Of particular importance was the greater role planned for contract staff in children's services and the movement towards the development of pre-placement contracts and approved lists on the model suggested by the Support Force (SFCRC 1995a). Gate-keeping panels were also a step in the right direction. Although set up chiefly as methods of financial control, these panels served to pool information about providers and develop a more coherent framework for monitoring and reviewing external placements. All these initiatives suggest moves towards a more systematic framework for contracting, one closer to the ideal of effective management outlined within the literature.

The general conclusion that can be drawn from the discussion so far is that while the majority of SSDs are moving towards developing more effective systems, there is still much work to be done. This conclusion has clear implications for our third set of concerns about what future changes are required in management systems.

Turning to recommendations, the message is that SSDs should continue to reform their management structures in the ways that most have already begun to do. This would include three main kinds of change. First, those SSDs that have not already done so should seek to develop central gate-keeping panels (preferably interagency) for the control of resources. Second, there should be a continuation of the trend whereby a clear role for managing external placements is established, preferably with the support of staff trained in contracting. This in turn would need to involve the development of information databases and other services to support social work staffs in making decisions about contract negotiation and monitoring. Lastly, SSDs should continue to move towards implementing the framework for contracting set out by the Support Force (SFCRC 1995a). This can be pursued either unilaterally (as in the case of Metro 1 and 3) and/or through collaboration with other authorities involved in regional consortia. All these changes should, over time, lead to substantial improvements in the management of external placements. They should result in more effective control over resources and in better safeguards for young people placed in non-local-authority provision.

So far it has been argued that if SSDs develop more sophisticated contract management systems this, in turn, will allow them to overcome many of the costs associated with externalisation. However, while this is generally the case, it is also important to make a number of qualifying remarks. In particular, it is necessary to identify certain obstacles that SSDs will face and which are likely to continue to stifle change. Two main issues need to be considered.

The first point follows from our earlier discussion about the possible transaction costs associated with managing contracts. It was stressed that some balance needed to be struck between the necessity for contract management systems and the costs involved in developing such systems. Such costs include additional staffing resources, clerical support, training for social workers and the time involved in activities such as conducting pre-checks on homes and monitoring. For large users of external provision, such as a number of our case SSDs (Metro 1, Shires 2 and 3), these costs can be justified. The major concern though is that they may suggest too high an expense for authorities that purchase only sporadically from the independent sector.

In the case of smaller SSDs, a choice needs to be made about just how far to invest in contract management systems and about what level of control is acceptable given limited resources. The implication is that if adequate controls can not be assured then these SSDs will either need to stop placing externally or pursue some alternative strategy. One alternative is to reduce the need for extensive controls by developing a high trust relationship or partnership with a select number of providers. This might be possible as authorities move towards the development of approved lists at a regional level. However, it also must be stressed that such trust-based relations are hard to maintain and may not offer appropriate safeguards.

A second set of issues relate to wider institutional constraints on the development of effective markets for children's residential care (Kirkpatrick *et al.* 2001). As we have seen, a particular problem is that a majority of SSDs are forced to place young people out of area. Although contrary to the goals of the Children Act 1989, this may be unavoidable. A key reason for the reliance on out-of-area placements is the lack of localised markets in many parts of England and Wales. The worry is that in the past a number of factors have worked against the development of markets in every locality and may continue to do so. The most obvious difficulty is that the demand for residential care nationally is probably not large enough to encourage the development of localised markets in every local area. There is also considerable uncertainty about future demand for residential care. A last obstacle appears in the high barriers to entry into the market. These barriers are created by (necessarily) high registration thresholds and by difficulties associated with real estate values and opposition to new developments in some areas.

All these factors imply a market with numerous structural problems. This means that while SSDs may improve their own management systems, certain problems will remain beyond their control. Above all, it will remain extremely difficult to reconcile the demand for localised placements in accordance with the *Children Act 1989* and the decision to use the independent sector.

10
Conclusion

Introduction

This study has been concerned with one of the less-researched areas of social care – the external management of children's homes. As will be clear by now, the sample of authorities presents a mixed pattern of achievement in solving the problems of externally managed residential homes for children. Nevertheless, as the findings show, there exists the potential to address such difficulties through fresh thinking about management and the exploration of new uses of accepted practices.

The attempt to investigate current practice in England and Wales was informed by a key decision. The research design chosen relied on an intensive, comparative examination of a limited number of cases. Similar organisational settings were identified with the intention of uncovering differing managerial choices and organisational outcomes within residential care. The sample contained different categories of local authority (Metropolitan, Shire, London Borough and Unitary) spread across most regions. Local policy choices were represented in the cases chosen and their contrasting records of residential care, scale of operations and structures. The project deliberately included one authority that relied on external placement for its total residential provision. A research design of this character has obvious limitations. The intensive approach required to build an initial understanding of management in this context was to an extent at the expense of breadth. Although we have related our findings to wider experiences throughout, an evidential base comprising 12 authorities, together with the earlier pilot and sector data, means that care is required in assessing the conclusions.

The purpose of the following pages is to highlight the study's main findings and observations on the general approach to management found in this area and to summarise our observations covering each part of the external management process. In addition, attention is paid to discussing the relevance of the results of the study to recent policy initiatives. Space is also given to cover the implications of our conclusions for the wider body of knowledge on public services.

10.1   The external management of children's homes

The main aims which have guided this study were fourfold: (i) to provide an understanding of the conceptions of management which inform the conduct of social services departments (SSDs) in the external management of children's homes; (ii) to evaluate the appropriateness of the forms of management currently in use and to suggest approaches which might help to solve key problems; (iii) to discover how far techniques of monitoring performance and of remedial intervention exist; and (iv) to develop a framework for examining the external management of children's homes which incorporates the distinctive character of social services and those involved in the process.

How the study has met its four core aims can be shown by reviewing its results in relation to each of those intentions.

1. Models of management and the external management of children's homes
Constructing a broad understanding of the nature of management in the external management of children's homes required separate attention. The distinctive nature of the setting was paramount. Building that understanding started by posing two questions: what is management and what is the nature of management goals in children's residential care? They were answered by first distinguishing management as a process of obtaining control and co-ordination in order to achieve organisational goals. Management goals in children's residential care are by no means straightforward. There are often competing goals between public, service, professional, family and child interests. Management has to ensure effective controls and safeguards, often derived from legislation. It has also to maximise the quality and effectiveness of residential provision by achieving a match between assessed needs and available resources, informed by research and the results of official inquiries.

The study also found that these competing goals within children's residential care were overlain by the organisational form that dominates social services – the professional bureaucracy. Its character was examined in more detail in Chapter 2. The importance for management is that control and co-ordination, in order to achieve organisational goals within a professional bureaucracy, are difficult. Occupational groups have subgoals governed by their professional communities. Decision making is often highly decentralised. Management techniques that are appropriate in other sectors are likely to be less effective in a social services department if imported without regard to their assumptions.

These findings are consistent with the conclusions of others who have pointed to the limited impact of new management approaches on professional work in local government social services departments more generally. From the late 1980s, SSDs have faced pressure to reform management practice, especially in the form of new legislation and guidance. This has called for a stronger strategic role for senior professionals, more emphasis on explicit rationing and tighter control over the practice of front-line staffs. From the available evidence it seems that there has been some movement towards the establishment of new management practices in SSDs. For example, senior professionals now take on a wider range of management responsibilities, including areas such as personnel management, contracts and strategy. There are also signs of a move towards the delegation of budgetary responsibilities to lower level staffs. There is evidence of more bureaucratic control being established over rank and file professionals and moves towards greater standardisation of decision making (Wistow *et al.* 1996; Lewis and Glennerster 1996; Means and Smith 1998).

While many in the sector have emphasised such changes, as our results show, the move to enhance management practices in the area of children's services have been uneven and contested. New forms of control have not been fully implemented. There has also been little fundamental change in occupational cultures or in personnel management practices. There is much evidence, consequently, of continuity between the ways these services were managed in the late 1990s and in the late 1970s (see also Clough 1998: 95 on the uncertainties amongst social workers as to their core activities and professional boundaries). This lack of radical change is explained by the way that SSDs remain professionally dominated, local government departments in which the scope for top management innovation has been limited (Ackroyd 1995). Many senior professionals in SSDs have retained their old 'custodial orientations' and have sought to negotiate and interpret official guidance in their own way. Above all, SSDs have been faced with contradictory imperatives, not least the pressures to establish new management systems and respond to more complex legislation and guidance while, at the same time, being forced to implement cuts in resources and staff establishments.

Our results from studying the external management of children's homes also overlap with other research which point to a gap between the rhetoric and reality of management in SSDs. Other studies have found that SSDs have been 'slow to realise the importance of investing in increased strategic capacity' (Lewis and Glennerster 1996: 71), due partly to inertia and a lack of high-level management skills to implement new systems and procedures (Walsh *et al.* 1997). A more serious problem however has been the lack of resources to invest in non-operational management posts and to set up new information systems (Wistow *et al.* 1996). A study by the LGMB/CCETSW (1997: 45–6) reached a similar conclusion, finding that between 1993 and 1995, the number of central support staff in SSDs had increased by only 4.3 per cent. The number of senior managers actually fell by 9.7 per cent over the same period. In the context of local government reorganisation (LGR), the signs are that this problem of insufficient management resources to engage in strategic planning has become worse (Craig and Manthorpe 1998: 203). While there is more emphasis on strategy, the capacity of management to deliver remains weak and, by and large, SSDs continue to be operationally driven professional organisations.

In the light of these constraints, the general reaction to management and managerial approaches to certain problems in social care has been mixed. As Parton puts it, the managerial approach to quality in social care and its 'increased emphasis on management, evaluation, monitoring and constraining professionals to write things down, is itself a form of government for them' (1994: 96). Who establishes the norms for guiding practice, especially following the creation of the General Social Care Council (see Section 10.2), and develops professional, standards and competencies remains an issue. The resource constraints on managers make their work problematic. Nevertheless, the opportunity exists for managers in the residential care and social care sector as a whole to create their own sense of a distinctive type of management.

Management approaches derived from the private sector may be relevant to social care but they have to be transformed in their application (Stewart and Ranson 1998: 55). On the strength of the management activity witnessed in children's residential care, people working there are becoming more skilled at tuning the need to manage with the essential features of their everyday practices. It is clear that engagement with the broad range of management theory and techniques is growing, one that has moved on beyond the rejection of simplistic notions of 'excellence' or 'managing culture'. As Sheldon and Chilvers (2000) point out, understanding what actions are effective is as old as social work itself. The notion of critical practice is particularly relevant. Brechin (2000: 44) uses the term to point to the practitioner as 'reflexive and engaged', an active participant in the processes of creating meaning and prepared to address alternative ideas and belief systems. At one level the assertion holds true for the relationship between practitioners and clients. This study argues that the same could be applied to the way in which professionals relate to the act of managing and the potential for reflexivity and, ultimately, the creation of the sector's own form of management knowledge. The potential for innovation is high where critical practice and wider reflection are joined.

One example is the problem of implementation. In one sense the child care sector is adept at reviewing and synthesising the varieties of operational level activity which arise from major legislation (e.g., Aldgate and Statham's 2001 overview of research on the Children Act). The emphasis in such activity is on refining how the techniques of care are carried out. What the field lacks, by contrast, is a comparably developed sense of its ability to manage SSDs and others so that such types of care are implemented appropriately (for an exception see Horvarth and Morrison 2000). There is a clear opportunity to create such a sense of the collective capacity of the sector to handle the process of implementation rather than concentrating on the technical content of the wealth of guidelines which they receive (cf. Martin and Henderson 2001).

2. Evaluating approaches to the external management of children's residential care   Armed with an appreciation of the organisational context and the general approach to management in SSDs, it was possible to appreciate the precise form of management involved in residential care. In order to make an assessment of how children's homes are externally managed, as Chapters 4–9 show, a composite notion of evaluation is required. This involved combining two types of criteria. The first concerned measures of management and organisational effectiveness taken from the appropriate literatures. Each chapter made use of specialist writing drawn from the management and related fields. The second set of criteria came from legislation and related research, centred on the extent to which residential services were matched with and met the assessed needs of clients.

The results of the project are grouped around six processes which we believe to be central to the external management of children's homes: strategy and implementation, child placement, line management, managing staff, monitoring and control (dealt with separately below in Section (iii)), and the management of external placements. The findings include both instances of innovation and the persistence of ingrained problems. Although some conclusions echo the results of earlier inquiries and research, the lack of change in some aspects of the management of residential care is an important observation in itself.

Strategy and implementation

The sample of authorities confirms the difficulties confronting anyone wishing to take a strategic view of local government and SSDs. The relationship between policy and planning, financial regulations and information systems are beset by uncertainties.

Applying concepts that may be new to the sector produced useful findings. The experience of six authorities showed that building a systematic view of children's services and how to reconstruct those services is possible. They were able to conceive of a planned approach that embraced implementation and where specialisation of residential care was achieved. It is apparent that such a capacity to join needs analysis and strategy creation and, in turn, to translate the resulting decision into operational form, pays huge dividends. None of our case examples had solved all the problems associated with such a capacity. Indeed, as Aldgate and Statham (2001: 141) point out, 'the search for a common understanding of the definition of need remains'. Yet in striving towards this approach, the leading group of SSDs were able to assess and incorporate the recommendations of Utting, LAC or matching needs and services as part of their strategic thinking – not as isolated projects.

It would be helpful to all the major parties concerned in managing social services and residential care (including the Department of Health and SSI) if they took a fresh look at their assumptions about strategy (cf. Baier *et al.* 1994 on implementation and ambiguity). As Chapter 4 showed, strategy and planning are not the same thing. Above all, a body of knowledge is emerging, which could prove to be extremely helpful in expanding the orthodoxy amongst planners and managers in children's services. The opportunity for a sector-wide initiative would seem timely. This conclusion is echoed by the report of the Waterhouse Inquiry which recommended that 'local authorities in Wales should ... give particular attention to the development of skills in strategic planning, [and] policy implementation, (Lost In Care 2000: 224).

The management of child placement

The legislation, research and guidance that was reviewed suggests that the process of child placement affects both the quality of placements and the extent to which SSDs are able to match needs and services. The aim was to look specifically at how placement decisions, that are constrained by factors such as the limited supply and specialisation of resources, contribute to the achievement of better outcomes. We conclude that, whilst these constraints ensure that placement decisions alone can never be decisive, effective management practices can improve outcomes.

This study has shown that few SSDs had effectively differentiated in-house supply. In only two of our cases was the specialisation of homes based upon a comprehensive evaluation of needs. Most of the other cases were characterised by high proportions of unplanned admissions and high occupancy rates. These conditions create low levels of slack in the system which further reduce the options available within the placement decision-making processes. Against this background, most SSDs have centralised the placement decision-making process in some way. This has usually been achieved either through placement officers or inter-professional panels. Neither of these arrangements fully prevents unplanned admissions into more specialised children's homes. The process of gate-keeping resources through the implementation of panels was found to be a highly political process. It appears that the political dynamics may become ends in themselves and sometimes the whole process remains resource, rather than needs driven.

Evidence from this study indicates that better placements are more likely to occur when senior managers have attempted to specialise the purpose of children's homes. This involved, for example, the development of buffer units with quick throughput to reduce overspill into other homes. These systems do, however, increase the risk of placement decision making being resource-led. The establishment of central panels with clear decision-making procedures, requiring that Field Social Workers (FSW) develop care plans and check alternatives prior to requesting placements, was significant in a number of cases.

By contrast to these elements of better practice, ineffective placement decision making involving high levels of unplanned admissions were more likely where less effort had been made by senior management to specialise residential provision. In a similar way, the absence of a central panel or placement officer often leads to the direct placement of children by FSWs. In many cases, this was shown to result in inappropriate placements and demoralised unit managers. This has led to inter-professional conflict in which both sides pursue their own sub-goals to the detriment of corporate interests.

Line management

The findings show that change has occurred and that new management practices are gradually being adopted. Many SSDs had started to create more specialist line manager posts and devolved responsibilities (especially for budgets) to unit managers. Around half of the sample had created policies which specified the frequency and content of staff supervision. All were investing more in management training and development.

Yet while management restructuring is apparent, the pattern is uneven. This general slowness is in contrast to progress elsewhere in UK public services. The practice of supervision, for example, remains dominated by a 'custodial' approach. Many of the obstacles to controlling and monitoring practice persist. Such problems are common to any professional bureaucracy and financial retrenchment has helped to slow the pace of change. The case SSDs also appear to reflect the wider problem in public services where managers face competing demands and find it difficult to protect activities such as supervision. Extra resources might help but justifying this type of investment will be hard given the scepticism of some practitioners who consider management as an overhead and who still query how far supervision enhances service quality.

It is clear that different models of line management exist. The conventional wisdom has led to the appointment of specialist line managers, able to perform a range of functions including supervision, monitoring and general support. It was apparent, however, that many line managers found it hard to combine these different tasks. It may be useful, therefore, to explore alternative models of line management, including the separation of the 'practice' and 'management' aspects of supervision and the development of appropriate support functions.

The results also point to the connection between line management reform and policies on children's residential care. Lack of clarity over objectives will constrain the ability of line managers to support and engage in practices such as performance appraisal. Developing line management practice will hinge on the clarity of the broader strategies which determine the purpose and level of specialisation in children's homes.

Managing and developing staff

In the area of managing people it is vital to appreciate the broader character of local authorities and their SSDs. The influence of traditional institutions weighs heavy. Personnel departments in the public sector are the recipients of conflicting expectations about their role and function. Change though is occurring, both across the public sector and in the social care field. Employment relations in the public services as a whole appear to be moving towards a position where the personnel function is becoming 'more strategic than administrative', employment practices are more flexible rather than standardised and the state is relinquishing its model employer status (Farnham and Horton 1996). The specific promptings and advice of official reports on children's care in the 1990s have produced a dual impact.

Detailed recommendations on recruitment and selection of residential staff, for example, may have been targeted primarily at residential care. Yet it has been the standards of conventional personnel management that informed such inquiries as Wagner (1988), Warner (DH 1992) and the Support Force (1995a–e) that have influenced local authorities.

The result from this study is that the case authorities are moving towards a human resource management approach. As a consequence, the potential for linking personnel planning and assessments of need is clearly visible. Over half the sample have personnel functions which now act as enablers of line managers and others. At the same time, personnel and children's services planning has become much clearer with benefits to both residential care and personnel professionals. More flexible employment arrangements have facilitated the redeployment upon which the redesign of children's services depends. The fuller adoption of an HRM approach could have multiple benefits. The planning of training for residential staff would thereby become a logical element of wider policy development. Not only training but also redeployment would, therefore, be thought through as part of needs analysis and care reviews, not afterwards as currently often happens.

The management of external residential placements

The study examined the management arrangements for contracting-out children's residential services to the independent sector. Effectiveness was defined in terms of the extent to which management information systems, contract development and monitoring helped to support both value for money from contracts and appropriate standards of quality. Our research shows that, since the publication of the Support Force guidance, decision-making frameworks, information systems, contract arrangements and monitoring have all developed along a number of significant paths.

In terms of decision making, most SSDs had moved towards more centralised structures through the introduction of gate-keeping panels. The general picture is, therefore, one of greater senior management oversight than in the past. Many key decisions for organising placements and contracts still lie with FSW staffs who are often provided with limited support. In information systems, there remains amongst our authorities, considerable reliance on informal sources such as word-of-mouth and advertisements placed in *Community Care*. We have shown, however, that some SSDs are beginning to make regular use of regional databases and about half of the sample had developed some kind of file or library of information held centrally. Panels can be helpful in terms of cross-referencing and pooling information between staff and between agencies about providers. With regard to contract arrangements, a large number of SSDs still use open-ended spot contracts. Most were, however, either developing more effective contracts in the form of pre-placement agreements developed unilaterally, or through consortia. The use, in some authorities, of block and management contracts may offer a means of securing good quality local services. There is still a heavy reliance placed upon FSWs with respect to contract monitoring. This has led to tensions emerging between the traditional role of FSW as manager of the care plan and the emergent role of contract compliance officer.

In sum, whilst we are able to report some improvements in management systems for contracting, most SSDs are still unable to collect and utilise the information required for the task. This means most are losing money and are unable to ensure the quality of placement that they purchase. In the light of these findings, SSDs are faced with a stark choice between two options. They should either invest more in the development of management systems or reduce their dependency upon external placements. In those authorities that are larger users of independent sector provision, it may be necessary to establish an in-house contracts unit. SSDs should continue to participate in regional consortia to improve contracting practices. They should also develop closer links with a small number of approved providers that meet the particular local needs. In the longer term, the development of high-trust relationships may be costly but necessary to ensure greater security in terms of standards of care and fee levels.

3. Monitoring performance and remedial intervention   In order to address the third key aim of the study – to discover how far techniques of monitoring performance and of remedial intervention have been developed – led us to examine the modes of inspection across the 12 SSDs. Two issues were dominant: the degree of compliance with offical policy and guidelines found in internal inspections regimes and the effectiveness of these systems.

The results show a far from uniform or even picture. Policy and guidance, was followed most noticeably in the creation of R&I units and new apparatus for the conduct of arm's length inspections. In other respects, action has not conformed with policy and guidance, especially in the case of regulation 22 visits where marked operational differences stand out. It is important though to recognise the shifts in practice which took place. New systems were established in most SSDs and inspection became an integral part of the work of front-line staff.

The overall purpose of inspection regimes was to ensure control and accountability but also to help improve services. The results show that the amount of information available to senior managers increased, practices in children's homes were more directly monitored and poor performance was more likely to be exposed. Yet questions persist about the standard of the resulting information that was produced from inspections and how it was used by senior managers in SSDs or committee members. Inspection was able to facilitate service improvement, in particular where R&I units used a 'developmental' approach which built in advice to managers. In addition, implementation of the recommendations made in inspection reports depended partly on resource constraints but were informed by the relationships between R&I units, local managers and committee members.

The findings also raise broader questions for policy makers and practitioners alike. The responsibilities of inspectors and line management in children's residential care are often problematic. Whilst official guidance assumes that the need to support managers via inspection was high, attempts to compensate any shortcomings in line management may give rise to other difficulties. These include the danger of inspection overload and possible cynicism among staff resulting in inspection becoming detached from practice. Given the need for arm's length inspection, the resources devoted to other forms of inspection could be used to create a more conducive setting for supervison based on trained managers and more robust performance appraisal. Adjusting the balance between regulatory and developmental inspection could also lead to the ongoing improvement of services by offering advice to unit managers and extra support for staff. Such developmental approaches may not sit so comfortably, however, in the larger national or regional inspection structures which have been created more recently.

4. A framework for understanding the external management of children's homes   In summary, our approach to understanding the external management of children's homes is holistic in character. The aim has been to capture the key parts that might add up to a more complete whole (cf. Bullock *et al.* 2001: 27). The results of this study point to a three-part framework.

The first component is an 'inclusive' orientation to the problem of external management (see Chapters 2 and 3). Inclusivity means going beyond the relationship between the children's home and the immediate line manager. Building an understanding of the external management of children's homes needs to encompass not only the home and line manager but also residential staff, service and resource managers, fieldworkers, senior managers, support staff, other professionals, those responsible for inspection, and members of social services committees. It also requires recognition of the distinctive setting of SSDs and the social care sector (see Section I).

While this inclusive view pays attention to the context in which external management occurs, the second element of our framework concentrates on the how the process of management operates. Six core aspects of management activity inform the external management found in the sample SSDs: strategic management, the management of child placement, line management, the management of staff, monitoring and control and the management of external placements. It is the choices made and actions taken in these areas which facilitate or constrain how external management operates at the level of practice within the distinctive context of SSDs described in Chapter 2.

The third part of the framework for understanding the external management of children's homes emerged from the attempt to employ different specialisms in order to evaluate the outcomes of this management process and its setting. The contention is that both the assumptions and practices of external management require exploration in terms of the extent to which they: meet the requirements and standards set not just by legislation, the Department of Health, and relevant professional bodies but also in the light of recognised measures found across the management literature.

Taking the experience of the authorities in this study as a whole, gives rise to a last general observation. Throughout our study many respondents, from residential staff to members of the SSI repeated an accepted nostrum: that social services in England and Wales remain in a state of continual turbulence. Yet the diversity of backgrounds, professional interests and responsibilities involved in the external management of children's homes can be both a strength and a weakness. What appears to maximise these potential advantages is how departments are integrated. The theme runs through each element of our inclusive framework. Research across sectors has shown that the more diverse and dynamic the environment, the more the effective organisation is able to be both differentiated and integrated.

The same seems to hold true for local authorities and the external management of children's homes. The pressures for differentiation are powerful, coming from legislation and outside pressures. The need for specialisation is a case-in-point. The character of the professional groups in social services adds to the potency of that differentiation. What our framework has tried to offer is a way that integration could be achieved; not just by developing a strategic capacity but also through management systems and placement arrangements. The framework is an early attempt at examining the management aspects of the external management of children's homes. The hope is that it may contribute to what has been termed (Audit Commission 1994) the balance needed between the different needs and service aspects of the residential care system.

10.2   Emerging policy and guidelines

Given the problems in the management of children's care and the operation of SSDs, outlined in Chapters 4–9, it is unsurprising that the government has produced a recent cluster of additional policy documents and guidelines. These extend from new overall objectives to specific requirements on training. The dominant emphasis is on setting standards for social services together with an enhanced recognition of the role of management. The findings from this study of the external management of children's homes speak to these new policy initiatives in a number of ways.

The programmes entitled *Quality Protects*, in England, and *Children First*, in Wales, began in late 1998 and early 1999 respectively, both with the aim of establishing outcome-based objectives in children's services. These were further developed in *The Government's Objectives for Children's Services* later in 1999, involving 11 aspects of practice of children's care and their management. The creation of a research programme which is evaluating these initiatives as they unfold is timely and could be an excellent means of supporting the emergence of critical practice linked to a reflective management discussed earlier (see Section 10.1). The Department of Health's annual statistical returns have been modified accordingly. Yet as the experience of the LAC documents reported in the previous chapters show, for example, a major effort will be required to secure the generation of sound data let alone its routine inclusion in management decision making (cf. Ward 2001: 8–9). The success of this effort will hinge greatly on the impact of the Department of Health's *Information Strategy for Social Care* and related *Core Information Requirements for Children's Services*.

The government has also devoted considerable attention to standards in social services. Broad action on social care includes the Best Value programme and the work of the Audit Commission. More specific steps stem for the White paper *Modernising Social Services* and the *Care Standards Act 2000*. These include the creation of the Commission for Care Standards, which replaces local inspection units with independent national inspectorates and regulators, and the establishment of a General Social Care Council. One of the aims of the Council is to create and maintain standards for all social care staff. Clearly such projects are consistent with many of the messages from our research on the management of staff and the areas of monitoring and control. It is not clear, at this stage, how far these new arrangements will address the problems which we highlighted of the relationship between staff and inspectorate and the crafting of a developmental exchange (see Chapter 8).

The Children's Services Planning Guidance 2000 seeks to aid the co-ordination in the planning process with the delivery of better outcomes for children in need. It is worth remembering that the order under the *Children Act 1989*, which obliged local authorities to plan for children's services in order to achieve better outcomes, only came into force in 1996 (Aldgate and Statham 2001: 11). The activity of planning, therefore, has enjoyed a relatively brief existence to-date. A major emphasis, however, of *Modernising Social Services* is what Langan terms a drive for accountability (Langan 2000: 161). The Department of Health (DH) will carry out annual reviews of social services' performance plans, aided by independent inspection from the SSI, which will also conduct joint reviews with the Audit Commission every five years. Successful local authorities will be able to apply for 'beacon status', while the government will intervene where services are failing.

In the light of our research, the DH would do well to temper its understandable emphasis on accountability with an appreciation of the need for new behaviour and practices that will facilitate improved planning and management. The skills of implementation and co-ordination discussed in Chapters 4 and 5 are cases in point.

What the government policies and DH guidelines seem to miss is one of the central messages from our research. The need for a new approach to the management of social services, and children's homes in particular, cannot rest only on fresh targets and objectives. There is an equal requirement for the inculcation of innovative thinking in managing such services which builds on the potential of the community of practice which exists but one which is prepared to challenge its accepted beliefs. An example may be instructive. Practitioners are bringing their own skills and experiences to bear on management issues and regarding them anew. (Pinnock and Dimmock 2003: 280) reports on the way North Lincolnshire social and housing services produced a Quarterly Performance Review (known affectionately in-house as the 'quick prod round') which avoided:

> 'highly rational planning ... Experience had taught them that over-elaborate planning systems consume a disproportionate amount of resources and usually produced disappointing results. Instead they have tried to see planning as a process of organisational learning, thereby focusing their limited capacity on delivering better results rather than on simply servicing an ever more elaborate planning system'

Such innovative thinking on managing children's services may qualify for the label of a 'wicked issue' (Clarke and Stewart 2000: 2). In other words, such problems are not easily tamed and there is no immediate and obvious solution. They call for the ability to derive new approaches and challenge existing patterns of order. The problem is unlikely to belong to a single group but will implicate many. The process of resolution will be iterative, not immediate. As we have argued throughout the previous chapters, the unquestioning import of management techniques has produced little benefit to such services. Yet the critical adaptation and reworking of management approaches by reflective practitioners and managers as they address the problems of planning, placement or outcomes, can pay off. The spirit of their activity sits comfortably with the so-called 'new production of knowledge' (Gibbons *et al.* 1994) or what Lewis calls 'knowledge-based change' in social care (Lewis 2002). Relying on local information and evidence from one's professional sphere alone is insufficient. As she argues, social care organisations can be managed in ways that encourage appropriate change through the generation of relevant knowledge. We maintain that the creation of such knowledge should encompass both the hitherto specialist fields of management and care practice to their mutual benefit.

10.3   Implications for UK public services

So far, much has been made of the direct relevance of the study's results for practitioners and policy makers in SSDs. To concentrate, however, on this aspect alone would be to ignore the wider significance of the findings concerning the nature of management in UK public services. The aim of this final section is to address this issue.

In recent years the new public management (NPM) has come to be regarded as a revolutionary movement, almost a paradigm shift away from traditional approaches towards public administration (Osbourne and Gaebler 1992). It is argued that public services in the United Kingdom, from central government to health, education and social services are now being transformed as a consequence of the NPM. However, while this claim is made there remains some doubt about how far new forms of management have actually been implemented. In addition, there has been a tendency to isolate certain kinds of changes, mainly in high profile sectors such as the NHS and central government. With some exceptions (Wistow *et al.* 1996; Harris 1998) far less attention has been paid to local authority SSDs. Given these deficiencies it is useful to draw out the implications for NPM of our own study of external management of children's residential care. More specifically, how does the experience of this under-researched sector add to an understanding of the NPM more generally?

In responding to this task, the proceeding section is divided into three parts. In the first section a definition of NPM is offered and the arguments concerning its implementation are summarised. The second considers how NPM practices have been introduced in the context of UK SSDs. The last returns to our data and looks at how the experience of external management in children's residential care can shed light on the key elements of the NPM project, such as strategy in professional services, control and regulation, and contract management.

The new public management

The NPM has been defined in a variety of ways (Osbourne and Gaebler 1992; Pollitt 1993; Ferlie *et al.* 1996). The ideal type model of NPM set out by Hood (1991, 1995; Dunleavy and Hood 1994) is a useful starting point because it treats NPM as an 'administrative doctrine' that attempts to combine a number of diverse elements.

Hood suggests that the NPM can be distinguished from traditional public administration (TPA) in two main ways. First, NPM implies a convergence of public and private sector management styles. Under NPM it is assumed that the gap between the private and public sectors will be removed, with the public sector emulating many of the same structures and practices. According to Hood (1995) such a change would involve: moving from centralised, vertically integrated bureaucracy towards more decentralised structures characterised by quasi business units (Hoggett 1996); greater use made of contracts and market mechanisms as a method of co-ordinating and planning service delivery; and a growing emphasis on financial management criteria and on achieving efficiency gains (Pollitt 1993).

The second fundamental change implied by NPM away from TPA relates to the question of 'how far managerial and professional discretion should be fenced in by explicit standards and rules' (1995: 95). According to Hood, an NPM agenda means greater empowerment for managers, stressing the 'right to manage' with fewer constraints such as those imposed by formal procedures and rules. The NPM implies a greater emphasis on the monitoring and control of outputs from services, and less concern with managing the process for its own sake.

In much of the literature it is common for such changes to be represented as being both inevitable and desirable (Hood 1998; Pollitt and Boukaert 2000). Governments and policy makers claim that management reforms are necessary to 'modernise' public services and likely to result in better service outcomes such as improved user satisfaction and efficiency gains. In particular, NPM may be a solution to many of the problems associated with traditional public administration. This has been perceived to be inefficient, dominated by the provision of existing services and lacking the capacity to respond to change (Osborne and Gaebler 1992).

Despite the enthusiasm for NPM expressed in some quarters there has also been criticism. Three issues are commonly discussed in the literature. The first are theoretical concerns about whether or not NPM does represent a coherent model of management. It is argued that the NPM seeks to reconcile ideas about management that are fundamentally incompatible (Hood 1995; Ferlie *et al.* 1996; Pollitt 1993: 11). One example is the policy rhetoric of decentralisation set beside simultaneous calls for increased centralisation of resources and regulatory procedures (Hoggett 1996; Thomas and Dunkerly 1999).

A second set of questions concerns the feasibility of NPM ideas. A key issue is whether, given existing organisational structures and the strength of opposition from entrenched interests, the NPM can ever be fully implemented (Hood 1998). While central government has been successful in restructuring parts of the public service, there have been limitations on how far it has been possible to impose directly new forms of management in areas such as education. In practice, changes associated with the NPM may be subject to the same 'widespread, "built in" and possibly inevitable limitations and trade off's' that have plagued earlier waves of administrative reform (Pollitt and Bouckaert 2000).

The third source of criticisms of the NPM relate to its appropriateness. Many have questioned the assumption that management ideas are portable from the private to the public sector (Stewart and Ranson 1988;

Harrow and Wilcocks 1990; Stewart and Walsh 1992). It is argued that the convergence argument is flawed because of 'important and irreducible differences between the assumptions, values and environmental conditions underpinning management activity in the public and in the private sectors' (Kessler and Purcell 1996: 217).

The implication of these critical accounts is that, at best the NPM will be hard to implement and worst, that it will be extremely costly and counter-productive. According to Power (1997: 92–3), because NPM 'puts itself as doctrine beyond question' this has led to a marked 'insensitivity to side-effects and empirical consequences'.

NPM in SSDs

According to some observers the process of management reform in SSDs began almost from the date of their establishment in the early 1970s (Howe 1986). However, outside periodic calls for increased management training for senior professionals (Younghusband 1978: 313; LGMB 1988), central government made little attempt to impose change until the late 1980s. Since then pressures on SSDs to reform their management arrangements have been intensified. Partly this has followed legislation (the NHS and Community Care Act for example) but it has also arisen from budgetary constraints and the more influential role played by regulatory bodies, such as the Social Services Inspectorate and Audit Commission (Henkel 1991).

Over the past decade there have been clear moves to implement aspects of the NPM model described above. One can see a number of ways in which private sector forms of management have been promoted. Most notably this has occurred through the shift towards purchaser–provider splits and the way key services in community care are contracted out. Turning to increased management discretion, one can also see attempted changes. There have been efforts to extend local management responsibility for strategy, with far greater emphasis on identifying local needs and developing new services to match them.

As we saw in Chapter 2 pressures to reform management in SSDs have generally been strongest in services for adults (Harris 1998). By contrast to the NHS and Community Care Act, the Children Act 1989 says very little about what organisational or management arrangements are necessary to improve standards (Berridge and Brodie 1997). Yet external pressures to reform the management in children's services have been visible in three areas. First, there has been considerable guidance requiring SSDs to develop a more strategic approach towards the planning and allocation of various services. As noted in Chapter 4, this goal is made explicit through the Children Act 1989 and the guidelines summarised in Section 10.2. Second, a great emphasis has been placed on establishing tighter forms of control and regulation over the decision making of front-line professionals (Bilton 1998: 201). This has necessitated more active supervision and more frequent inspection and the new *Looking After Children* assessment and care planning procedures (Ward 1995). Third, although largely unplanned, there has been a shift towards the externalisation of much residential and other provision with an expectation that SSDs will establish effective commissioning and contract management (SFCRC 1996).

It is apparent that in SSD children's services, as in other parts of the public sector, there has been an attempt to promote aspects of the NPM model. It remains unclear though how far these aspects of the NPM have been implemented in practice. There is also uncertainty over the new forms of management and whether they help or hinder the delivery of effective services. To-date there has been little research on SSDs that addresses these questions directly. It is timely, therefore, and useful to consider the findings produced in our own study of external management and their wider implications for current knowledge about NPM.

NPM and children's residential care

We highlight three areas of management change in SSD children's services that carry wider implications for the NPM: strategy, the control and regulation of front-line staffs and the management of contracts and markets.

Strategy

As noted earlier, one of the main goals of the NPM is to ensure that public organisations have clear objectives and that they engage in strategic planning to ensure the most effective allocation of services. In the past, professional services were much criticised for being too operationally driven and lacking clear strategic leadership (Langan and Clarke 1994: 75).

Our results show that in some of the case SSDs, there had been a determined effort to transform the strategic management. This has centred on the development of a matching needs and services approach. The aim has been to develop effective management information systems for the identification of local need and to use them in planning future services. The ability of SSDs to differentiate in-house residential services, establish statements of purpose and function, and procedures for placement planning has been slow to appear. The SSDs present a mixed picture in terms of developing an effective strategic capacity and planning for the long-term development of specialised services that meet the needs.

These results underline the difficulty of creating long term strategy in public organisations that are politically controlled. Political control may result in increased ambiguity over strategic goals and a tendency for compromise. Local political contingencies such as changing voter priorities can make it hard for professionals/managers to pursue long-term strategies (Keen and Scase 1998). While there have been attempts to give management boards greater executive powers (e.g. in TECs or FE colleges) (Ferlie *et al.* 1996), this did not apply to SSDs. In effect, SSDs remained under the formal control of local government, with limited independent executive powers being delegated to managers. The obstacles to strategy formulation in professional service organisations are also well known (cf. Mintzberg 1993; Hinings *et al.* 1991).

Our study points to far deeper obstacles facing strategic management than have been recognised in the literature. A key problem stems from the lack of resources and time devoted to strategic management and planning in SSDs. Partly this was due to cuts in the number of middle and senior managers, especially in post LGR authorities (Craig and Manthorpe 1998). It is also due however to the proliferation of demands facing managers in this sector, seen in new legislation, guidance and almost periodic restructuring of departments (Means and Smith 1998; Packman and Hall 1996). This points to a significant gap between the rhetoric of being more strategic and the reality of stretched professional managers lacking in adequate training. A similar contradiction between policy goals and resources has meant that SSDs are unable to protect the specialised statements of purpose and function of their residential resources (see Chapter 5 on placement planning). These types of contradictions are noted in the NPM literature (Pollitt and Bouckaert 2000), but are rarely analysed in detail. The wider implication that conventional strategy making may be almost impossible under these conditions is rarely discussed. NPM experts also fail to recognise how the successful development of a strategic management capacity in the private sector is far from common (Whipp 2002).

External markets

The NPM literature assumes that 'contract based competitive provision' is a superior mechanism to bureaucracy for organising the delivery of public services (Hood 1995: 96). The NHS and Community Care Act 1990 insisted that local authorities contract out a significant proportion of residential care and other services for adult clients. In children's services there was no formal requirement to externalise provision, although as we saw in Chapter 9, a significant number of local authorities have done so.

According to our results, most SSDs had not invested in effective systems of contract management, although there were some moves to improve practice. The main conclusion was that relying on the market had become a very costly option for SSDs, both in economic and policy terms. Our findings are similar to those of other studies that have looked at the development of contract management in other parts of the public sector. Studies of the community care market for adults reveal many of the same difficulties (Wistow *et al.* 1996; Walsh *et al.* 1997; Lewis and Glennerster 1996; Means and Langan 1996; Johnson *et al.* 1998; Leat and Perkins 1998; Wistow and Hardy 1999). Our research also indicates a trend towards a 'third way' (between markets and bureaucracy) of greater collaboration between purchasers and providers and attempts to develop a framework for obligational or relational contracting (Sako 1992). Similar developments have also been noted in health, social care and local government (Flynn *et al.* 1996; Audit Commission 1997; Milne 1997).

Our study though raises more fundamental questions about the role of contracts and markets in complex social care markets. The conditions which characterise children's services ensure that market mechanisms are likely to be a costly alternative to local authority managed provision (also see Petrie and Wilson 1999). Difficulties arise from the complex and uncertain nature of the services provided, which are consequently hard to specify and monitor, and from the legislative demands placed on local authorities. The conclusion that markets do not work well in this sector challenges the NPM doctrines that assume markets will always be a superior mechanism for co-ordinating the delivery of goods and services. Our data offer support for the proposition that 'social care is different from other goods and services ...' and that it is 'inappropriate to bring market relationships into a context where users were vulnerable and outcomes difficult to define or measure' (Wistow and Hardy 1999: 183).

A further implication of our study is that it suggests that, while many authorities will seek to overcome the problems of markets through relational contracting, some will also return to bureaucratically controlled provision. Such a result is a counterpoint to the dominant assumptions found in the NPM literature. The general view seems to be that 'traditional bureaucratic authority ... is no longer appropriate and is best seen as the historical starting-point from which radical change has become necessary' (Leach *et al.* 1994: 2). The alternative to bureaucracy, it is argued, is either the market or some form of hybrid, network organisation

(Rhodes 1996; Kirkpatrick 1999). By contrast, our findings suggest that a reliance on local authority owned and managed provision may be a valid option in this sector.

Accountability and control

As noted earlier, a key goal of the NPM is to establish more effective control over front-line staffs through a variety of mechanisms, including regular supervision, formal procedures and audit/inspection. This implies that, a 'key function' of professional managers will be to 'monitor (overtly or discreetly) the practice of other professionals, and to institute corrective action where it is deemed necessary' (Causer and Exworthy 1999: 85). In the context of local authority children's services this objective was reinforced by the Children Act 1989 and given added importance by a stream of reports and abuse scandals pointing to inadequacies in management control (Howe 1992; Berridge and Brodie 1996). The trend, it seems, is towards 'tighter managerial control over practitioners, with more emphasis on procedures for child protection ...' (Rushton and Nathan 1996: 372).

In Chapters 6 and 8 (on supervision and inspection) we saw how there had been moves in SSDs to establish more effective supervision and monitoring of practice. The main finding, however, was that most SSDs had not established very effective management information systems with a tendency for older practices and traditions – based on collegial control – to prevail. Two points seem especially relevant.

There is clear evidence of an expansion of audit and monitoring in SSDs, as in the rest of the UK public sector (Power 1997). Nevertheless, our findings also suggest that while there has been an increase in audit activity, this has not necessarily interfered with professional autonomy. There is a tendency to 'go through the motions' of audit/inspection and to conform, somewhat ritualistically, to dominant expectations. Furthermore, our study points to the very uneven way in which new forms of direct supervision and performance management have emerged in this sector. Older patterns of custodial supervision had survived and, in some cases, had been extended. This raises serious doubts about any gradual shift towards more bureaucratic, or neo-Taylorist forms of control over professionals in this sector (Pollitt 1993; Hoggett 1996). There is a question about whether such forms of control will ever become dominant in SSDs, given the problem of increasing demands on line management and declining resources; what Ackroyd (1995: 8) describes as the 'unpalatable incompatibilities in government policies' relating to NPM.

Resolutions to such issues in UK children's residential social work will be shaped by the distinctive features of management in SSDs. Yet while other areas of the UK public sector may provide lessons for the future of management in SSDs, it may be instructive to examine developments in social work settings further afield. Given the influence of North American policy and practice in many areas of UK public service, a brief look towards the United States could be useful in order to assess its possible relevance to UK children's residential social work.

Following the contingent perspective adopted throughout this study, it is important to emphasize that UK and US public services have very different structures and agendas for change. Structurally, as this study has emphasized, the UK system is still relatively centralised and relies on public financing (tax) and service provision. In contrast, the United States operates a fragmented system of decentralised state markets that vary in the extent to which state governments devolve budgetary and regulatory responsibilities to local (city and county) administrations. Each of the 51 state markets for public services comprises a complex mixture of purchasing agencies (typically government and not-for-profit) and service providers (not-for-profit, for profit and some government).

In terms of the broader policy agenda in the United States, Osbourne and Gaebler's (1992) prescription to 'reinvent' government has been more influential than the ideas of NPM described in this study. At first glance, the two reform concepts display common characteristics that might encourage the view that reinvention offers a natural extension of NPM. The two reform projects do share some basic tenets, including an emphasis on top-down change and a belief in the efficacy of (and capacity to implement) commercial models of welfare provision. Both agendas have attracted support from influential policy-makers and researchers. While NPM continues to dominate UK public policy research, a recent annual meeting of the American Society of Public Administration was devoted to the theme of reinvention. Osbourne was enlisted as a special adviser to the National Performance Review (NPR) of US government functions during President Clinton's first term. Several NPR recommendations bore the hallmark of reinventing ideology, especially those concerning procurement (Kellough 1998). In the face of limited evidence of improvements to emerge from either NPM or reinvention (Frederickson 1996), critiques on both sides of the Atlantic emphasise comparisons with 'traditional' public administration to show that reinvention and NPM underplay equity and the political nature of administration (Gabris *et al.* 1998).

Beyond these shared features, there are at least three critical points of contrast between NPM and reinvention against which any attempt to apply the latter to the United Kingdom should be considered. First, the ideological basis of reinvention rests on a set of prototypically American ideas concerning the efficacy of markets for social provision and anti-statist concerns about the exercise of government authority. Second, reinvention places a much clearer and more prescriptive emphasis on themes of entrepreneurship, privatisation and consumerism. Third, empirical support for reinvention is largely restricted to local cases taken from limited functional areas such as solid waste disposal and human resource management. A dearth of research into the impact of reinvention in US children's welfare services provides no evidence base to support its future adoption in the United Kingdom (Cohen 2002).

The distinctive system of US public administration is reproduced within a federally mandated child welfare system that annually consumes $19 billion in federal and state expenditures (Child Welfare League of America [CWLA] 2004). As in other fields of US public administration, the CWS is organised through 51 loosely-coupled state markets in which various tiers of governments exert limited regulatory oversight over fragmented collections of government and private purchasing and provider agencies. While the national child welfare system is dominated by foster care, residential providers include custodial facilities, orphanages and specialised facilities for children with behavioural and cognitive difficulties. The most similar organisations to UK children's homes are the 4500 'group homes' that are typically licensed by state governments to provide 24-hour non-medical and supervised care to children needing more restive environments than foster care (CWLA 2004).

Despite the structural and policy differences between the systems of children's residential care in the United States and the United Kingdom, they share a number of common themes. First, periods of relative calm are punctuated by local scandals that typically progress through cycles of intense media attention followed by state government investigations issuing reports that cite issues including limited resources and the problems of 'controlling' professional social workers who demand autonomy from management. In a second similarity, there is increasing recognition in the United States that social work practice, research and policy are 'languishing' and in need of the development of a unique approach to management. While the development of national policy concerning group homes remains limited, in the late 1990s most states entered a 'compact' of protocols governing out-of state placements; a phenomenon beset with similar problems associated with out-of county/local authority placements in the United Kingdom.

Beyond these similarities, the periodic investigations of problems in US child's 'out of home' welfare provision consistently draw attention to inadequate state oversight, limited resources and issues associated with the use of non-governmental agencies purchasing services from a fragmented array of providers (Kennedy School of Government 1996). While policy responses have been left to purchasing agencies at the state level, their capacity for strategic response are limited by an ongoing battle to survive by fund-raising and grant writing (Hopkins and Hyde 2002).

Within this basic framework, in California and most other states, the vast majority of the child welfare cases (73 per cent) in any month (c. 90,000) are located in the state's 14,500 licensed foster homes. Of the 11 per cent of children in care who live in the state's 1800 groups homes, the average stay is only 12 months and there is a far higher proportion of probation cases (as opposed to child welfare cases) compared with foster care (43 per cent compared with 6 per cent). This, and the higher costs of facility care, help to explain why group homes consume almost half ($45 million) of the total monthly care costs of nearly $100 million (California Department of Social Services [CDSS] 2001).

In 1997, CDSS introduced a new automated case management system that allows more than 16,000 users to access the system at 294 computer locations (CDSS 2002a). The formal outputs of this system provide case plans for clients, case history reviews for social work supervisors, and comprehensive programme statistics for policy-makers and senior managers. Administrative costs approach 20 per cent of the average costs per child in care. Such programme data were used as the basis for the development of a strategic plan for service 'Redesign' that began with a comprehensive needs assessment (CDSS 2003). Despite the new case management system and strategic plan, an independent study reported that group homes suffered from many of the same problems identified in our UK study; this included 25 per cent of children being placed inappropriately, poor service co-ordination, workforce problems and limited strategic capacity (CDSS 2002b).

This brief examination of the US system indicates a number of possible future policy directions and avenues for further investigation for counterparts in the United Kingdom. In terms of policy development, it may not be long before there are attempts to explore the ideology of reinvention as both an appropriate and effective reform agenda for UK public services. For any government that takes evidence-based policy seriously, this review provides two reasons for pause. First, the reinvention movement is based on a set of ideas about the nature of public service that is not well established in the United Kingdom. Second, despite powerful support and presentation there remains limited local evidence of quality and cost improvements in the United States in general, and the persistence of budgeting and human resource issues in child welfare services (Green and Walters 1999; Hopkins and Hyde 2002).

In terms of practical lessons concerning the basic structure of child welfare systems, the US example presents a worrying picture of what could result from any extension of the embryonic marketisation reported in our UK study. In particular, the US market generates high transaction/administration costs (20 per cent of expenditures in California). Similar basic problems not only persist (e.g. matching needs and services) but these are exaggerated by fragmentation and poor co-ordination between agencies. Three examples of practical developments in the United States, however, that may warrant further consideration are: the protocols developed for inter-state referrals, the greater emphasis placed on foster care and the development of advanced strategic capacity in some states systems.

After considering the NPM and reinvention projects though, it is important to be clear on not just the wider relevance of what this study has found but to consider how that position has been reached. Commentary on the general character and changes in social care is readily available. Intensive research on the problem of managing specific areas such as children's homes is, by contrast, rare. Hopefully, both our general conclusions relating to the sector as a whole and the specific findings on local practice point to the rewards to be had in engaging with the problems of supposedly minority fields such as residential care.

The benefits include not just the opportunity to gauge the extent of the challenges which staff face but the chance to appreciate the potential for creative outcomes. The difficulties of managing residential care are as multilayered and contradictory as those found in any part of the contemporary private sector. Working with those responsible for shaping this emerging management form has highlighted the scope for fresh combinations of theory and technique, whether it be in allying the management and social care fields or joining unfamiliar academic frameworks with policy guidelines and practice instincts. It appears that practitioners have left behind the cliches of managerialism and monolithic notions of management. Instead, those involved are shaping their own version of management knowledge which is rooted in their experience of managing as they build a managed service.

Appendix 1

Fieldwork *pro forma*

The interviews, observation and document inspection were guided by a *pro forma* directed at the following people and themes:

Social Services Directors, Senior Management and Support/Advisory Staff – departmental policy towards residential care, strategic planning and the connections between residential care and other child care services, profile of residential care, organisational structure, placement planning, contracting, operational integration between fieldworkers and residential care, line management, personnel policies, inspection and regulation.

External Managers of Children's Homes – background, managerial responsibilities, approach to the line management of children's homes, relations with senior management, role in placement planning, training and staff development, inspection.

Unit Managers of Children's Homes – background, aims of the home, role and responsibilities of the UM, relations with external-management, contribution to placement planning and wider integration, staff training and development, impact of inspection and regulation.

Field Social Work Teams – backgrounds, jobs and roles, team purpose, position within departmental structure, understanding of placement, monitoring of children's progress, relationship with residential staff, operational issues which arise between FSWs and other groups.

Inspection and Registration Staff – backgrounds, organisation of unit, nature of the inspection process, evaluation and data used, information generated, results of poor inspections, independent homes.

Appendix 2

Table 1 Interview data record

Case	Senior AD/ director	Middle management field social work	Middle management resources	Line managers	Contracts managers/ placements officers	Planning develop- ment staff	Members	Inspectors	Unit Managers	Other managers	Personnel/ training managers	Total per case
Metro 1	3	3	2	6	3	2	1	3	5	3	–	31
Metro 2	3	4	1	3	1	2	1	2	10	2	1	30
Metro 3	2	3	2	–	1	–	1	1	4	2	1	17
Shire 1	2	2	1	1	1	–	1	2	4	1	–	14
Shire 2	2	2	4	5	1	2	–	1	13	2	1	33
Shire 3	2	2	2	1	1	1	1	1	4	2	1	18
London 1	1	2	4	2	–	1	1	1	4	–	2	18
London 2	2	2	3	2	1	–	2	1	6	2	1	22
London 3	2	5	2	–	3	2	1	3	3	3	–	24
Unitary 1	2	1	1	1	–	1	3	1	1	1	–	12
Unitary 2	3	2	3	3	–	3	1	1	6	2	1	25
Unitary 3	1	2	3	2	1	1	1	2	3	–	1	17
Sub totals	25	30	28	26	12	15	14	19	63	20	9	261

Bibliography

Ackroyd, S. 1995. 'The new management and the professionals: assessing the impact of Thatcherism on the British public services', Working Paper No. 24, Work Organisation – Economy Working Paper Series, Stockholm University.

Ackroyd, S., J. A. Hughes and K. Soothill. 1989. 'Public sector services and their management', *Journal of Management Studies*, 26, 6: 603–19.

Advancement of Residential Child Care (ARCC). 1995. *The Management of Residential Child Care*. London: ARCC.

Aldgate, J. 1978. 'The advantages of residential care', *Journal of Adoption and Fostering*, 92: 29–33.

Aldgate, J. and Statham, J. 2000. *The Children Act Now: Messages from Research*. London: The Stationery Office.

Aldrich, H. 1971. 'Organisational boundaries and interorganisational conflict', *Human Relations*, 24: 279–87.

Andrews, K. R. 1971. *The Concept of Corporate Strategy*. Georgetown, Ontario: Irwin.

Ashburner, L. and Ferlie, E. 1994. 'Organisational transformation and top-down change: the case of the NHS'. Mimeo: Centre for Corporate Strategy and Change, University of Warwick.

Association of Directors of Social Services. 1993. *Children's Homes are for Living In*. London: ADSS.

Association of Directors of Social Services. 1997. *ADSS News*. 5, 4, April.

Audit Commission. 1994. *Seen but not Heard: Co-ordinating Child Health and Social Services for Children in Need*. London: HMSO.

Audit Commission. 1997. *Take Your Choice*. London: Audit Commission.

Ayre, P. 2001. 'Child protection and the media: lessons from the last three decades', *British Journal of Social Work*, 31, 6: 864–87.

Bach, S. 1999. 'Personnel managers: managing to change' in Corby, S. and White, G. (eds), *Employee Relations in the Public Services: Themes and Issues*. London: Routledge, 177–98.

Baier, V., J. March and H. Soetren. 1994. 'Implementation and ambiguity', in McKevitt, D. and Lawton, A. (eds), *Public Sector Management: Theory, Critique and Practice*. London: Sage, 160–70.

Ballard, R. 1994. 'Double trouble', *Community Care*. 1–7 September.

Balloch, S., J. Phal and J. McLean. 1998 'Working in social services: job satisfaction, stress and violence', *British Journal of Social Work*, 28: 329–50.

Bartlett, W. and J. LeGrand. 1993. 'The theory of quasi-markets', in LeGrand, J. and Bartlett, W. (eds), *Quasi-Markets and Social Policy*. Macmillan: Basingstoke.

Berridge, D. 1985. *Children's Homes*. Oxford: Basil Blackwell.

Berridge, D. and I. Brodie. 1996. 'Residential child care in England and Wales: the inquiries and after', in Hill, M. and Aldgate, J. (eds), *Child Welfare Services: Developments in Law, Policy, Practice and Research*. London: Jessica Kingsley.

Berridge, D. and I. Brodie. 1997. *Children's Homes Revisited*. London: Jessica Kingsley.

Berry, J. 1975. *Daily Experiences in Residential Life: A Study of Children and their Caregivers*. London: Routledge and Kegan Paul.

Billis, D. 1984. *Welfare Bureaucracies*. London: Heinemann.

Bills, D., G. Bromley, A. Hey and R. Rowbottom. 1980. *Organising Social Services Departments*. London: Heinemann.

Bilton, K. (1998). 'Child and family social work: organisational context and identity', *Child and Family Social Work*, 3: 197–203.

Blau, P. and W. Scott. 1963. *Formal Organisations: A Comparative Approach*. New York: Basic Books.

Blom-Cooper, L. 1986. *A Child in Trust*. London: London Borough of Brent.

Blom-Cooper, L. 1987. *A Child in Mind*. London: London Borough of Greenwich.

Bovaird, T. and P. Davis. 1997. 'Learning to manage within limited resources: coping strategies and learning breakthroughs'. Paper presented to the 2nd International Research Symposium on Public Services Management, Aston University. 11–12 September 1997.

Brechin, A., H. Brown and M. Eby. 2000. *Critical Practice in Health and Social Care*. London: Sage.

Brown, M. and S. Payne. 1990. *Administration in Britain*. London: Routledge.

Bryson, J. M. 1998. *Strategic Planning for Public and Non Profit Organizations*. San Francisco: Jossey-Bass.

Bull, R. 1980. 'Social services department structures and the organisation of residential social work' in Walton, R. G. and Elliott, D. (eds), *Residential Care: A Reader in Current Theory and Practice*. London: Pergamon.

Bullock, R., M. Little and S. Millham. 1993. *Residential Care for Children: A Review of the Research*. London: HMSO.

Bullock, R., J. Randall and A. Weyts. 2001. 'Social work effectiveness: evaluating the contributions of social workers to interventions with children in need'. Dartington Social Research Unit.

Burgner, T. 1996. *The Regulation and Inspection of Social Services*. London: Department of Health and Welsh Office.

Burns, T. and J. M. Stalker. 1962. *The Management of Innovation*. Oxford: Oxford University Press.

Burton, J. 1993. *The Handbook of Residential Care*. London: Routledge.

Burton, J. 1998. *Managing Residential Care*. London: Routledge.

Butler-Sloss, E. Lord Justice. 1988. *Report of the Inquiry into Child Abuse in Cleveland*. Cm 412. London: DHSS.

California Department of Social Services (CDSS). 2001. *Child Welfare Services, Children in Group Homes Characteristics*. Sacramento, CA: CDSS.

California Department of Social Services (CDSS). 2002a. *Child Welfare Services/Case Management System: Strategic Plan*. Sacramento, CA: CDSS.

California Department of Social Services (CDSS). 2002b. *Re-examination of the Role of Group Care in a Family-Based System of Care: A Status Report*. Report to the Legislature, 16 August. Sacramento, CA: CDSS.

California Department of Social Services (CDSS). 2003. *CWS Redesign: The Future of California's Child Welfare Services*. Final Report, September. Sacramento, CA: CDSS.

Care Base. 1997. *Annual Report Computerised Placement Matching Service*. London Research Centre.

Causer, G. and M. Exworthy. 1999. 'Professionals and managers across the public sector', in Exworthy, M. and Halford, S. (eds), *Professionals and the New Managerialism in the Public Sector*. Buckingham: Open University Press.

Central Council for Education and Training in Social Work and Department of Health Expert Group. 1992. *Quality Standards for Residential Care*. London: CCETSW.

Centre for Policy on Ageing. 1994. *Home Life*. London: CPA.

Challis, L. 1990. *Organising Public Social Services*. Harlow: Longman.

Chandler, A. D. 1962. *Strategy and Structure: Chapters in the History of American Industrial Enterprise*. Cambridge, MA.: MIT Press.

Child, J. 1985. *Organisation: A Guide to Problems and Practice*. London: Harper and Row.

Child Welfare League of America (CWLA). 2004. *National Data Analysis System*. http://www.cwla.org/programs/researchdata/default.htm. Accessed 5 February.

CIPFA. 1996. *Personal Social Services Statistics 1995–96* (estimates).

CIPFA. 1997. *Personal Social Services Statistics 1996–97* (estimates).

Clare, M. 1988. 'Supervision, role strain and social services departments', *British Journal of Social Work*, 18: 489–507.

Clarke, J. 1988. 'Social work in the welfare state', in Clarke, J. (ed.) *Social Problems and Social Welfare*. Milton Keynes: Open University Press.

Clarke, J. 1995. 'After social work?', in N. Parton (ed.) *Social Theory, Social Change and Social Work*. London: Routledge.

Clarke, J., and J. Newman. 1997. *The Managerial State*. London: Sage.

Clarke, J., A. Cochrane and E. McLaughlin (eds). 1994. *Managing Social Policy*. London: Sage.

Clarke, M. and J. Stewart. 2000. 'Handling the wicked issues', in Davies, C., Finlay, L. and Bullman, A. (eds), *Changing Practice in Health and Social Care*. London: Sage and Open University, 377–86.

Clough, R. 1998. 'Social services', in Laffin, M. (ed.), *Beyond Bureaucracy? The Professions in the Contemporary Public Sector*. Aldershot: Ashgate.

Cohen, B. 2002. 'Alternative organizing principles for the design of service delivery', *Administration in Social Work*, 26, 2: 17–26.

Cohen, P. 1987. 'Testing out the care manager', *Social Work Today*, 20, 7: 7.

Collshed, V. 1990. *Management in Social Work*. Basingstoke: Macmillan.

Craig, G. and J. Manthorpe. 1998. 'Small is beautiful? Local government reorganisation and the work of social services departments', *Policy and Politics*, 26, 2: 189–207.

Dartington Social Research Unit. 1995. *Matching Needs and Services: The Audit and Planning of Provision for Children Looked after by Local Authorities*, London, Support Force for Children's Residential Care.

Dartington Social Research Unit. 1996a. *Structure and Culture in Children's Homes*. Dartington: Dartington Social Research Unit.

Dartington Social Research Unit. 1996b. *Matching Needs and Services: The Audit and Planning of Provision for Children Looked after by Local Authorities*. Dartington: Dartington Social Research Unit.

Dartington Social Research Unit. 1997a. 'Organisation, services and outcomes in personal services for children and families'. Mimeo: Dartington: Dartington Social Research Unit.

Dartington Social Research Unit. 1997b. 'Early intervention and children in need'. Mimeo: Dartington Social Research Unit.

Davidson, J. and J. Grieves. 1996. 'Developing quality in local government'. Paper presented to the ISO 9000 and TQM conference, De Montfort University, 10–12 April.

Day, P. and R. Klein. 1987. 'The Business of Welfare', *New Society*, 19: 11–13.

Day, P. and R. Klein. 1990. *Inspecting the Inspectorates*. York: Joseph Rowntree Trust.

Deal, T. and A. Kennedy. 1982. *Corporate Cultures*. Reading, MA: Addison Wesley.

Denis, J. L., L. Lamothe, A. Langley and A. Valette. 1999. 'The struggle to redefine boundaries in health care systems', in Brock, D. M., Hinings, C. R. and Powell, M. J. (eds), *Professional Organisations: Toward a New Archetype*. London: Routledge.

Denzin, N. and Y. Lincoln. 1994. *Handbook of Qualitative Research*. London: Sage.

Department of Health (DH). 1989. *An Introduction to the Children Act 1989*. London: HMSO.

Department of Health (DH). 1990. *Caring for People – Community Care in the Next Decade and Beyond: Policy and Guidance*. London: HMSO.

Department of Health (DH). 1991a. *Children in the Public Care: A Review of Residential Care*. London: HMSO (Utting Report).

Department of Health (DH). 1991b. Children Act, 1989 Guidance and Regulations, Volume 4: Residential Care. London: HMSO.

Department of Health (DH). 1991c. *Patterns and Outcomes in Child Placement – Messages from Current Research and their Implications*. London: HMSO.

Department of Health (DH). 1992. *Choosing with Care: The Report of the Residential Staffs Inquiry into the Selection, Development and Management of Staff in Children's Homes*. (Warner Report). London: HMSO.

Department of Health (DH). 1993a. *Children Looked After by Local Authorities, 14 October 1991 – March 1993, England*. London: HMSO

Department of Health (DH). 1993b. *Child Care Research Strategy 1993/4 Initiative on Residential Child Care*. Progress bulletin, Autumn. London: HMSO.

Department of Health (DH). 1994a. *Children Act Report 1994*. Cm 2878. London: HMSO.

Department of Health (DH). 1994b. *Moving Forward*. London: HMSO.

Department of Health (DH). 1995. *Looking After Children: Research into Practice*, (ed.) Ward, H. London: HMSO.

Department of Health (DH). 1996 and various years. *Children Looked After by Local Authorities, Year Ending 31 March 1996 (England)*. London: HMSO.

Department of Health (DH). 1997. *People Like Us: The Report of the Review of the Safeguards for Children Living Away from Home*. (The Utting Report) London: The Stationery Office.

Department of Health (DH). 1998a. *Caring for Children Away From Home: Messages from Research*. Chichester: Wiley.

Department of Health (DH). 1998b. *Modernising Social Services*. London: Department of Health.

Department of Health (DH). 1999a. *The Government's Objectives for Children's Services*. London: Department of Health.

Department of Health (DH). 1999b. *Modernising Children's Services*. Cm 4169.

Department of Health (DH). 2000. *New Children's Services Planning Guidance.* London: Department of Health.

Department of Health Local Authority Circular 1998. *Quality Protects Circular: Transforming Children's Services.* LAC(98)28.

Department of Health and Welsh Office. 2000. *Lost in Care. Report of the Tribunal of Inquiry into the Abuse of Children in Care in the Former County Council Areas of Gwynedd and Clwyd since 1974* (The Waterhouse Report).

Department of Health and Social Security (DHSS). 1976. *Some Aspects of Residential Care.* London: HMSO.

Department of Health and Social Security (DHSS). 1982. *Child Abuse: A Study of Inquiry Reports, 1973–81.* London: HMSO.

Department of Health and Social Security (DHSS). 1985. *Review of Child Care Law: Report to Ministers of an Interdepartmental Working Party.* London: HMSO.

Department of Health and Social Security. 1988. *Report of Inquiry into Child Abuse in Cleveland.* Cmnd.412. London: HMSO.

Department of Health and Social Security Inspectorate. 1989. *Inspection of Nine Birmingham Children's Homes.* London: HMSO.

Dingwall, R., J. Eekalaar and T. Murray. 1983. *The Protection of Children: State Intervention in Family Life.* Oxford: Blackwell.

Donzelot, J. 1980. *The Policing of Families: Welfare versus the State.* London: Hutchinson.

Downey, R. 1995. 'Home today, gone tomorrow', *Community Care*, 14 December, 14–15.

Dunleavy, P. and C. Hood. 1994. 'From old public administration to new public management', *Public Money and Management*, July–September, 9–16.

Farnham, D. and S. Horton. 1996. *Managing People in the Public Services.* London: Macmillan.

Fayol, H. 1949/1990. 'General and industrial management', in D. S. Pugh (ed.), *Organisation Theory.* London: Penguin.

Ferlie, E., L. Ashburner, L. Fitzgerald, and A. Pettigrew. 1996. *The New Public Management.* Oxford: Oxford University Press.

Fisher, M., P. Marsh, D. Phillips and E. Sainsbury. 1994. 'Rethinking child care policy', in S. Morgan and P. Righton (eds), *Child Care: Concerns and Conflicts.* London: Hodder and Stoughton.

Fisher, M., P. Marsh, D. Phillips, and E. Sainsbury. 1986. *In and Out of Care: The Experience of Children, Parents and Social Workers.* London: Batsford/BAAF.

Flynn, R., G. Williams and S. Pickard. 1996. *Markets and Networks: Contracting in Community Health Services.* Buckingham: Open University Press.

Foster, D. and P. Hoggett. 1999. 'Changes in the benefits agency: empowering the exhausted worker?' *Work, Employment and Society*, 13, 1: 19–39.

Foster, P. and P. Wilding. 2000. 'Whither welfare professionalism?', *Social Policy and Administration*, 34, 2: 143–59.

Frederickson, H. G. 1996. 'Comparing the reinventing government movement with the new public administration', *Public Administration Review*, 56: 263–71.

Freidson. E. 1978. *Professionalism Reborn: Theory, Prophecy and Policy.* Cambridge: Polity Press.

Friedson, E. 1994. *Professionalism Reborn: Theory, Prophecy and Policy.* Cambridge: Polity Press.

Gabris, G., K. Grenell, and J. Kaatz. 1998. 'Reinventing local government human services management: a conceptual analysis', *Public Administration Quarterly*, 22, 1: 74–98.

Gersick, C. 1991.'Revolutionary change theories: a multilevel exploration of the punctuated equilibrium paradigm', *Academy of Management Review*, 16: 10–36.

Gibbons, M., C. Limoges, H. Nowotny, S. Schwartzman, P. Scott and M. Trow, 1994. *The New Production of Knowledge: The Dynamics of Science and Research in Contemporary Societies*. London: Sage.

Gregory, R. 1989. 'Political rationality or incrementalism', *Policy and Politics*, 17, 2: 139–53.

Green, P. 1995. 'Managing for care: the external management of children's homes', in *Interface or Interference: The First Line Management of Residential Care for Children and Young People*, SSI and SFCRC. London: Department of Health.

Green, R. and S. Waters. 1999. 'The potential effects of welfare reform on state's financing of child welfare services', *Children and Youth Services Review*, 21, 10: 865–80.

Greenwood, R. and B. Hinings. 1988. 'Organizational design types, tracks and the dynamics of strategic change', *Organization Studies*, 9, 3: 293–316.

Greenwood, R. and J. D. Stewart. 1986. 'The institutional and organisational capabilities of local government', *Public Administration*, 64: 35–50.

Hall, C. 1997. 'Organisation and outcomes in personal social services for children and Families'. Mimeo: Dartington Social Research Unit.

Hallett, C. 1982. *The Personal Social Services in Local Government*. London: George Allen and Unwin.

Hallett, C. 1991. 'The Children Act 1989 and Community Care: comparisons and contrasts', *Policy and Politics*, 19, 4: 283–91.

Hammer, M. and J. Champy. 1993. *Re-engineering the Corporation*. London: Nicholas Brearly.

Harding, L. M. F. 1994. 'Two value positions in recent child care law and practice', in Morgan, S. and Righton, P. (eds), *Child Care: Concerns and Conflicts*. London: Hodder and Stoughton.

Harrow, J. and L. Wilcocks. 1990. 'Public services management: activities, initiatives and limits to learning', *Journal of Management Studies*, 27, 3: 281–304.

Harris, J. 1998. 'Scientific management, bureau professionalism, new managerialism: the labour process of state social work', *British Journal of Social Work*, 28: 839–62.

Hatch, M. J. 1997. *Organizational Theory: Modern, Symbolic and Postmodern Perspectives*. Oxford: Oxford University Press.

Hearn, B. 1994. 'The purchaser/provider split 15 years on', *Concern*, 88: 8–9.

Henkel, M. 1991. 'The new evaluative state', *Public Administration*, 69, spring: 121–36.

Heyes, J. 1996. 'An Investigation into the impact of change on social work after more than a decade of ideological shifts and legislative reforms', Unpublished Research Report. University of Central Lancashire.

Hill, M. and J. Aldgate. 1996. *Child Welfare Services: Developments in Law, Policy, Practice and Research*. London: Jessica Kingsley.

Hills, D., C. Child, J. Hills and V. Blackburn, 1998. *Evaluating Residential Care*. London: Tavistock Institute.

Hinnings, C. R., Brown, J. and Greenwood, R. 1991. 'Change in an autonomous professional organisation', *Journal of Management Studies*, 28: 375–94.

Hoggett, P. 1996. 'New modes of control in the public service', *Public Administration*, 74, 1: 9–25.

Holman, B. 1993. *A New Deal for Social Welfare*. Oxford: Lion Publishing.

Hood, C. 1991. 'A public management for all seasons?', *Public Administration*, 69: 3–19.

Hood, C. 1995. 'The "New Public Management" in the 1980s: variations on a theme', *Accounting, Organisation and Society*, 20, 2/3: 93–109.

Hood, C. 1998. *The Art of the State: Culture, Rhetoric and Public Management*. Oxford: Clarendon Press.

Hood, S. 1997. 'Purchaser-provider separation in child and family social work: implications for service delivery and for the role of the social worker', *Child and Family Social Work*, 2: 25–35.

Hopkins, K., and C. Hyde. 2002. 'The human service managerial dilemma: new expectations, chronic challenges and old solutions', *Administration in Social Work*, 26, 3: 1–14.

Horvarth, J. and T. Morrison. 2000. 'Identifying and implementing pathways for organizational change – using the *Framework for the Assessment of Children in Need and their Families* as a case example', *Child and Family Social Work*, 5: 245–54.

Howe, D. 1986. *Social Workers and their Practice in Welfare Bureaucracies*. Aldershot: Gower.

Howe, D. 1992 'Child abuse and the bureaucratisation of social work', *Sociological Review*, 40, 3: 491–508.

Howe, E. 1992. *The Quality of Care: A Report of the Residential Staffs Inquiry*. London: Local Government Management Board.

Huczynski, A. and D. Buchanan. 1997. *Organisational Behaviour*. London: Prentice Hall.

Iles, P. and R. Auluck. 1993. 'Team building, inter-agency team development and social work practice', in Mabey, C. and Mayon-White, B. (eds), *Managing Change*. London: Open University and Harper and Row.

James, A. 1994. *Managing to Care*. Harlow: Longman.

Johnson, G. 1987. *Strategic Change and the Management Process*. Oxford: Basil Blackwell.

Johnson, N., S. Jenkinson, I. Kendall, Y. Bradshaw and M. Blackmore. 1998. 'Regulating for quality in the voluntary sector', *Journal of Social Policy*, 27, 3: 307–28.

Jones, A, and K. Bilton. 1994. *The Future Shape of Children's Services*. London: National Children's Bureau.

Kahan, B. 1994. *Growing Up in Groups*, NISW: HMSO.

Keen, L. and R. Scase. 1998. *Local Government Management*. Buckingham: Open University Press.

Kennedy School of Government. 1996. *Partners in Child Protection Services: The Department of Social Services and La Alianza Hispana (Epilogue)*. Kennedy School of Government, Case Program C10–96–1327.1. Cambridge, MA: John F. Kennedy School of Government, Harvard University.

Kessler, I., and J. Purcell. 1996. 'Strategic choice and new forms of employment relations in the public service sector: developing an analytical framework', *International Journal of Human Resource Management*, 7, 1: 206–29.

Kirkpatrick, I. 2000. 'The worst of both worlds?: public services without markets or bureaucracy', *Public Money and Management*, 19, 4: 7–14.

Kirkpatrick, I., M. Kitchener and R. Whipp. 2001 'Out of sight, out of mind? The uncertain development of markets in local authority children's services', *Public Administration*, 79, 1: 49–71.

Kirkpatrick, I., M. Kitchener, D. Owen and R. Whipp. 1999. ' "Un-chartered territory": experiences of the purchaser/provider split in local authority children's services', *British Journal of Social Work*, 29: 707–26.

Kirkwood, A. 1993. *The Leicestershire Inquiry 1992*. Leicester: Leicestershire County Council.

Kitchener. M. and R. Whipp. 1997. 'Tracks of change in hospitals: a study of quasi-market transformation'. *International Journal of Public Sector Management*, 10, 1/2: 47–62.

Kitchener, M., I. Kirkpatrick and R. Whipp. 1999. 'Decoupling managerial audit: evidence from the local authority children's homes sector', *International Journal of Public Sector Management*, 12, 4: 338–50.

Kitchener, M., I. Kirkpatrick and R. Whipp. 2000. 'Supervising professional work under new public management: evidence from an invisible trade', *British Journal of Management*, 11, 3: 213–26.

Knapp, M. and Lowin, A. 1997. 'The economics of child social care: a review of evidence and possibilities'. Mimeo: Personal Social Services Research Unit, London School of Economics and Political Science.

Langan, M. 2000 'Social services: managing the third way', in Clarke, J., Gerwitz, S. and McLaughlin, E. (eds), *New Managerialism. New Welfare?* London: Sage and Open University.

Langan, M. and J. Clarke. 1994 'Managing in the mixed economy of care', in Clarke, J., Cochrane, A. and McLaughlin, E. (eds), *Managing Social Policy*. London: Sage.

Larson, M. S. 1977. *The Rise of Professionalism: A Sociological Analysis*. London: University of California Press.

Lawler, J. and J. Hearn. 1997. 'The managers of social work: the experiences and identifications of third tier social services managers and the implications for future practice', *British Journal of Social Work*, 27: 191–218.

Lawrence, P. and J. Lorsch. 1967. *Organisation and Environment*. Cambridge, MA: Harvard University Press.

Leach, S., J. Stewart and K. Walsh. 1994. *The Changing Organisation and Management of Local Government*. Macmillan: London.

Leach, S. 1997. 'The vision thing', *Community Care*, 27 November–3 December: 2–3.

Leat, D. and E. Perkins. 1998. 'Juggling and dealing: the creative work of care package purchasing', *Social Policy and Administration*, 32, 2: 166–81.

LeGrand, J. and W. Bartlett. 1993. *Quasi-Markets and Social Policy*. Basingstoke: Macmillan.

Levy, A. and B. Kahan. 1991. *The Pindown Experience and the Protection of Children*. Stafford: Staffordshire County Council.

Lewis, J. 2002. 'The contribution of research findings to practice change', Managing Community Care, 10: 1.

Lewis, J. and H. Glennerster. 1996. *Implementing the New Community Care*: Buckingham: Open University Press.

Lewis, J., P. Bernstock, V. Bovell, and F. Wookey. 1997. 'Implementing care management: issues in relation to the new community care', *British Journal of Social Work*, 27: 5–24.
Local Government Management Board. 1988. *The Development of Senior Managers within Social Services Departments*. LGMB.
Local Government Management Board (LGMB) and Central Council for the Education and Training of Social Work (CCETSW). 1997. *Human Resources for Personal Social Services*, London: LGMB and CCETSW.
Lyles, M. 1990. 'A research agenda for strategic management in the 1990s', *Journal of Management Studies*, 27, 4: 363–75.
Martin, V. and E. Henderson. 2001. *Managing in Health and Social Care*. London: Routledge.
Means, R. and J. Langan. 1996. 'Charging and quasi-markets in community care: implications for elderly people with dementia', *Social Policy and Administration*, 30, 3: 244–62.
Means, R. and R. Smith. 1998. *Community Care: Policy and Practice*. London: Macmillan.
Meyer, J. W. and B. Rowan. 1991 'Institutional organisations: formal structure as myth and ceremony', in Powell, W. W. and DiMaggio, P. J. (eds), *The New Insititutionalism in Organisational Analysis*. Chicago: University of Chicago Press.
Millham, S., R. Bullock and K. Hosie. 1978. *Locking Up Children*. Aldershot: Farnborough: Saxon House.
Millham, S., R. Bullock, K. Hosie and M. Haak. 1986. *Lost in Care: The Problem of Maintaining Links between Children in Care and their Families*. Aldershot: Gower.
Milne, S. 1997. *Making Markets Work: Contracts, Competition and Co-operation*. London: ESRC.
Mintzberg, H. 1993. *Structure in Fives: Designing Effective Organisations*. London: Prentice Hall.
Mintzberg, H. 1994. *The Rise and Fall of Strategic Planning*. Hemel Hempstead: Prentice Hall.
Morgan, J. and P. Righton. 1994. *Child Care: Concerns and Conflicts*. London: Hodder and Stoughton.
Morrison, T. 1997. *Staff Supervision in Social Care*. Brighton: Pavilion Publishing.
Nutt, P. C. and R. W. Backoff. 1992. *Strategic Management of Public and Third Sector Organizations*. San Francisco: Jossey-Bass.
Orme, J. 2001. 'Regulation or fragmentation? Directions for social work under new labour', *British Journal of Social Work*, 31: 611–24.
Osbourne, D. and T. Gaebler. 1992. *Reinventing Government: How the Entrepreneurial Spirit is Transforming the Public Sector*. Reading: Addison Welsey.
Ouchi, W. G. 1980. 'Markets, bureaucracies and clans', *Administrative Science Quarterly*, 25, 129–41.
Packman, J. and C. Hall. 1996. *The Implementation of Section 20 of the Children Act, 1989*. Dartington: Dartington Social Research Unit.
Packman, J., with J. Randal and N. Jaques. 1986. *Who Needs Care ? Social Work Decisions about Children*. Oxford: Basil Blackwell.
Page, R. and G. Clark. 1977. *Who Cares ? Young People in Care Speak Out*. London: National Children's Bureau.
Pahl, J. 1994. 'Like the job – but hate the organisation: social workers and managers in social services', in Page, R. and Baldock, J. (eds), *Social Policy Review*: 191–210.

Parker, J. 2000. 'These are the children we crush', *The Guardian*, 15 February: 19.
Parker, R., H. Ward, S. Jackson, J. Algate and P. Wedge. 1991. *Looking After Children: Assessing Outcomes in Child Care*. London HMSO.
Parsloe, P. 1981. *Social Services Area Teams*. London: George Allen and Unwin.
Parton, N. 1993. *Governing The Family*. Basingstoke: Macmillan.
Parton, N. 1994. 'The nature of social work under conditions of (post) modernity', *Social Work and Social Sciences Review*, 5, 2: 93–112.
Payne, C. and R. Douglas. 1980. 'The right method of supervision revisited', *Social Work Today*, 11, 40: 25.
Penna, S., I. Paylor, and K. Soothill. 1995. *Job Satisfaction and Dissatisfaction: A Study of Residential Care Work*. London: National Institute for Social Work.
Perrow, C. 1986. *Complex Organisations*. Dallas: Scott Foresman.
Petrie, S. and Wilson, K. 1999. 'Towards the disintegration of child welfare services', *Social Policy and Administration*, 33, 2: 181–96.
Pettes, D. E. 1976. *Supervision in Social Work*. London: Allen and Unwin.
Pettigrew, A. and R. Whipp. 1991. *Managing Change and Competitive Success*. Oxford: Basil Blackwell.
Peters, T. J. and R. H. Waterman. 1982. *In Search of Excellence*. London: Harper and Row.
Pinnock, M. and B. Dimmock. 2003. 'Outcomes are us?' ch. 11 in Seden, J. and Reynolds, J. (eds), *Managing Care in Context*. Milton Keynes: Open Univeristy Press.
Pithouse, A. 1989. *Social Work: The Social Organisation of an Invisible Trade*. Aldershot: Avebury.
Patti, R. 2003. 'Reflections on the state of management in social work', *Administration in Social Work*, 27, 2: 1–11.
Platt, D. 1994. 'Split decisions', *Community Care*, 14 May: 30–2.
Pollitt, C. 1993. *Managerialism and the Public Services: The Anglo American Experience*. London: Macmillan.
Pollitt, C. 1990 'Doing business in the temple? Managers and quality assurance in the public services', *Public Administration*, 68, Winter: 435–52.
Pollitt, C. and Bouckaert, G. 2000. *Public Management Reform: A Comparative Analysis*. Oxford: Oxford University Press.
Power, M. 1997. *The Audit Society*. Oxford: Oxford University Press.
Quinn, J. B. 1980. *Strategies for Change: Logical Incrementalism*. Homewood, Illinois: R. D. Irwin.
Quinn, J. B. 1982. 'Managing strategy incrementally', *Omega*, 10: 6.
Raelin, J. A. 1992. *The Clash of Cultures*. Boston MA: Harvard Business School Press.
Redman, T., E. Snape, D. Thompson and F. Ka-ching Yan. 2000. 'Performance appraisal in an NHS hospital', *Human Resource Management Journal*, 10, 1: 48–62.
Reed, M. 1996. 'Expert power and control in late modernity: an empirical review and theoretical synthesis', *Organisation Studies*, 17, 4: 473–598.
Residential Care Association. 1982. *Middle Management in Residential Social Work*. (The Ollerton Report). London: RCA.
Rhodes, R. A. W. 1996. 'The new governance: governing without government', *Political Studies*, XLIV: 652–67.
Rose, D., G. Marshall, H. Newby and C. Volger. 1987. 'Goodbye to supervisors', *Work Employment and Society*, 1/1:7–24.
Rowe, J. and L. Lambert. 1973. *Children Who Wait*. London: ABAA.

Rowlands, J. 1995. 'Corporate planning for childrens and young people in children's homes', in Interface or Interference. Mimeo: DoH.

Rushton, A. and J. Nathan. 1996. 'The supervision of child protection work', *British Journal of Social Work*, 26: 357–74.

Sako, M. 1992. *Prices, Quality and Trust: Inter-firm Relations in Britain and Japan*. Cambridge: Cambridge University Press.

Sanderson, I. 2001. 'Performance management, evaluation and learning in "modern" local government', *Public Administration*, 79, 2: 297–313.

Schwenk, C. R. 1989. 'Linking cognitive, organisational and political factors in explaining strategic change', *Journal of Management Studies*, 26, 2: 177–87.

Scott, W. R. 1965. 'Reactions to supervision in a heteronomous professional organisation', *Administrative Science Quarterly*, 10: 65–81.

Seebohm Report. 1968. *Report on the Committee on Local Authority and Allied Social Services*. Cmnd 3703. London: HMSO.

Shaw. I. 1995. 'The quality of mercy: the management of quality in the personal social service', in Kirkpatrick, I. and Lucio, M. (eds), *The Politics of Quality in the Public Sector*. London: Routledge.

Sheldon, B. and R. Chilvers. 2000. *Evidence-Based Social Care: a Study of Prospects and Problems*. Lyme Regis: Russell House.

Simm, M. 1995. 'Aiming high', *Community Care*, November, 16–17.

Sinclair, I. 1975. 'The influence of wardens and matrons on probation hostels', in J. Tizard *et al*. (eds), *Varieties of Residential Experience*. London: Routledge and Kegan Paul.

Sinclair, I. 1987. 'Literature review on residential care'. Draft summary presented to The Overview of the Department of Health's Residential Child Care Research, Dartington Hall, 17–19 November.

Sinclair, I. and I. Gibbs. 1996. 'Quality of care in children's homes'. Mimeo: Department of Health report (Ref 370/0317).

Sisson, K. (ed.), 1989. *Personnel Management in Britain*. Oxford: Blackwell.

Skinner, A. 1992. *Another Kind of Home*. Edinburgh: HMSO.

Smale, G. 1996. *Mapping Change and Innovation*. London: HMSO.

Social Services Committee. 1984. *Children in Care*. (HC 360). London: HMSO.

Social Services Inspectorate. 1986. *Inspection of the Supervision of Social Workers in the Assessment and Monitoring of Cases of Child Abuse when Children, Subject to Court Order, Have Been Returned Home*. London: DHSS.

Social Services Inspectorate. 1988a. *Key Indicators of Local Authority Social Services: A Demonstration Package by R. William Warburton*. London: DHSS.

Social Services Inspectorate. 1988b. *Decentralisation of Social Service Departments: Project Papers*. Nos. 1–6. London: DHSS.

Social Services Inspectorate. 1988c. *Inspection of Cleveland Social Service Department's Arrangement for Handling Child Sexual Abuse*. London: DHSS.

Social Services Inspectorate. 1991a. *Managing to Care: A Study of First Line Managers in Social Services Departments in Day and Domicillary Care*. London: SSI.

Social Services Inspectorate. 1991b. *Review of Residential Child Care Services in Southwark, March 1991*. London: Department of Health.

Social Services Inspectorate. 1993. *Corporate Parents: Inspection of Residential Child Care Services in Eleven Local Authorities (November 1992 to March 1993)*. London: SSI.

Social Services Inspectorate. 1994a. *Inspecting for Quality: Standards for Residential Care*. London: HMSO.

Social Services Inspectorate. 1994b. *How Well are Children Being Looked After?* London: Department of Health.

Social Services Inspectorate. 1995a. *Interface or Interference?* London: Department of Health.

Social Services Inspectorate. 1995b. *Small Unregistered Children's Homes.* London: Department of Health.

Social Services Inspectorate. 1996a. *Organisation of Children's Services Project.* London: HMSO.

Social Services Inspectorate. 1996b. *Organisation Structure of Children's Services.* Report of seminar held at Skipton House, London, 12 September.

Social Services Inspectorate. 1997. *Introducing the Inspection Division.* London: SSI/DoH.

Social Services Inspectorate. 1998. *Someone Else's Children: Inspections of Planning and Decision Making for Children Looked After and The Safety of Children Looked After.* London: Department of Health.

Social Services Inspectorate Wales and Social Information Services (SSIW). 1991. *Accommodating Children: A Review of Children's Homes in Wales.* Cardiff: Welsh Office.

Social Services Inspectorate Wales. 1995. *Quality Care in Children's Homes in Wales.* Cardiff: Welsh Office.

Social Services Inspectorate Wales. 1997. *Inspection of Children's Homes Provided by Rhondda Cynon Taff County Borough.* SSIW: Cardiff.

SOCITM. 1994. Local government IT trends. Mimeo, Society of Information Technology Managers.

Stewart, J. and S. Ranson. 1988. 'Management in the public domain', *Public Money and Management*, Spring/Summer: 13–19.

Stewart, J. and K. Walsh. 1992. 'Change in the management of public services', *Public Administration*, 70: 499–518.

Strauss, A., Schatzman, L. D. Ehrlich, D. Bucher and M. Shashin. 1973. 'The hospital and its negotiated order', in G. Salaman and K. Thompson (eds), *People in Organisations.* London: Open University Press.

Support Force for Children's Residential Care (SFCRC). 1994. *Out of Authority Placements: Checklist of Information to be Obtained.* London: Department of Health.

Support Force for Children's Residential Care. 1995a. *Contracting for Children's Residential Care.* London: Department of Health.

Support Force for Children's Residential Care. 1995b. *The Use and Development of Databases of Residential Child Care Resources.* London: Department of Health.

Support Force for Children's Residential Care. 1995c. *Staff Supervision in Children's Homes.* London: Department of Health.

Support Force for Children's Residential Care. 1995d. *Good Care Matters – Ways of Enhancing Good Care Practice in Residential Child Care.* London: Department of Health.

Support Force for Children's Residential Care. 1995e. *Strategic Planning Framework: Part 2 – Implementing Change.* London: Department of Health.

Support Force for Children's Residential Care. 1996. *Residential Care for Children and Young People – A Positive Choice?: Final Report to Secretary of State for Health.* London: Department of Health.

Syrett, V., M. Jones and N. Sercombe. 1997. 'Implementing community care: the congruence of manager and practitioner cultures', *Social Work and Social Sciences Review*, 7, 3: 154–69.

Thomas, R. and D. Dunkerley. 1999. 'Janus and the bureaucrats: middle management in the public sector', *Public Policy and Administration*, 14, 1: 28–41.

Thomas, R., S. Hardy and A. Davies. 2000. 'Gender, restructuring and new public management: changing managerial identities in three public service organisations', paper presented at the British Academy of Management Annual Conference, 13–15 September, University of Edinburgh.

Thompson, A. 1997. 'Into the breach', *Community Care*, 13, 19: 22–23.

Thompson, N., S. Stradling, M. Murphy and P. O'Neill. 1996. 'Stress and organisational culture', *British Journal of Social Work*, 26, 5, 647–66.

Thurley, K. and H. Wirdenius. 1973. *Supervision: A Reappraisal*. London: Heinemann.

Tizard, B. 1977. *Adoption: A Second Chance*. London: Routledge.

Tizard, J., I. Sinclair, and R. Clarke. 1975. *Varieties of Residential Experience*. Oxford: Routledge and Keegan Paul.

Townley, B. 1997. 'The institutional logic of performance appraisal', *Organisation Studies*, 18, 2: 261–85.

Trice, H. M. and J. M. Beyer. 1986 'The concept of charisma', *Research in Organisational Behaviour*, 8, New York: JAI Press.

Triseliotis, J. and J. Russell. 1984. *Hard to Place*. London: Heinemann Educational.

Utting, W. 1991. *Children in the Public Care: A Review of Residential Child Care*. London: HMSO.

Utting, W. 1997. *People Like Us: The Review of the Safeguards for Children Living Away From Home*. Summary report. London: HMSO.

Vernon, J. and D. Fruin. 1986. *In Care: A Study of Social Work Decision-Making*. London: National Children's Bureau.

Wagner, G. 1988. *Residential Care : A Positive Choice*. London: HMSO.

Waine, B. 2000. '*Managing Performance through pay*', in Clarke, J., Gerwitz, S. and McLaughlin, E. (eds), *New Managerialism New Welfare? London: Sage.

Walby, C. 1993. 'The contract culture', *Children and Society*, 7, 4: 343–56.

Walsh, K., N. Deakin, P. Smith P. Spurgeon and N. Thomas, 1997. *Contracting for Change: Contracts in Health, Social Care, and Other Local Government Services*. Oxford: Oxford University Press.

Ward, H. (ed.). 1995. *Looking After Children: Research into Practice.* London: HMSO.

Ward, H. 2001. 'Current initiatives in the development of outcome-based evaluation of children's services in the UK', Mimeo, Loughborough University.

Warner, N. 1997. 'Muddled thinking', *Community Care*, February–March: 25.

Waterhouse, L. 1988. 'Residential child care: matching services with needs', in Wagner, G. *Residential Care: A Positive Choice*. London: HMSO.

Webb, A. and G. Wistow. 1987. *Social Work, Social Care and Social Planning: The Personal Social Services since Seebohm*. London: Longman.

Weick, K. E. 1976. 'Educational organisations as loosely-coupled systems', *Administrative Science Quarterly*, 21: 1–16.

Welsh Office. 1994. *Citizen's Charter: Inspecting Social Services in Wales*. September: 68/94. Cardiff: Welsh Office.

Welsh Office. 1994. *Inspection of Community Homes*. 7/94. January. Cardiff: Welsh Office.

Welsh Office 1999. *The Children First Programme in Wales: Transforming Children's Services 20/99*. Cardiff: Welsh Office.

West Riding Social Services Department. 1973. 'The Role of Liaison Officers to Residential Establishments'. Mimeo: West Riding Social Services Department.

Whipp, R., R. Rosenfeld, and A. Pettigrew. 1989. 'Culture and competitiveness', *Journal of Management Studies*, 26, 6: 26–282.

Whipp. R. and A. Pettigrew. 1992. 'Managing change for competitive success: bridging the strategic and the operational', *Industrial and Corporate Change*, 1, 1: 205–33.

Whipp, R. 1992. 'Human resource management, strategic change and competition: the role of learning', *International Journal of Human Resource Management*, 2, 2: 165–92.

Whipp, R. 1998. 'Qualitative methods: technique or size?' in Whitfield, K. and Strauss, G. (eds), *Researching the World of Work*. Ithaca: Cornell University Press, 51–63.

Whipp, R. 2002. 'Managing strategic change', in Faulkener, D. and Campbell, A. (eds), *The Oxford Handbook of Strategic Management*. Oxford: Oxford University Press.

Whipp, R., B. Adam and I. Sabelis (eds), 2002. *Making Time: Time and Management in Modern Organizations*. Oxford: Oxford University Press.

White, G. and B. Hutchinson. 1996. 'Local government', in Farnham, D. and Horton, S. (eds), *Managing People in the Public Service*. London: Macmillan.

Whittaker, D., L. Archer, and L. Hicks. 1996. *The Prevailing Cultures and Staff Dynamics In Children's Homes*. London: HMSO.

Whittaker, D., L. Archer and L. Hicks. 1998. *Working in Children's Homes: Challenges and Complexities*. Chichester: Wiley.

Whittington, R., T. McNulty and R. Whipp. 1995. 'Market-driven change in professional services: problems and processes', *Journal of Management Studies*, 31, 6.

Wilding, P. 1982. *Professional Power and Social Welfare*. London: Routledge.

Wilding, P. 1994. 'Maintaining quality in human services', *Social Policy and Administration*, 28, 1: 43–57.

Williams, A. 2001. 'Ready for take-off', *Community Care*, August, 2.

Wistow, G., M. Knapp, B. Hardy and C. Allen. 1994. *Social Care in a Mixed Economy*. Milton Keynes: Open University Press.

Wistow, G., M. Knapp, B. Hardy, J. Forder, J. Kendall, and R. Manning. 1996. *Social Care Markets*. London: Open University Press.

Wistow, G. and Hardy, B. 1999. 'The development of domiciliary care: mission accomplished?' *Policy and Politics*, 27, 2: 173–186.

Woodward, J. 1965. *Industrial Organisation: Theory and Practice*. London: Oxford University Press.

Worall, L, C. Collinge and T. Bill. 1996. 'The strategic process in local government', Mimeo: Management Research Centre, University of Wolverhampton.

Younghusband, E. 1978. *Social Work in Britain 1950–1975, Volumes I and II*. Surrey: George Allen and Unwin.

Zucker, L. G. 1987. 'Normal change or risky business: Institutional effects on the "hazard" of change in hospital organisations, 1959–1979', *Journal of Management Studies*, 24, 6: 671–700.

Index